PROPERTY TAX REFORM IN DEVELOPING COUNTRIES

PROPERTY TAX REFORM IN DEVELOPING COUNTRIES

by

JAY K. ROSENGARD

Harvard Institute for International Development
and
International Tax Program
Harvard University

Published in association with

INTERNATIONAL TAX PROGRAM
HARVARD UNIVERSITY

KLUWER ACADEMIC PUBLISHERS
BOSTON / DORDRECHT / LONDON

Distributors for North America:
Kluwer Academic Publishers
101 Philip Drive
Assinippi Park
Norwell, Massachusetts 02061 USA

Distributors for all other countries:
Kluwer Academic Publishers Group
Distribution Centre
Post Office Box 322
3300 AH Dordrecht, THE NETHERLANDS

Library of Congress Cataloging-in-Publication Data

A C.I.P. Catalogue record for this book is available from
the Library of Congress.

Printed on acid-free paper

Printed in the United States of America

ad miseram contribuentem plebem

Contents

About the Author

JAY K. ROSENGARD is a Development Associate at the Harvard Institute for International Development (HIID), Harvard University. He has over twenty years of experience in the design, implementation, and evaluation of development policies, programs, and projects throughout Asia, Africa, and Latin America. Dr. Rosengard's areas of expertise include: municipal finance and management; intergovernmental fiscal relations; banking and financial institutions development; microenterprise financing; tax reform; management information systems; monitoring and evaluation; human resource development; and public administration. He has worked for a wide variety of multilateral and bilateral donors, as well as directly for host governments and private sector clients. His experience combines significant accomplishments while managing complex overseas implementation activities, interspersed with internationally recognized applied policy research and teaching at leading development institutions in the United States.

Foreword

Developing countries experiencing high rates of urbanization and facing increased demands for the provision of municipal services have had great stress put on their budgets at the state and local levels of governments. In their search for an appropriate source of revenues to finance these services, governments have been turning to the property tax as a potential revenue mechanism. Although property taxation in some form has often had deep historical roots, it is a form of taxation that in more recent years has been neglected because of its political sensitivity and the difficulties faced by the tax authorities to implement it in a fair and stable manner. Pressures for special exemptions, multiple rates, and an inadequate design to account for inflation have eroded the property tax faster over time than most other components of revenue systems.

The response of many professionals in this area has been to try to implement ever more sophisticated, and expensive, mapping and computerized geographical information systems. To date the results of this approach have been dismal, at best. Dr. Rosengard has taken a different approach by studying in depth the experiences of a series of countries that have made major efforts at implementing property tax systems. From this research he has tried to identify what elements lead to success and what have failed. In addition, he is a practitioner who has worked for several years as an advisor in Indonesia on one of the few successful implementation experiences to be found in developing countries.

The Harvard Institute for International Development was given the privilege to assist the Ministry of Finance of the Government of Indonesia from the design stage through to its final implementation. As a member of that team, Dr. Rosengard was able to get first hand experience on the identification of factors that are critical for success.

The International Tax Program (ITP) at Harvard University is delighted to have been able to support this research effort, and to be identified with the publication of this book. The ITP has been able to do this because of the generous financial support it has received from the Lincoln Institute of Land Policy to undertake research on such topics. I am confident that the findings of Dr. Rosengard that are presented in this book will be of great interest to both academics and practitioners in this important area of applied public finance.

Glenn P. Jenkins
Director,
International Tax Program
Harvard University
Cambridge, Massachusetts

Author's Preface

The principal strengths and weaknesses of property taxation in developing countries are not well understood. Thus, governments attempt to use property taxes to achieve unrealistic policy objectives. At the same time, they miss promising opportunities to exploit property taxation effectively. Governments try to remedy a multiplicity of economic, political, and social ills via property tax reform, while they fail to optimize the financial potential of property taxation.

The cost of these fundamental misperceptions is compounded as technocrats and foreign advisors attempt to reform misunderstood property tax systems by misapplying scarce resources to achieve inappropriate ends. The results are not encouraging. Revenue generation routinely falls well short of needs. Ancillary objectives are seldom achieved. Tax bases are narrow and quickly eroded. Coverage is inequitable. Administration is arbitrary and corrupt. Unduly large amounts are spent on overly complex data collection and property valuation activities. Taxpayer compliance is low. Popular resentment is high.

Property Tax Reform in Developing Countries presents practical guidelines for the design and implementation of property tax reform in developing countries, based on an innovative conceptual framework and intensive field investigations. This book reviews the underlying fundamentals of the property tax, examines the common misperceptions that have led to so many unsuccessful attempts at property tax reform, analyzes the experiences of Indonesia, Chile, Jamaica, and the Philippines in depth to highlight what works and what does not work, and concludes with detailed suggestions for future property tax reform initiatives.

Property Tax Reform in Developing Countries emphasizes that the ***purpose*** of property tax reform in developing countries should be to ensure the long-term generation of adequate local government discretionary resources. This book makes a compelling argument that property taxation is an inappropriate policy tool and poor administrative mechanism for guiding allocative decisions, achieving social goals, recovering the cost of capital investments, or pricing private goods.

Property Tax Reform in Developing Countries also stresses that the fundamental ***principals*** of property tax reform in developing countries should be administrative and allocative efficiency, horizontal and vertical equity, and system sustainability. This book demonstrates that, unlike the norm in property tax improvement efforts, reforms can minimize the costs and maximize the longevity of reform by: increasing coverage through establishment and maintenance of a broad tax base; emphasizing simplicity through promotion of transparent policies and administrative clarity; and enhancing buoyancy through routine indexing and periodic non-traumatic revaluations.

To translate these concepts into operational practices, *Property Tax Reform in Developing Countries* explains why the ***process*** of property tax reform in developing countries should be one which stresses utilization of personal and institutional incentives, dissemination of public information, an integrated perspective, and selective implementation. This contrasts sharply with the usual approach to property tax reform, which usually ignores the incentives required for personal and institutional behavioral change, the importance of public awareness, the need for a holistic approach, and the wisdom of approaching change incrementally.

Acknowledgments

I am deeply indebted to many who have assisted me during preparation of this study.

First and foremost, my family has maintained its faith and confidence in me throughout the ordeal, and their support has been both a comfort and an inspiration. I am also grateful for the wise counsel of the Gang of Four: William A. Doebele, José A. Gomez-Ibañez, Glenn P. Jenkins, and Karl E. Case. Our discussions have been spirited and intense, with seldom a dull moment to anesthetize our deliberations. Suggestions have been taken in the constructive spirit offered: sometimes accepted, sometimes rejected, but never ignored. The adept facilitation of Carl Steinitz is also appreciated. Of course, ultimately I am responsible for the product, so I adhered to an old Yiddish expression: *Barat zich mit vemen du vilst; un tu miten aigenem saichel* - Ask advice from everyone, but act your own mind.

I am most appreciative of the financial support provided by the Graduate School of Design for the past two years, and by the International Tax Program for field work undertaken in preparation of the case studies.

I have benefited immensely from my Harvard Institute for International Development colleagues both in Cambridge and in the field, particularly those I have had the pleasure of working with most closely in Indonesia: Richard Patten, St. Clare Risden, Marco Montes, and Roy Kelly.

Finally, the credibility of this study is greatly enhanced by the insights of taxpayers and tax officials in Jamaica, the Philippines, Chile, and Indonesia who graciously subjected themselves to repeated questioning regarding their thoughts and actions.

Although it is not feasible to thank all those who have helped me understand their countries better, I would like to express my appreciation to those who have subjected themselves to the most abuse in the course of my research: Commissioner of Land Valuations Elizabeth A. Stair of the Ministry of Finance and Public Service in Jamaica; Director of the Bureau of Local Government Finance's Special Projects Management Service Erlito R. Pardo of the Department of Finance in the Philippines; and Valuation Subdirector Roger Lowick Russel Alvarez of the Internal Tax Service in Chile.

I am especially grateful to Property Tax Director Karsono Surjowibowo of the Ministry of Finance in Indonesia, who has been a close friend, respected professional colleague, and demanding client, often all at the same time. We have certainly both learned a lot while working together to improve property.

1

INTRODUCTION

An indefinable something is to be done, in a way nobody knows how, at a time nobody knows when, that will accomplish nobody knows what.

Thomas B. Reed,
Letter to Sereno E. Payne,
December 2, 1902

CONCEPTUAL FRAMEWORK

Summary

The principal strengths and weaknesses of property taxation in developing countries are not well understood. Thus, governments attempt to use property taxes to achieve unrealistic policy objectives. At the same time, they miss promising opportunities to exploit property taxation effectively.

Governments try to remedy a multiplicity of economic, political, and social ills via property tax reform, while they fail to optimize the financial potential of property taxation. Property taxes are commonly believed to be a dominant factor in investment and consumption decisions over which they have negligible influence, rather than as a viable means for funding the local provision of public goods.

The cost of these fundamental misperceptions is compounded as technocrats and foreign advisors attempt to reform misunderstood property tax systems by misapplying scarce resources to achieve inappropriate ends. Selective vision focussed on erroneous targets encourages introduction of complex, expensive, unfeasible, and unsustainable valuation and assessment techniques as the elixir of property tax reform. Outdated and insufficient tax roll data are blamed for the failings of property tax systems, so property tax reform is pursued as a quest to answer everything you always wanted to know about property but could never afford to ask.

Alternative reform strategies are not considered. Weaknesses regarding tax object discovery, tax roll maintenance, tax base buoyancy, and tax collections are not addressed. Administrative feasibility is not evaluated rigorously. The political economy of taxation is not given due consideration. The importance of behavioral change is not acknowledged. The idiosyncracies of developing country environments are not accommodated.

The results are not encouraging. Revenue generation routinely falls well short of needs. Ancillary objectives are seldom achieved. Tax bases are narrow and quickly eroded. Coverage is inequitable. Administration is arbitrary and corrupt. Unduly large amounts are spent on overly complex data collection and property valuation activities. Taxpayer compliance is low. Popular resentment is high.

It is within this context that the following conceptual framework for property tax reform in developing countries has been formulated (see Figure I-1):

> The **purpose** of property tax reform in developing countries should be to ensure the long-term generation of adequate local government discretionary resources. This entails providing local government with more revenue where the property tax yield is insufficient, and strengthening the future viability of property taxation by improving administrative cost-effectiveness, economic neutrality, and operational fairness whether or not revenue adequacy has already been achieved. Property taxation is an inappropriate policy tool and poor administrative mechanism for guiding allocative decisions, achieving social goals, recovering the cost of capital investments, or pricing private goods.
>
> Accordingly, the fundamental **principles** of property tax reform in developing countries should be administrative and allocative efficiency, horizontal and vertical equity, and system sustainability. This will ensure that revenue will be generated in a financially viable, economically non-distortive, politically fair, socially just, and temporally enduring manner. Reformers can minimize the costs and maximize the longevity of reform by: increasing coverage through establishment and maintenance of a broad tax base; emphasizing simplicity through promotion of transparent policies and administrative clarity; and enhancing buoyancy through routine indexing and periodic non-traumatic revaluations.
>
> To translate these structural tenets into operational practices, the **process** of property tax reform in developing countries should be one which stresses utilization of personal and institutional incentives, dissemination of public information, an integrated perspective, and selective implementation. This will facilitate changes in tax policies, administrative systems, and human

[1]The following discussion is based on interviews with Elizabeth Stair (Commissioner of Land Valuations), Norma Dixon (Commissioner of Inland Revenue), and Dennis Larman (Managing Director of Fiscal Services (EDP) Ltd.).

behavior. Reformers can minimize public, governmental, and political obstruction, misperception, and risk, and thus maximize cooperation by: improving service; applying sanctions; promoting meritocracies; mounting multimedia campaigns; linking policies and practices as well as all subsystems of field operations; phasing implementation activities; and upgrading existing systems.

Elaboration

Purpose of Property Tax Reform

The first element of this framework is that the property tax is best suited to generating revenue to finance relatively modest public expenditures, and thus, *the purpose of property tax reform should be to ensure the long-term generation of adequate local government discretionary resources.*

The property tax in developing countries is a wealth tax on fixed assets to help finance local government provision of public facilities and services. Just like other taxes, it is "a compulsory transfer of money . . . from private individuals, institutions or groups to the government. . . . [as] one of the principal means by which a government finances its expenditure."[2] A property tax can do no more, but can certainly do considerably less.[3]

The evidence supporting this premise is primarily historical. Property taxation traditionally has been the primary producer of local government own-source discretionary revenue for provision of public services, as well as operation and maintenance of physical and administrative infrastructure. In contrast, the property tax has been a poor tool for guiding allocative decisions, achieving social objectives, cost recovery of capital investments, or pricing of private goods.

[2]Graham Bannock, R.E. Baxter, and Evan Davis, The Penguin Dictionary of Economics, 4th ed. (London: Penguin Books, 1987), 398.

[3]Property taxes are generally defined as ad valorem ("according to the value" tax, as opposed to a unit tax), in rem ("against an object" tax, as opposed to a personal or in personam tax) levies on the ownership, occupation, or development of land and/or buildings. Property taxes usually are assessed annually upon the capital value of a property, or upon proxies for capital value such as presumed or actual rental income. Taxes not confined to immovable property, such as net wealth taxes and general capital gains taxes, are not commonly classified as property taxes.

FIGURE I-1:

CONCEPTUAL FRAMEWORK FOR PROPERTY TAX REFORM

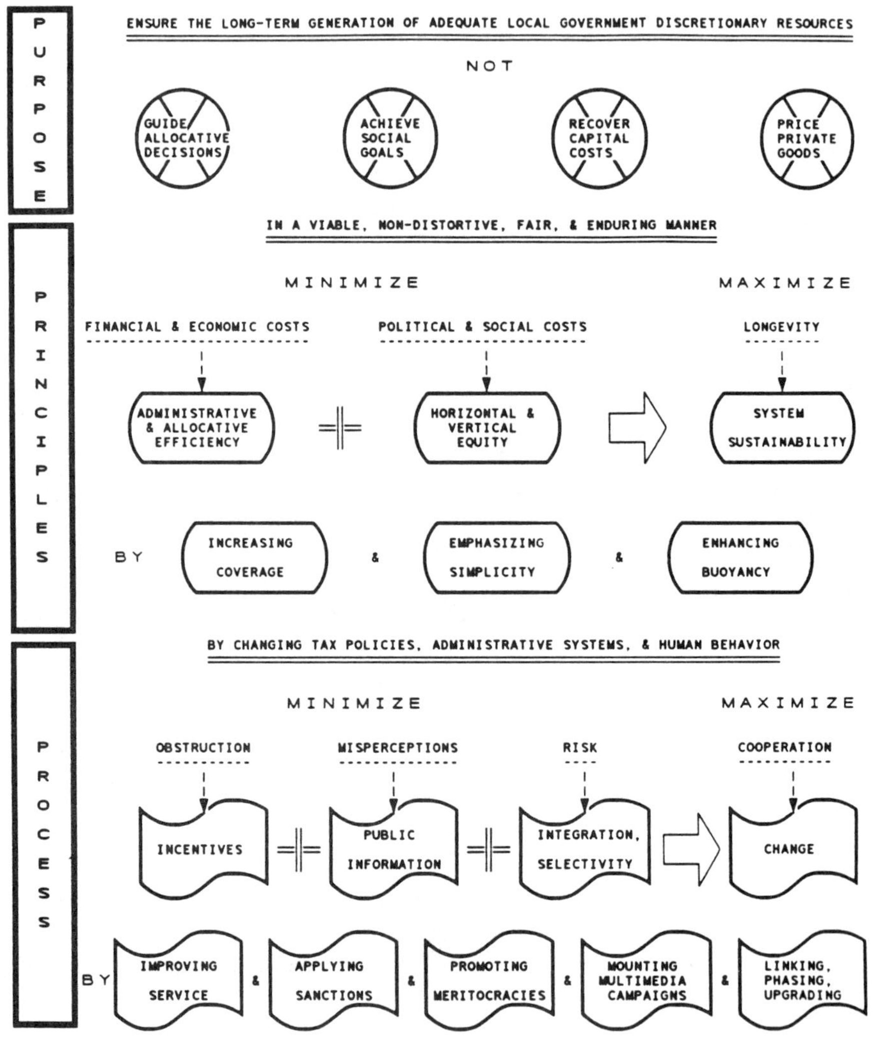

Source: Author's formulation.

TABLE I-1: MUNICIPAL RELIANCE ON PROPERTY TAXATION

	Property Taxes As Percent Of:	
Country/City	**Taxes**	**Total Revenue**
BRAZIL	40%	8%
Sao Paulo	38%	16%
Rio de Janeiro	31%	12%
COLOMBIA	46%	6%
Bogota	32%	18%
INDIA	40%	24%
Bombay	22%	17%
Calcutta	92%	36%
Madras	82%	41%
INDONESIA	43%	12%
Jakarta	10%	5%
KENYA	99%	36%
Nairobi	92%	36%
KOREA	27%	19%
Seoul	21%	18%
MEXICO	55%	12%
Mexico (DF)	59%	6%
NIGERIA	n.a.	n.a.
Lagos	70%	22%
Ibadan	13%	3%
PAKISTAN	8%	6%
Karachi	13%	12%
Lahore	13%	12%
PERU	n.a.	n.a.
Lima	57%	17%
PHILIPPINES	70%	20%
Manila	59%	36%

TUNISIA	28%	9%
Tunis	n.a.	14%
MEDIAN		
Countries	42%	12%
Cities	35%	17%

Source: Dillinger, *Urban Property Taxation in Developing Countries*, 3; no year cited for data in original source.

Most developing countries have some sort of property tax, primarily to finance local government expenditures.[4] Although local government dependence on property taxation varies considerably, property taxes usually comprise a plurality, if not a majority, of municipal tax revenues in developing countries.[5] Property taxes constitute 40 to 50 percent of aggregate municipal tax revenues in four of the most populous developing countries: Mexico, Brazil, India, and Indonesia (see Table I-1). Dependency on property taxation tends to be even more pronounced for secondary cities and small towns. When measured as a percentage of *total* municipal recurrent revenue, however, the contribution of property taxes is considerably smaller, due primarily to the prominent central government role in financing key municipal services.[6]

Property taxation is appealing to governments in developed countries because it is: hard to avoid legally, due to the high visibility and relative immobility of property; economically efficient, again because of asset immobility; a potential money machine, given the high income elasticity of property ownership characteristic of developed countries; relatively stable, as well as amenable to slight adjustments and incremental rate changes; clearly enforceable through seizure and liquidation of property; an enhancer of local autonomy through elicitation of a greater responsiveness to local priorities; a proxy for a local income tax because of the close relationship between property values and long-term income levels; roughly correlated with benefits received when used to finance local public goods; and generally progressive for residential property[7] (see Table I-2).

---

[4]Vito Tanzi, "Quantitative Characteristics of the Tax Systems of Developing Countries," in The Theory of Taxation for Developing Countries, ed. David Newbery and Nicholas Stern (New York: Oxford University Press, 1987), 206-17.

[5]William Dillinger, Urban Property Taxation in Developing Countries, WPS 41 (Washington, D.C.: World Bank, Office of the Vice President, Development Economics, August 1988), 2.

[6]Dillinger, Urban Property Taxation in Developing Countries, 3; no year cited for data in original source.

[7]Most economists now agree that: 1) the land portion of the property tax is borne by existing landowners through lower land prices, as the supply of land is finite and immobile, and given the distribution of land ownership by income classes, is progressive; 2) if there is a single national tax rate, the improvements portion of the property tax is borne by the owners of capital (see below), who experience lower returns similar to those

The property tax also has several glaring weaknesses: its large number of statutory taxpayers magnifies the political impact of even slight tax increases; its high visibility, accentuated by active payment mechanisms (unlike income tax withholding) and lumpy disbursements (in contrast to minuscule sales tax payments), amplifies awareness and intensifies resentment of the tax burden; its purported non-objective basis of assessment is commonly perceived as arbitrary and unsubstantiated; it sometimes lacks relationship with ability to pay because of mismatches of wealth in real property and income; in countries where rates and expenditures are determined locally, it tends to exacerbate regional disparities in wealth as rich jurisdictions grow richer while poor jurisdictions become poorer; and the tax's very existence is often seen as a threat to the sanctity of private property, thus evoking hostile visceral reactions well beyond the magnitude of the tax itself (see Table I-2).[8]

---

caused by a corporate profits tax and, given the distribution of capital ownership by income classes, is also progressive; and 3) if there is no national rate but a variety of local rates, and capital is mobile, the interjurisdictional differentials affect product prices and factor returns like an excise tax, and are therefore regressive. Incidence is also dependent on the mix of property types, the nature and composition of export and local industry, a variety of elasticity and mobility characteristics, and whether annual measured income or lifetime income standards are used. For example, if the owners of capital are not the consumers of the taxed service, as in industrial real estate used to produce tradeable goods, the tax tends to be regressive as wage rates are driven down.

[8]This summary of the generic strengths and weaknesses of the property tax draws heavily on the author's field experience, as well as on: Jensen, Property Taxation in the United States; and Netzer, Economics of the Property Tax. Property tax capitalization, incidence, and efficiency are explored at length in: Peter Mieszkowski, "The Property Tax: An Excise or a Profits Tax?," Journal of Public Economics 1 (April 1972): 73-96; Dick Netzer, "The Incidence of the Property Tax Revisited," National Tax Journal 26 (December 1973): 515-35; Henry Aaron, "A New View of Property Tax Incidence," American Economic Review 64 (May 1974): 212-21; and Charles E. McLure, Jr., "The Relevance of the New View of the Incidence of the Property Tax in Less Developed Countries," in The Taxation of Urban Property in Less Developed Countries, ed. Roy W. Bahl (Madison: University of Wisconsin Press, 1976), 51-76.

TABLE I-2: GENERIC CHARACTERISTICS OF THE PROPERTY TAX

Strengths

- Hard to avoid legally. Property is highly visible and relatively immobile, and thus, can neither be easily concealed nor moved in the short-run to another location to escape taxation.
- Economically efficient. Asset immobility minimizes interference in the allocation of resources.

- Potential money machine. Given the high income elasticity of property ownership characteristic of developed countries, the property tax can be a tremendous revenue generator.

- Relatively stable. The property tax is amenable to slight adjustments and incremental rate changes, thereby reducing tax tension and enhancing revenue predictability through residual financing.

- Powerful enforcement mechanism. Property can be seized and sold to satisfy delinquent taxes.

- Supports local autonomy. The property tax enhances responsiveness to local priorities, and helps in budgeting discipline by relating additional expenditures to their tax costs.

- Proxy for a local income tax. The close relationship between property values and long-term income levels for owner-occupied residences allows the property tax to substitute for a local tax on multiyear average earnings.

- Roughly correlated with benefits received. When used to finance local public goods, the property tax corresponds somewhat to consumption of these goods.

- Generally progressive. Given the distribution of land and capital ownership by income classes, incidence is predominantly progressive, except for the excise effects of interjurisdictional rate differentials, and cases where the owners of capital are not the consumers of the taxed service.

Weaknesses

- Large number of statutory taxpayers. While a broad tax base enhances equity and allocative efficiency, it also magnifies the political impact and popular resistance of even slight tax increases.

- High visibility. Active payment mechanisms (rather than withholding like a payroll income tax) and lumpy payments (instead of negligible increments like a sales tax) amplify awareness and intensify resentment of the property tax burden.

- Non-objective basis of assessment. Estimates of stock value or imputed rental value are commonly perceived as arbitrary and unsubstantiated, and poor administration often leads to glaring horizontal inequities.

- No direct relationship with ability to pay. An incongruity of wealth in real property and income can result in a taxpayer being asset rich and cash poor.

- The potential to exacerbate regional disparities in wealth. In countries where rates and expenditures are determined locally, rich jurisdictions tend to grow richer while poor jurisdictions become poorer.

- A perceived threat to the sanctity of private property. The very existence of a property tax is often seen as a menace to a family's principal lifetime capital investment, thus evoking hostile visceral reactions well beyond the magnitude of the tax itself.

Sources: Draws heavily on the author's field experience, as well as on: Jens P. Jensen, *Property Taxation in the United States* (Chicago: University of Chicago Press, 1931); Dick Netzer, *Economics of the Property Tax* (Washington, D.C.: The Brookings Institution, 1966); and William A. Doebele, "The Interaction of Land-Based Taxation and Land Policy: A Planning Perspective," in *International Conference on Property Taxation and Its Interaction with Land Policy: Plenary Session Papers* (Cambridge, Mass.: Lincoln Institute of Land Policy, September 1991), 101-12.

The property tax in developing countries has many unique characteristics, as it tends to: be uniform and nationally determined rather than comprise many local varieties, which minimizes economic distortion and simplifies administration, but reduces local autonomy; constitute a hybrid of rental, capital, and site value systems, making reform proposals based on traditional classifications ill-advised; appear unimportant because it generates an insignificant share of total national tax revenue, but is in fact critical to local jurisdictions as it is commonly the major source of discretionary local government revenue; respond poorly to income growth because of weak administrative capacity and strong political pressures; entail multiple and often contradictory goals, such as simultaneously maximizing revenue generation while serving as a proxy for a formal property registration and titling system; and be built on a highly skewed tax base, in keeping with the acutely uneven distribution of property ownership characteristic of many developing countries (see Table I-3).[9]

Thus, the generic features of property taxation, together with adaptations to developing country environments, make it a potentially effective mechanism for generating local government discretionary revenue for the provision of local public goods, but a poor instrument for the attainment of larger allocative, social, financing, and pricing objectives.

Many of these public policy goals should certainly be pursued to correct for market distortions and failures, ameliorate social inequities, promote financially viable development activities, and encourage the prudent production and utilization of scarce resources. However, property tax rates historically have been much too low to elicit desired behavior, and political sensitivities, particularly in regard to the cash flow constraints of many middle-class property owners, appear to preclude ever raising these rates to a level where they might significantly alter major investment and consumption decisions. Furthermore, even if policymakers could increase property tax rates substantially, they would needlessly risk jeopardizing net tax revenue and inducing unintended economic distortions that could reduce welfare and inhibit growth significantly, while alternative policy instruments could probably achieve the same objectives in a more fair and efficient manner.[10]

---

[9]Based on the author's field experience, as well as on Bahl, The Taxation of Urban Property in Less Developed Countries.

[10]Several papers presented at the International Conference on Property Taxation and Its Interaction with Land Policy (Cambridge, Mass., September 22-28, 1991) dealt with the effects of property taxation on non-revenue policy objectives, from a broad spectrum of viewpoints: William A. Doebele, "The Interaction of Land-Based Taxation and Land Policy: A Planning Perspective"; Oliver Oldman, "The Interaction of Land-Based Taxation and Land Policy: A Tax Perspective"; Karl E. Case, "Taxes and Speculative Behavior in Land and Real Estate Markets"; Koichi Mera, "Land Tax Reform of 1991 in Japan: Expected Impacts and Evaluation"; Vincent Renard, "Affecting Land Prices through Taxation: Perspectives from the French Experience"; Pekka Virtanen, "Land-Related Taxes in Finland and Their Effects on Land Policy"; and Connie Hughes, "Tax Policy and Its Effect on Urban Land Uses."

TABLE I-3: CHARACTERISTICS OF THE PROPERTY TAX IN DEVELOPING COUNTRIES

***Uniform*:**	Usually a standardized national system with uniform national rates, administered by local government, in contrast to the more than 75,000 jurisdictions and property tax systems in the United States. This minimizes distortion and simplifies administration, but reduces local autonomy.
***Hybrid*:**	The classic trichotomy of property tax types (annual/rental value, capital value, site/land value) greatly oversimplifies actual system types, which are often hybrids. Moreover, many countries/cities are either switching from annual value systems to capital value systems, or resorting to the use of capital value assessment to a considerable extent. This complexity is sometimes overlooked when formulating reform programs.
Local Revenue:	Typically contributes a relatively insignificant portion of national tax revenue, but is commonly the major source of discretionary local government income. This often causes policymakers to misjudge the strategic importance of property taxation to local jurisdictions.
***Static*:**	Relatively inelastic revenue growth with respect to income, due mainly to administrative inability and political reluctance to maintain an assessment roll at current market values, and to collect taxes from those on the tax roll.
Mixed Goals:	Often adjusted in a piecemeal fashion to achieve allocative and equity goals, with unintended and contradictory results. Payment of property taxes is often used as a basis for tenure claims, given the poor functioning of formal property registration and titling systems.
***Skewed*:**	A very small percentage of properties, usually high-value urban buildings, traditionally provide the bulk of property tax income, in keeping with the uneven distribution of property ownership characteristic of many developing countries. Consequently, the majority of tax assessments cost more to collect than the revenue they generate.

Sources: Based on the author's field experience, as well as on Bahl, *The Taxation of Urban Property in Less Developed Countries.*

For example, the property tax has been a clumsy, inefficient tool to guide allocative decisions such as:

- construction of industrial plants in remote areas;
- siting of businesses in targeted secondary cities;
- promotion of special districts or strategic sectors;
- intensification of urban land use; and
- encouragement of private home ownership.

A location's comparative disadvantage depends less on the property tax than on infrastructure siting and quality, distance from suppliers, access to markets, availability and cost of factor inputs, and return on alternative investments, all of which have been major deterrents to industrial and commercial growth in relatively remote regions of developing countries. Likewise, an economic sector's lack of financial viability in terms of the high prices or inferior quality of its products has been the main obstacle to rehabilitating uncompetitive businesses. Property tax rates are seldom cited by investors as a major impediment to the potential success of such ventures.[11]

Higher tax rates on vacant urban land, despite their conceptual attraction, are of dubious efficacy in practice. Such a policy often entails a direct tradeoff between land use and revenue generation objectives. If the tax on undeveloped land is high enough to encourage landowners to put vacant land to more intensive use, revenue will often decline given the traditionally large tax rate differential between vacant and developed land. If the tax fails to alter behavior, revenue might increase but vacant land will remain underutilized. Moreover, a tax on vacant land is often unenforceable. Not only does it usually constitute an implicit challenge to the politically powerful owners of prime urban sites, but it is also prone to considerable abuse because the distinction between vacant and developed land often is blurred sufficiently to allow token *pro forma* development rather than substantial investment in land development.[12]

Preferential property tax rates for owner-occupied residential properties is a common practice to encourage private home ownership and to ease cash flow

---

[11]This is true throughout Asia, Africa, and Latin America, for example in eastern Indonesia, northeastern Thailand, northern Nigeria, western Kenya, northern Chile, and northeastern Brazil. A collection of theoretical papers and case studies regarding the effects of property taxation on economic development is assembled in: Arthur P. Becker, ed., Land and Building Taxes: Their Effect on Economic Development (Madison: University of Wisconsin Press, 1969).

[12]For example, see: W. A. Clark, The Impact of Property Taxation on Urban Spatial Development, Institute of Government and Public Affairs Report no. 187 (Los Angeles: University of California, 1974); and Frederick D. Stocker, "Property Taxation, Land Use, and Rationality in Urban Growth Policy," in Property Taxation, Land Use, and Public Policy, ed. Arthur D. Lynn, Jr. (Madison: University of Wisconsin Press, 1969), 187-94.

difficulties associated with the property tax. Although this practice is quite popular politically, the actual economic impact of property taxation as an incentive for home ownership tends to be much smaller than home financing options and income tax treatment of mortgage interest, and cash flow constraints might better be addressed by reducing the lumpiness of tax payments rather than adopting differential tax rates.[13] The property tax has also been ineffective in achieving social objectives such as:

- income redistribution;
- decrease in land speculation;
- reduction of environmental degradation; and
- the legitimatizing of land tenure.

The property tax is already somewhat progressive because of the distribution of land and building ownership by income classes. Efforts to build further progressivity into property tax rates have often been counterproductive: instead of promoting income redistribution and raising more revenue, they have encouraged taxpayers and tax officials to manipulate the property values and classifications of wealthy real estate owners to lower effective tax rates, and thus, reduce tax liabilities. This decreases rather than augments progressivity.[14]

Land speculation is usually fueled by the attractive return offered by rapidly increasing land prices, along with the availability of affordable financing to buy and trade real estate. The inefficacy of curbing land speculation through property tax policies is not restricted to developing country cities such as Bangkok and Jakarta; Tokyo and Vancouver provide two recent examples of the same phenomenon in developed countries.[15]

Environmental degradation, such as air and water pollution, deforestation, and erosion is best dealt with via regulatory and pricing mechanisms. For example, the proposal to set overall pollution limits and allow polluters to trade their pollution quotas within these limits is now attracting considerable attention in the United States.[16]

---

[13]For example, see: Netzer, Economics of the Property Tax, 67-85.

[14]See the case studies on Jamaica (Chapter Two) and the Philippines (Chapter Three) for vivid examples of this phenomenon.

[15]For example, see: "Japanese Finance," Economist, special survey, December 8, 1990; and the International Conference on Property Taxation and Its Interaction with Land Policy series referenced earlier.

[16]More traditional policies are examined in: Douglas N. Jones, "Property Taxation, Land Use, and Environmental Policy: The Alaska Case," in Property Taxation, Land Use, and Public Policy, ed. Lynn, 167-85; and Frederick D. Stocker, ed., The Role of Exactions in Controlling Pollution, Tax Policy Roundtable Property Tax Papers Series no. TPR-15 (Cambridge, Mass.: Lincoln Institute of Land Policy, 1987).

While attempts to use property taxation as a system of establishing land tenure rights are sometimes relatively successful in achieving this secondary objective, such efforts greatly compromise the cost-effectiveness of generating tax revenue. There tends to be an positive correlation between property value and certainty of tenure, resulting in the expenditure of scarce administrative resources on those properties least likely to produce significant tax receipts.[17]

Large-scale infrastructure financing is another inappropriate policy objective for property taxation. Despite the intense desire of lending agencies and borrowing countries to the contrary, property tax revenue cannot begin to recover a significant portion of capital investments in rural irrigation systems or in urban health, utility, and transport infrastructure. Land readjustment schemes, as well as betterment or exaction charges, have been much more successful in achieving the requisite levels for meeting capital cost recovery objectives.[18]

Finally, the property tax is a poor instrument for determining the price and quantity of publicly-financed private goods such as water, electricity, and telephone services.[19] Whether such facilities ultimately are provided publicly or privately, cost recovery and conservation objectives are more appropriately met via user charges set equal to the marginal cost of providing an additional unit of service than through property taxation. Properly determined user charges not only raise revenue more efficiently and equitably, but can also be a better means of encouraging efficient provision and usage of scarce resources.[20]

In short, there are more effective public policy instruments than property taxation for guiding allocative decisions, achieving social goals, recovering capital costs, and pricing private goods: targeted investments in infrastructure, selective but enforced zoning codes, personal and corporate taxes, interest rates, credit

---

[17]See the case studies of Jamaica (Chapter Two) and Indonesia (Chapter Five) for detailed descriptions of this practice.

[18]For example, see: William A. Doebele, ed., Land Readjustment: A Different Approach to Financing Urbanization (Lexington: Lexington Books, 1982); W.A. Doebele, O.F. Grimes, and J.F. Linn, "Participation of Beneficiaries in Financing Urban Services: Valorization Charges in Bogota, Colombia," Land Economics 55 (February 1979): 73-92; Jorge Macon and Jose Merino Manon, Financing Urban and Rural Development Through Betterment Levies: The Latin American Experience (New York: Praeger, 1977); and Roger S. Smith, "Financing Cities in Developing Countries," in International Monetary Fund Staff Papers, no. 21 (Washington, D.C.: IMF, July 1974), 329-88.

[19]In contrast to private goods, public goods are best paid for out of general revenue because they are non-rival in consumption and their benefits are non-excludable and non-rejectable. Locally provided public goods are appropriately financed by property tax receipts because of the close relationship between property values and long-term income levels, as well as the rough correlation between property tax liabilities and benefits received from local public expenditures.

[20]For example, see: Richard E. Wagner, ed., Charging for Government: User Charges and Earmarked Taxes in Principle and Practice (New York: Routledge, 1991); and World Bank, Lessons of Tax Reform (Washington, D.C.: World Bank, 1991), 20.

availability, technical assistance for product development, environmental regulation and pricing mechanisms, simplified property registration and titling procedures, land readjustment, special assessments, linkage fees, and user charges.[21]

Principles of Property Tax Reform

The second element of this conceptual framework is that *the principles of efficient, equitable, and sustainable local revenue generation can best be attained by maximizing coverage, simplicity, and buoyancy.*

The evidence for this contention is based on logic and observation. *Administrative and allocative efficiency* is important to maintain a reasonable relationship between revenue generated and the financial and economic cost of raising these funds. While it is common to increase gross tax receipts when substantial resources are allocated to the task, it is much more difficult to increase net tax revenue, both in strictly financial terms and after accounting for losses due to resultant economic distortions.[22] In short, it costs more to tax most properties in developing countries than the net revenue they generate.[23]

As Adam Smith wrote more than two hundred years ago:

> *Every tax ought to be so contrived as both to take out and to keep out of the pockets of the people as little as possible, over and above what it brings into the public treasury of the state. A tax may either take out or keep out of the pockets of the people a great deal more than it brings into*

---

[21]Several of these policy tools are explored at length in: Harold B. Dunkerly, ed., Urban Land Policy: Issues and Opportunities_(New York: Oxford University Press for the World Bank, 1983); and Richard A. Musgrave and Peggy B. Musgrave,_Public Finance in Theory and Practice, 5th ed. (New York: McGraw-Hill Book Company, 1989).

[22]"Economic efficiency costs," sometimes called "excess burden" or "deadweight loss," refers to tax-induced distortions to the economy which reduce the real income of taxpayers by more than the amount of revenue that is transferred to the government. These costs occur when firms and households make decisions that are not socially efficient because they are based more on their tax implications than on their inherent economic virtues, such as modifying behavior in an attempt to reduce tax burdens or spending resources to evade taxes. For a more detailed explanation, see: World Bank, Lessons of Tax Reform, 21-22.

[23]Since this is certainly true in financial terms, consideration of economic efficiency costs simply increases the magnitude of the loss. While reliable estimates of the allocative costs of taxation in developing countries are not available, a recent study for the United States concluded that in the early 1980s, a one percent increase in all existing tax rates would have led to incremental efficiency costs ranging from 17 to 56 cents for each extra dollar of revenue raised. See: Charles L. Ballard, John B. Shoven, and John Whalley, "General Equilibrium Computations of the Marginal Welfare Costs of Taxes in the United States," American Economic Review 75 (March 1985): 128-38.

> *the public treasury, in the four following ways. First, the levying of it may require a great number of officers, whose salaries may eat up the greater part of the produce of the tax, and whose perquisites may impose another additional tax upon the people. Secondly, it may obstruct the industry of the people . . . Thirdly, by the forfeitures and other penalties which those unfortunate individuals incur who attempt unsuccessfully to evade the tax, it may frequently ruin them . . . Fourthly, by subjecting the people to the frequent visits and the odious examination of the tax-gatherers, it may expose them to much unnecessary trouble, vexation, and oppression. . . .*[24]

Horizontal and vertical equity is critical if the political economy of property tax reform is to be addressed. The political fallout of a system of property taxation which is perceived to be unfair greatly exceeds the economic dividends of such a system. It is difficult to instill a moral imperative of voluntary compliance for the public good when, to paraphrase George Orwell, some taxpayers are more equal than others.[25]

The ability-to-pay principle, or economic capacity, is used most often to evaluate the fairness of a property tax. According to this principle, the burden of the property tax is tied to the value of a taxpayer's real property.

Expressed in terms of horizontal and vertical equity, similar properties should have similar tax liabilities assessed and paid, while relative differences in property value should be reflected in comparable relative differences in property tax assessments and payments.[26]

---

[24]Adam Smith, An Inquiry Into the Nature and Causes of the Wealth of Nations, 2nd. ed. (London: W. Strahan and T. Cadell, 1778), 778-79.

[25]In George Orwell's Animal Farm, "All animals are equal, but some animals are more equal than others."

[26]This definition of vertical equity is quite different from the traditional notion of income-based progressivity, whereby the greater one's income, the greater one's proportionate tax burden. The definition of vertical equity used throughout this study is based on empirical observation of the most successful property tax systems in developed and developing countries, although there is no obvious explanation why taxpayers seem to demand progressive income taxes but resist progressive property taxes. The fundamental principle of "richer" citizens paying more taxes than their "poorer" compatriots is still applied, but the tax base is defined in terms of real estate value by plot rather than income by person, and fair tax burdens are perceived to be uniform levies on fixed stocks of unaggregated wealth rather than differential levies on total income flows.

Equity also entails the clear, consistent, and unsubjective application of widely understood and accepted policies and procedures:

> To be fair, taxes should be imposed according to general and objective rules that are recognized as reasonable and just. The amount of taxes to be paid should be certain and should not be set by negotiation or arbitrary exaction.[27]

The principle of certainty to ensure equity in taxation and the consequences of uncertainty are put rather more colorfully by Adam Smith:

> *The tax which each individual is bound to pay ought to be certain, and not arbitrary. The time of payment, the manner of payment, the quantity to be paid, ought all to be clear and plain to the contributor, and to every other person. Where it is otherwise, every person subject to the tax is put more or less in the power of the tax-gatherer, who can either aggravate the tax upon any obnoxious contributor, or extort, by the terror of such aggravation, some present or perquisite to himself. The uncertainty of taxation encourages the insolence and favours the corruption of an order of men who are naturally unpopular, even where they are neither insolent nor corrupt. . . .*[29]

System sustainability is necessary because of the recurrent nature of local public expenditures traditionally financed by property tax revenue: local government requires a stable source of revenue to develop and maintain a desired level of local services and facilities. To be sustainable, a system of property taxation must balance dynamism and flexibility with stability and consistency, so that it is both adaptable to changed circumstances and predictable in its application. The most critical element of sustainability is a well-functioning management information system to minimize the gap between policy and practice.

Wide *coverage* is essential if property taxation is to be efficient, equitable, and sustainable.[30] Coverage is important because the most grievous inequities and

---

[27]Richard Goode, Government Finance in Developing Countries (Washington, D.C.: The Brookings Institution, 1984), 77.

28Richard Goode, Government Finance in Developing Countries (Washington, D.C.: The Brookings Institution, 1984), 77.

[29]Smith, The Wealth of Nations, 778.

[30]Wide coverage clearly supports equity by broadening the tax net. Moreover, although counterintuitive, an explicit goal of wide coverage can also increase efficiency by obviating complex and expensive administrative procedures in order to include more property with the same resources.

greatest foregone revenue have been due to narrow tax bases, either as formally defined (statutory) or actually administered (effective). Tax rolls generally comprise a small portion of taxable property, and thus, when revenue needs rise, in the absence of expanded tax rolls, a self-defeating cycle of higher assessments, decreased compliance, smaller effective tax base, lower revenue, and again increased assessments is generated. However, even comprehensive and accurate tax rolls will not produce a broad tax base in practice without an effective collection system.

The statutory property tax base is often so narrowly defined that it prevents the property tax from becoming a significant revenue source. This is done in a number of ways: numerous special property categories or locations either are exempted entirely or not taxed when below a minimum value; low assessment ratios drive a significant wedge between nominal and effective tax rates; and multiple assessment ratios and tax rates introduce the complexity and discretion that often encourages property misclassification in the field.

In addition, a narrow tax base increases the need for a relatively high tax rate. Not only is this economically inefficient because deadweight loss from land improvements rises at the square of the tax rate, but it is also socially inequitable because it increases the tax burden of those few citizens whose property is not excluded from the tax base.

Even where there is a broad statutory property tax base, poor administration often results in a much narrower effective base. Property tax rolls are notorious for their omissions and inaccuracies. Moreover, coverage and value are often inversely related.

These problems are compounded by map-based strategies for establishing and maintaining fiscal cadastres. Not only are such strategies expensive and time consuming, but they rely heavily on outside contractors, who have tremendous incentives to perpetuate their task indefinitely, while at the same time "overlook" parcels of particular sensitivity.

However, given the high concentration of wealth in relatively few urban areas, tax officials can identify most high-value property without maps. Concurrently, local communities can gather sufficient property-related data for mid- to low-value property to provide comprehensive, if rudimentary coverage without incurring the tremendous cost and considerable time lag entailed in most mapping projects.

Emphasis should be given to plugging gaping holes in coverage before embarking on fine tuning of minor inaccuracies; given low effective tax rates, the most grievous property tax inequities arise from omissions or intentional misrepresentation, not good faith estimates.

A comparable effort should be made to improve collections, if coverage is not to be eroded at the final stage of property tax administration. Good collection performance depends on the reliable delivery of tax bills, the timely payment and efficient processing of tax liabilities, and the routine imposition of sanctions if a taxpayer fails to comply voluntarily.

Simplicity in both design and execution accommodates institutional and resource constraints, and hinders subjective, arbitrary, and corrupt tax administration.

Simplicity in property tax design entails broad-based taxation at uniform rates across properties. Although this is in stark contrast to the dictates of optimal taxation theory, both optimal and uniform taxation nonetheless strive to enhance economic efficiency - they only differ in the prescription for accomplishing this objective.[31]

"Optimal taxation" attempts to minimize excess burden with differential tax rates based on income-derived social welfare functions and correlative anticipated responses of taxpayers to tax-induced relative price changes - the stress is on progressive tax rates and vertical equity.

In contrast, "uniform taxation" rejects optimal taxation both as speculative theory, and as an approach whose product is too complex to implement even if based on sound analysis:

> . . . it neglects entirely the tax administration component of tax reform by assuming perfect tax administration, analogous to the physicist's simplifying assumptions of a frictionless world."[32]

Thus, uniform taxation seeks to limit the efficiency costs of taxation by recommending simple structures of broad-based taxes that allow the use of lower *effective* marginal rates, thereby reducing the level of tax-induced distortions.[33]

---

[31]For a detailed critique of the theory of optimal taxation, see: Joel Slemrod, "Optimal Taxation and Optimal Tax Systems," Journal of Economic Perspectives 4 (Winter 1990), 157-78.

[32]Wayne Thirsk, Lessons from Tax Reform: An Overview, Policy, Research, and External Affairs Working Paper Series 576 (Washington, D.C.: World Bank, January 1991), 4.

[33]Kindly note the emphasis on effective rather than nominal marginal rates. High nominal tax rates are sometimes combined with low assessment ratios to increase the political acceptability of property taxes. The effective tax rate thereby remains low, fostering economic efficiency, while taxpayers tend to focus on the "underassessed" value of their property, simultaneously appealing and difficult to appeal. This tactic is based on the following relationships:

$MV * r$	$= AV$	when	MV	=	Market Value
$AV * t_n$	$= T$		AV	=	Assessed Value
$r * t_n$	$= t_e$		r	=	Assessment Ratio
T □ MV	$= t_e$		T	=	Tax
			t_n	=	Nominal Tax Rate
			t_e	=	Effective Tax Rate

Uniform taxation also exploits the high degree of complementarity between the allocative efficiency gains of economic neutrality, the social benefits of horizontal equity, and the administrative advantages of design simplicity:

> If tax bases are broader and tax rates are lower and more uniform, there is a greater likelihood that households in the same economic circumstances prior to the application of taxes will continue to resemble each other after taxes have been applied. Lower tax rates reduce the rewards for rent seeking, evasion and tax incentive relief, thereby improving the odds that equals are treated equally. Moreover, if differential tax treatment is ruled out and various distinctions among taxpayers and different sources of income are swept aside, it is possible to simplify and streamline the operation of the tax system.[35]

Simplicity in property tax administration enhances both the cost-effectiveness and fairness of tax policy implementation. Simple property tax procedures are quickly understood by tax officials and taxpayers, so they are relatively easy and inexpensive to administer - abuses are also transparent to both parties. Moreover, streamlined operations allow greater coverage with limited resources, and encourage voluntary taxpayer compliance by improving service.

Tax *buoyancy*, or increased property tax revenue in response to rising real estate values as well as discretionary changes in tax policies, is critical to maintain and enhance the real value of property tax revenue over time. The rapid increase in land values and high inflation rates typical of many developing countries quickly and drastically erode the value of property tax receipts unless simple indexing and revaluation techniques are applied. Considerable efforts are often devoted to parcel-by-parcel updating of property-related data, an expensive, time-consuming, and low-return activity, but scant attention is given to simply maintaining the value of roughly accurate data - this is relatively easy to do while offering immediate and

---

[34]Kindly note the emphasis on effective rather than nominal marginal rates. High nominal tax rates are sometimes combined with low assessment ratios to increase the political acceptability of property taxes. The effective tax rate thereby remains low, fostering economic efficiency, while taxpayers tend to focus on the "underassessed" value of their property, simultaneously appealing and difficult to appeal. This tactic is based on the following relationships:

$MV * r = AV$	when	MV	=	Market Value
$AV * t_n = T$		AV	=	Assessed Value
$r * t_n = t_e$		r	=	Assessment Ratio
T □ MV = t_e		T	=	Tax
		t_n	=	Nominal Tax Rate
		t_e	=	Effective Tax Rate

[35]Thirsk, Lessons from Tax Reform, 6.

substantial returns. Again, the motto should be approximately right rather than precisely wrong.

There are inevitable tradeoffs between many of these reform principles. While marginal cost-benefit analysis might indicate that it is administratively most efficient to concentrate efforts on large taxpayers, a broad tax base encompassing low value properties is nonetheless often necessary to accommodate popular perceptions of fairness. Simplicity might reduce costs, errors, and abuses, but might also reduce precision, entailing tradeoffs between administrative efficiency, general equity, and individual circumstances. Tying property values to the consumer price index might enhance overall tax buoyancy, but failure to capture relative price changes might decrease horizontal and vertical equity. The appropriate balance between sometimes conflicting principles is neither absolute nor static. Rather, it depends on the specific political, social, economic, and institutional context.

Process of Property Tax Reform

The third element of this conceptual framework is that *changes in tax policies, administrative systems, and human behavior are best facilitated through utilization of incentives, dissemination of public information, an integrated perspective, and selective implementation.*

The judicious use of *incentives* is critical to the process of fostering change. People and organizations must be rewarded for constructive contributions to reform and punished for efforts to obstruct reform. Positive and negative personal and institutional incentives are the key to inducing desired behavior and discouraging unwanted conduct.[36]

Improved service is the most effective encouragement for taxpayers to cooperate with tax reform measures. It should cost taxpayers less time, effort, and money to comply with reporting requirements and to follow payment procedures than before reform. Taxpayers should also be discouraged from noncompliance by a

---

[36]There is a considerable body of literature on taxpayer compliance, from a wide variety of perspectives: maximization of expected utility; bounded rationality; game theory; social sanctions; social networks; and guilt neutralization. The most comprehensive review of research to date on taxpayer compliance is: Jeffrey A. Roth, John T. Scholz, and Ann Dryden Witte, eds., Taxpayer Compliance, 2 vols. (Philadelphia: University of Pennsylvania Press, 1986).

37There is a considerable body of literature on taxpayer compliance, from a wide variety of perspectives: maximization of expected utility; bounded rationality; game theory; social sanctions; social networks; and guilt neutralization. The most comprehensive review of research to date on taxpayer compliance is: Jeffrey A. Roth, John T. Scholz, and Ann Dryden Witte, eds., Taxpayer Compliance, 2 vols. (Philadelphia: University of Pennsylvania Press, 1986).

credible threat that meaningful sanctions will be applied if they do not fulfill their duties on time.

Tax officials also need appropriate positive and negative incentives to perform their jobs as reformers desire. These officials must be provided at least partial compensation for personal income lost due to cleaner administration, and success in attaining key reform objectives should be the principal criterion for subsequent assignments and promotions. Likewise, violations of civil service codes and poor job performance should be penalized. A meritocracy should be developed whereby an institution and its officers are monitored and evaluated based on clearly articulated organizational objectives: the efficient, equitable, and sustainable generation of tax revenue.

Similar principles should be followed regarding government officials outside of the tax department, especially those in charge of administering local government. Not only must local government officials, whether elected or appointed, be fairly compensated for the burden of property tax administration, but they must be able to show their constituents the community benefits of expenditures made with property tax receipts. As with tax officials, graft and corruption must also be punished.

Public information is an important tool in preventing misperceptions of reform objectives, procedures, and results. Equity is in the eye of the beholder. Although government policymakers might believe they are instituting a politically fair and socially just property tax, poor communications with local government officials, tax officers, and taxpayers could result in staff resentment of misunderstood policies, as well as popular perceptions of subjective, arbitrary, and inequitable taxation. Such negative perspectives often heighten administrative sabotage and taxpayer noncompliance.

Senior executive and legislative officials, civil servants, and the general public must understand the nature and purpose of initiatives to reform property taxation. In addition, taxpayers must understand their rights and obligations, including their recourse to appeal and penalties for noncompliance. Campaigns utilizing print and electronic media, as well as personal appearances of influential political figures, are essential in enabling reform implementors and participants to make informed decisions regarding new tax policies and practices.

An *integrated perspective* is important because tax policy and field implementation are inseparable, and property tax administration is a complex chain of interdependent subsystems that is only as strong as its weakest link.

Reforms must focus on both policy and operational issues. Increasing the statutory level and the effective level of the property tax is complementary, and addressing one constraint while ignoring the other is counterproductive. Policy reform is often essential in realizing the full revenue potential of property taxes, but is promulgated under the assumption administrative capacity and political will are sufficient to ensure faithful implementation of the law - if not, revenue enhancing legislation only exacerbates current inequities. Likewise, improved implementation of weak property tax legislation might not generate enough revenue to justify tax administration costs.[38]

Most reform efforts that have a large implementation component have focussed on increasing the quality and quantity of property-related data, but neglect of collections and enforcement has produced impressive tax rolls that generate negligible new revenue. Conversely, if data base and valuation procedures are not eventually improved, tax reform will be confined to efficient collection of trivial amounts of money. It is necessary to focus on complete tax systems, from general tax policy to tax administration in the field, and on all stages of implementation.

Selective implementation, through the phased introduction of changes and the upgrading of existing systems, focusses application of scarce resources; provides tax officials and taxpayers with time to adapt their behavior to changed circumstances; and offers an opportunity to refine reforms via accommodation of unanticipated conditions and responses.

Phased tax reform through the gradual replication of pilot projects reduces the risk and increases the compatibility of reform efforts in economically, politically, socially, ethnically, and physically diverse environments.

Upgrading existing property tax systems reduces reform cost, risk, and lead-time. Fundamental system transformation entails considerable psychological barriers for the tax collector and the taxpayer, as we are all creatures of habit.

Consequently, requisite lead-time is longer, administrative conversion costs are greater, and windfall gains and losses resulting from responses to changed expectations are increased when reformers attempt to supplant a flawed tax system with a completely new system.

Except where there are few private property rights, almost every country has some form of tax on immovable property with elements upon which an improved system can be built, and no one property tax system has been proven inherently superior to another. Rental value, capital value, and site value systems, as well as hybrid variations, have exceeded expectations and been unmitigated disasters: success has been dependent on soundness of design and execution, rather than an intrinsic technical strengths or weaknesses.[39]

---

[38]Glenn P. Jenkins notes the following in "Tax Reform: Lessons Learned," in Reforming Economic Systems in Developing Countries, eds. Dwight H. Perkins and Michael Roemer (Cambridge, Mass.: Harvard Institute for International Development, 1991), 305: "While we have learned a great deal about how to design a modern tax structure, our knowledge of how to reform tax administrations is, at best, in its infancy. In the 1960s and 1970s the motto of many tax reform efforts could be summarized as 'Dead upon Publication.' At the current time, I am afraid that in a number of cases the motto is being changed to 'Death through Administration.'"

[39]An excellent review of the relative merits and weaknesses of each system can be found in Alan R. Prest, "Land Taxation and Urban Finances in Less-Developed Countries," in World Congress on Land Policy, 1980, ed. Matthew Cullen and Sharon Woolery (Lexington: Lexington Books, 1982), 369-406.

Thus, in most cases, reformers should heed the wisdom of Plautus (*Trinummus I.ii.*): "Keep what you have; the known evil is best." The primary objective of property tax reform should be similar, regardless of one's point of departure: to ensure adequate long-term revenue generation for local government in an efficient, equitable, and sustainable manner.

METHODOLOGY AND PRESENTATION

Overview

This is the kind of conceptual framework that is impossible to prove conclusively. Rather, the intention is to make the most compelling argument possible to persuade the reader as to its validity. *A model for property tax reform in developing countries is derived from a theoretical distillation of empirical experience.*

The model is constructed in four steps:

- First, the reader is propositioned - the model is formulated as a series of hypotheses based on a synthesis of general literature and observations.
- Second, this model is applied in a positioned reading of case studies of property tax reform.
- Third, points of congruence and dysjunction between the model and the cases are identified, to determine either model weaknesses or instances where the cases exceed the model's scope.
- Fourth, the model is reformulated in light of these case studies.[40]

Although elements of several modes of inquiry are employed, this study is *not* exclusively: a program review of current reform efforts in any one country; a

[40]For detailed discussions of alternative approaches to comparative methodologies, see: Adam Przeworski and Henry Teune, The Logic of Comparative Social Inquiry, reprint (Malabar: Robert E. Krieger Publishing Company, Inc., 1982); Charles C. Ragin, The Comparative Method: Moving Beyond Qualitative and Quantitative Strategies (Berkeley: University of California Press, 1987); and Arthur L. Stinchcombe, Constructing Social Theories (Chicago: University of Chicago Press, 1986).

[41]For detailed discussions of alternative approaches to comparative methodologies, see: Adam Przeworski and Henry Teune, The Logic of Comparative Social Inquiry, reprint (Malabar: Robert E. Krieger Publishing Company, Inc., 1982); Charles C. Ragin, The Comparative Method: Moving Beyond Qualitative and Quantitative Strategies (Berkeley: University of California Press, 1987); and Arthur L. Stinchcombe, Constructing Social Theories (Chicago: University of Chicago Press, 1986).

narrative description and historical recounting of the nature and evolution of property taxation; a theoretical exploration of models for optimal taxation; or an investigation of alternative means of financing local government.

The primary objective of this study is to establish, through logic, theory, and observation: what constitutes a good property tax system, for whom, under what conditions; why such a system works; and how inferior systems can be upgraded to approximate well-functioning systems.

Case Studies

The author visited each of the case countries between May and September 1991, to obtain:

- further documentation on reform efforts, including an enhanced understanding of reform dynamics; and
- updated information on the current status of property taxation.

Interviews were conducted both in the capital city and upcountry with tax officials, local government officials, and taxpayers. In addition, published documentation was reviewed and supplementary data were collected.

Jamaica, the Philippines, Chile, and Indonesia constitute a geographic, demographic, economic, and political cross-section of developing countries (see Table I-4).[42]

In terms of geographic distribution, Asia (the Philippines and Indonesia), Latin America (Chile), and the Caribbean (Jamaica) are all included; Africa and the Middle East are the only major developing country geographic regions not represented.[44] Total area ranges from an 11,000 square kilometer island (Jamaica) to a 1.9 million square kilometer archipelago (Indonesia), and comprises a wide variety of ecologies, ranging from the Chilean mountains and deserts to the Philippine and Indonesian terraced rice paddies and tropical rain forests.

---

[42]Statistics for this section are compiled from: World Bank, World Development Report 1991: The Challenge of Development (New York: Oxford University Press, June 1991), 193-290.

43Statistics for this section are compiled from: World Bank, World Development Report 1991: The Challenge of Development (New York: Oxford University Press, June 1991), 193-290.

[44]This is due primarily to lack of any documented attempts at sustained, nation-wide property tax reform in African and Middle Eastern countries.

TABLE I-4: COMPARATIVE PROFILE OF CASE STUDY COUNTRIES

Statistic	Jamaica	Philippines	Chile	Indonesia
1. Total Area (000s km^2)	11	300	757	1,905
2. 1989 Population				
a. Total (millions)	2.4	60	13.0	178.2
b. Urban (%)	52	42	85	30
c. <15 Years Old (%)	34	40	31	37
3. GNP Per Capita				
a. 1989 (US$)	1,260	710	1,770	500
b. 1965-89 Average Annual Growth (%)	-1.3	1.6	0.3	4.4
4. Ave. Annual Inflation Rate				
a. 1965-80 (%)	12.8	11.7	129.9	35.5
b. 1980-89 (%)	18.5	14.8	20.5	8.3
5. 1989 Development Assistance				
a. Total (US$ millions)	258	831	61	1,830
b. Per Capita/US$	8.3	13.8	4.7	10.3
c. Share of GNP/%	6.6	1.9	.2	1.9
6. 1989 External Debt				
a. Total (US$ billions)	4.3	28.9	18.2	53.1
b. Relation to GNP (%)	133.8	65.3	78.3	59.4
c. Service:Exports/%	26.4	26.3	27.5	35.2
7. Political System During Reform	Democracy	Martial Law; Democracy	Martial Law; Democracy	"Guided Democracy"

Source: World Bank, *World Development Report 1991: The Challenge of Development* (New York: Oxford University Press, June 1991), 193-290.

Demographically, total population ranges from 2.4 million (Jamaica) to 178 million (Indonesia), and from 70 percent rural (Indonesia) to 85 percent urban (Chile). These populations are characterized by racial, ethnic, and religious diversity; in addition, more than 30 percent of the population is less than 15 years old in all four countries.

Economically, Indonesia is classified as "low-income," while the other three countries are classified as "lower-middle-income."[45] Indonesia is also a member of the Organization of Petroleum Exporting Countries (OPEC). The 1989 gross national product (GNP) per capita ranges from $500 (Indonesia) to $1,770 (Chile), and the GNP per capita average annual growth rate from 1965 to 1989 varies from -1.3 percent (Jamaica) to 4.4 percent (Indonesia). The average annual inflation rate from 1965 to 1980 varies from 11.7 percent (Philippines) to 129.9 percent (Chile); comparable figures for 1980 to 1989 range from 8.3 percent (Indonesia) to 20.5 percent (Chile).

Dependence on development assistance varies considerably among the four case study countries. In 1989, Chile received only $61 million, while Indonesia received $1.8 billion. The variations are also quite large relative to the size of each country's population and economy: Chile received a low of $4.7 per capita while Jamaica received a high of $108.3 per capita; development assistance constituted only 0.2 percent of Chile's GNP but 6.6 percent of Jamaica's GNP.

These differences are reflected in the external debt burdens of the four case study countries. In 1989, external debts ranged from $4.3 billion (Jamaica) to $53.1 billion (Indonesia), and from 59.4 percent of GNP (Indonesia) to 133.8 percent of GNP (Jamaica). However, the 1989 ratio of external debt service to exports was in the mid-twenties for all but Indonesia, whose ratio was 35.2 percent. Finally, in terms of national political system during the period of property tax reform, regimes ranged from Jamaica's continuous parliamentary democracy after independence was achieved, to an executive-dominated "guided democracy" in Indonesia, to swings between democracy and martial law in the Philippines and Chile.

In sum, the case study countries are similar in that they are all classified as either low-income or lower-middle-income developing nations by virtue of their current economic status. Otherwise, they are more different than they are alike, whether it be in terms of: geographic location and area; natural and human ecology; population size and distribution; economic performance; reliance on development assistance; or national political system.

These differences highlight the importance of examining each property tax reform effort within the context of its specific geographic, ecologic, social,

[45]These classifications are used in: World Bank, World Development Report 1991, 193-290. The World Bank's main criterion to classify economies is gross national product per capita: "low-income economies" had per capita incomes of $580 or less in 1989; "lower-middle-income economies" had per capita incomes of more than $580 but less than $2,355 in 1989.

demographic, economic, and political environment. A proposal that might suit an island republic like Jamaica could be unmanageable in a country as large and diverse as Indonesia; a solution that might work in a place with a population as urbanized as Chile might be inappropriate for the predominantly rural Philippines.

However, these contrasts do not obviate the need to identify common elements of property tax reform despite national differences: all successful attempts to induce behavioral change have a similar need to provide appropriate incentives, in both design and execution, that elicit desired responses.

The case studies will facilitate an investigation into the behavior and motivations of developing country taxpayers and tax officials in response to property tax reform activities, as their diversity transcends environmental differences: each country's reform effort differs from the others in terms of reform objectives, reform principles and processes, or both (see Figure I-2).

Indonesia's experience to date is the closest to an appropriate model for property tax reform in developing countries. The explicit desire of Indonesian reformers to improve property taxation as a way of enhancing the generation of local government revenue is an appropriate objective for property tax reform, and most of the time, these reformers have adhered to the reform principles and processes described in the conceptual framework presented earlier.

Reform efforts in the Philippines represent an appropriate reform objective inappropriately pursued, while reform activities in Chile indicate the opposite - the noble pursuit of an unattainable objective. Philippine reformers have been trying to generate local government revenue in a manner which is unintentionally inefficient, inequitable, and unsustainable. In contrast, Chilean reformers risk undermining a well-functioning property tax system in their attempts to perfect it.

Jamaica's reform experience represents the unfortunate fourth cell in this property tax reform matrix. Revenue generation has not been a primary objective of Jamaican policymakers, and the design and implementation of the property tax have been complex, costly, and unfair.

PRESENTATION

The study is developed in three stages. First, a conceptual framework is presented in Chapter One for the formulation, implementation, and evaluation of property tax reform in developing countries. This framework draws on multidisciplinary theoretical literature, third-party empirical documentation, and the author's field experience.

Second, attempts to reform property taxation in four developing countries are examined in detail. The case studies are presented in Chapters Two through Five. Each case study focuses on three key issues: the formal structure and operations of a country's property tax system; attempts to change the system's design or execution; and the results of these reform efforts.

Presentations of the property tax systems are brief and primarily descriptive, while accounts of reform activities are essentially chronological and highlight key actors' roles and motivations. All four case studies are projected through the lens of the conceptual framework presented in Chapter One, and are assembled in parallel construction. This ensures a sharp and common focus by concentrating on the same underlying themes and investigative priorities, as well as enhances a subsequent cross-country evaluation by using comparable terminology and standards.

Finally, in Chapter Six, the results of the reform efforts described in the four case studies are evaluated and guidelines for reform are offered. Reform results are assessed both in light of their stated objectives, and the extent to which they enhanced the efficient, equitable, and sustainable generation of local government revenue. Key success variables examined comprise: the degree to which property tax reform activities increased coverage, emphasized simple policies and procedures, and enhanced buoyancy; and the extent to which the reform process utilized incentives, promoted public understanding, stressed an integrated perspective, and pursued implementation activities selectively. The study concludes with specific recommendations for reforming property tax systems in developing countries, based on the conceptual framework and synthesizing lessons of the case studies. Let us now explore efforts to improve Let us now explore efforts to improve property taxation in Jamaica, the Philippines, Chile, and Indonesia, keeping in mind Thomas Fuller's rumination in *Gnomologia*: "It is easier to bear what's amiss than go about to reform it."

FIGURE I-2:

TYPOLOGY OF PROPERTY TAX REFORM CASE STUDIES

	PRIMARY REFORM OBJECTIVE: GENERATE LOCAL GOVERNMENT DISCRETIONARY RESOURCES	PRIMARY REFORM OBJECTIVE: OTHER THAN LOCAL GOVERNMENT REVENUE GENERATION
REFORM PRINCIPLES AND PROCESSES SAME AS CONCEPTUAL FRAMEWORK	INDONESIA	CHILE
REFORM PRINCIPLES AND PROCESSES DIFFERENT FROM CONCEPTUAL FRAMEWORK	PHILIPPINES	JAMAICA

Source: Author's formulation.

2

JAMAICA CASE STUDY

What is't to us if taxes rise or fall?
Thanks to our fortune, we pay none at all.

Charles Churchill,
Night, 1762

THE JAMAICAN PROPERTY TAX IN PERSPECTIVE: CASE STUDY SNAPSHOT

Since 1956, government officials have tried to improve property tax policies and practices in Jamaica: reformers devoted eighteen years to switching from a system of taxation based on the capital value of real property to one based on the unimproved value of land, and they have spent the subsequent eighteen years trying to maintain and upgrade this new system of property taxation. Results have been mixed. Considerable progress has been made in compiling and automating a universal land valuation roll, despite limited resources and lack of a national legal cadastre upon which to build a fiscal cadastre. This valuation roll is indeed quickly dated, but the automatic, periodic application of an inflation index would keep property values relatively current.

However, a comprehensive register of property listings and their appraised values, even if indexed for inflation, does not a successful property taxation system make. Jamaican reformers have not been able to translate valuation achievements into significant tax revenue because:

- national policies which strive to use property taxation as an instrument to achieve a variety of political, economic and social objectives rather than attain and maintain revenue adequacy;

- an inefficient, inequitable, and unsustainable system of tax administration; and
- a reform process which has not provided effective incentives to induce desired behavior from taxpayers and tax officials.

The following study of the design, reform, and performance of property taxation in Jamaica will explore the nature, strengths, and weaknesses of property tax policies and practices over the past four decades.

THE JAMAICAN PROPERTY TAX IN LAW: SYSTEM DESIGN

Tax Base

All land in Jamaica is valued for the assessment of a national property tax on the land's unimproved value as defined in the Land Valuation Act.[1] Statutory relief is provided under the Land Taxation (Relief) Act for the following three types of property if the potential land use is higher than its existing use, presumably imposing a hardship on the landowner: bona fide agricultural land, private dwelling-houses, and approved organizations for approved purposes.[2] The Land Taxation (Relief) Act also provides for derating relief if land is used exclusively or principally for agriculture, a bona fide hotel enterprise, or for purposes of a hotel approved under the Hotel (Incentives) Act of 1968. Current derating allows a 75 percent reduction in the tax assessed for agricultural land and a 25 percent reduction in the tax assessed for hotel land.[3] Finally, the Land Taxation (Relief) Act allows the minister of finance to grant special discretionary tax relief. Such tax relief is most often granted for cases of genuine hardship where taxpayers such as pensioners, widows, and the elderly may find it burdensome or impossible to pay the property tax. Land used primarily for religious, social, cultural, educational, diplomatic, charitable, or benevolent purposes is usually exempt from property taxation.[4]

---

[1]The Land Valuation Act, Paragraphs 2 and 6(1).

[2]The Land Taxation (Relief) Act, Paragraph 5(1).

[3]The Land Taxation (Relief) Act, Third Schedule (Agricultural Land and Hotel Land) Derating Order, 1973.

[4]The Land Taxation (Relief) Act, Paragraph 5(4) and First Schedule.

Tax Rate

The property tax rate is progressive, and is applied uniformly throughout Jamaica. Residential, commercial, industrial, and agricultural property are all subject to the same tax schedule (see Table II-1).[5]

TABLE II-1: PROPERTY TAX RATES IN JAMAICA

Property Values (J$)		Rate (%)
>	*but* ≤	
0	6,000	$5 flat
6,000	10,000	1.00
10,000	16,000	1.50
16,000	25,000	1.75
25,000	50,000	2.00
50,000	100,000	2.25
100,000	-------	3.00

Source: Stair, *A Position Paper on The Property Taxation System*, 4.

Valuation

Under the Jamaican system, usually referred to as the site value system, valuations are based solely on the estimated market value of the land component of real property. Valuers attempt to ascertain the price of a land parcel in a competitive market[6] taking into account its size, location, quality, current use, and development potential. Improvements are excluded from the land's presumed value.[7]

[5]Elizabeth Stair, A Position Paper on The Property Taxation System (Kingston: Land Valuation Department, August 1990), 4.

[6]The price at which the land would be exchanged given a willing and bona fide seller and buyer.

[7]According to Paragraph 2 of The Land Valuation Act, improvements are "those physical additions and alterations thereto and all works for the benefit of the land made or done by the owner or any of his predecessors in title which . . . has the effect of increasing its value: Provided that -- (a) the destruction or removal of timber or vegetable growth; (b) the draining, filling, excavation or reclamation of the land; (c) the making of retaining walls or other similar works designed to arrest or prevent erosion or flooding of the land; or (d) the grading or levelling of the land, shall not be regarded as improvements. . . ."

Differential tax treatment is accorded land used for mining bauxite or laterite, so that in practice such land is valued as agricultural land if vacant and industrial land if there are structures on it.[8] The Land Valuation Act requires a comprehensive revaluation every five years, resulting in a new national valuation roll. However, the minister of finance has the power to alter the intervals between valuations, and the commissioner of land valuations has the authority to amend the valuation roll between valuations if: land is sub-divided;[9] a public work, service or undertaking is provided which changes land value; land is permanently damaged by natural disaster; a change of land rights or land use occurs which alters land value; or circumstances warrant revaluation to preserve or attain uniformity in values for comparable parcels of land.[10]

Collection

Upon completion of the valuation roll, the commissioner of land valuations transmits this new valuation roll to the commissioner of inland revenue, who in turn prepares a tax roll and issues individual tax assessment notices. Tax bills are delivered either by mail or field agents.[11] Property tax liabilities are due and payable on April 1 of each year to the revenue services center under whose jurisdiction the property falls.[12] Tax liabilities may be paid by registered mail (postage paid by the government) or in person. Payments may be made in single, quarterly or half-yearly installments.[13] Several housing finance institutions include property tax liabilities in monthly mortgage payments. All property tax receipts are paid into the national treasury as recurrent revenue for subsequent national

---

[8]According to Paragraph 7 of The Land Valuation Act, any increase in the capital value of land attributable to the presence of bauxite or laterite, "shall, for the purpose of determining the unimproved or the improved value of the land, be deemed to be limited to the value of any royalties payable to the owner of the land" and "the value of royalties payable to an owner of land in respect of bauxite or laterite shall . . . be deemed to be one-twentieth of the unimproved value of the land."

[9]According to Paragraph 11(4) of The Land Valuation Act, a variation of this is "where two or more parcels of unoccupied land adjoining each other are valued as one portion of land and one or more parcels of such land is or are sold or occupied . . ."

[10]The Land Valuation Act, Paragraph 4.

[11]The Property Tax Act, Paragraphs 3(2) and 3(3).

[12]The Property Tax Act, Paragraphs 3(1) and 4.

[13]According to Paragraph 5 of The Property Tax Act, "where the property tax due and payable in respect of any year does not exceed five dollars it shall be paid in full and no moieties or instalments [sic] shall be allowed in respect of such tax."

budgetary allocation.[14] If the property tax is not paid on time, the legal provisions for enforcement are both explicit and extensive.[15]

Tax liabilities are generally held to be valid for seven years (the current tax year plus six years of arrears) under the statute of limitations.

Administration[16]

Implementation of property taxation is shared by two departments in the ministry of finance: Land Valuation and Inland Revenue. The Land Valuation Department's primary responsibility is preparation and maintenance of a national valuation roll. It also provides valuation services to government ministries, departments, and statutory bodies for purposes ranging from land acquisition and disposal to determination of the value of a hotel extension for tax relief. The Inland Revenue Department is responsible for property tax billing and collection, including preparation of a national tax roll. It is also responsible for assessing and collecting several other domestic taxes, such as business related levies, motor vehicle fees, the hotel accommodation tax, and the retail sales tax. Both departments are supported by Fiscal Services (EDP) Ltd., a government-owned electronic data processing center comprising over 200 technical staff responsible for automating all revenue services. Fiscal Services is developing two computer systems to improve property tax administration: ELVIS (Enhanced Land Valuation Information System) for the Land Valuation Department and JAMTIS (Jamaica Tax Information System) for the Inland Revenue Department. ELVIS will be an on-line repository

---

[14]Formally, according to Paragraph 4 of The Property Tax Act, the property tax "shall be carried to the credit of the Consolidated Fund."

[15]The following points are based on discussions with Norma Dixon (Commissioner of Inland Revenue), as well as with staff at the Constant Spring Revenue Services Center in Kingston: 1) The taxpayer should first be reminded of the unpaid tax liability, either in person, by phone, or in writing. 2) If the tax remains unpaid, revenue field officers can then be issued levy writs, which empower them to serve demand notices (including a mandatory 10 percent penalty and an optional interest charge) for collection of tax liabilities or attachment of the property owner's personal property. 3) Legally, almost any asset on the taxpayer's premises may be levied to clear outstanding tax liabilities. 4) The government may also lodge a caveat, which would prevent a title transfer until the property tax is paid. 5) Unresolved disputes are taken to the Resident Magistrates Court. If the Court rules in the government's favor, individuals generally have 30 days to pay or face incarceration, while companies are served a warrant of distress. 6) According to The Property Tax Act, "until paid the said tax shall be a first charge and lien upon the real property liable thereto."

[16]The following discussion is based on interviews with Elizabeth Stair (Commissioner of Land Valuations), Norma Dixon (Commissioner of Inland Revenue), and Dennis Larman (Managing Director of Fiscal Services (EDP) Ltd.).

of land-related information for Land Valuation, while JAMTIS will assist Inland Revenue with its cashier, compliance, and tax information functions.

THE JAMAICAN PROPERTY TAX IN TRANSITION: SYSTEM REFORM

The Change Process: Policy

From 1956 to 1974, Jamaica switched from a system of taxation based on the capital value of real property to a system based on the unimproved value of land, commonly referred to as a "site value" or "land value" system of property taxation. Further, the system changed from one of self-declaration of property value ("ingivings") to land valuation by government officials.[17]

The principal objectives of this reform were to:

- use fiscal policy as a tool for agrarian reform by redistributing the relative tax burden from poor to wealthy landowners and discouraging the withholding of land from productive use in income- and job-generating activities; and
- create an updated and accurate valuation roll through external, professional assessments.

Initially, the Jamaican property tax reform was intended to be fiscally neutral.

The distribution of land in Jamaica has been highly skewed for as long as records have been kept, with a handful of families owning the bulk of Jamaica's prime land. The most recent figures available, from 1968, are indicative (see Figure II-1): 78 percent of all farms were less than five acres but accounted for only 15 percent of total farmland; 2 percent of all farms were 25 acres or more, but accounted for 63 percent of total farmland.[18]

---

[17]The site value system was introduced in Jamaica when The Land Valuation Act (Law 73 of 1956) took effect on January 18, 1957. A description of the pre-1956 evolution of the Jamaican property tax can be found in: O. St. Clare Risden, "A History of Jamaica's Experience with Land Taxation based on the Site Value System," paper prepared for the Conference of the Committee on Taxation, Resources and Economic Development held at the Lincoln Institute of Land Policy, Cambridge, Massachusetts, October 1976, 2-3.

[18]This inequitable distribution of land is even more dramatic than the above-cited figures might indicate, as roughly 53,000 of the 145,000 farms under five acres are actually less than one acre.

FIGURE II-1:
RURAL LAND DISTRIBUTION IN JAMAICA
IN 1968

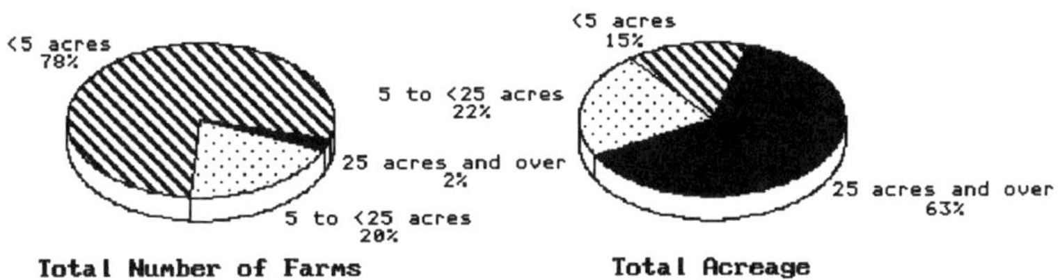

Source: Author's calculations.

Furthermore, there has traditionally been an inverse relationship between farm size and land quality: large-scale rural landowners are typically wealthy agribusinessmen, while small-scale rural landowners are mostly poor subsistence farmers. Prime Jamaican farmland is below 1,000 feet in elevation, usually located on the coastal plains, and is dominated by commercial plantations of export crops such as sugar and bananas; most of Jamaica's small-scale farmers tend small upland parcels with traditional technologies to provide food crops for home consumption.[19]

The Land Valuation Act was aggressively promoted and passed on the eve of Jamaica's independence by the majority party in Parliament, Norman Manley's People's National Party (PNP).[20] The PNP prided itself on advocacy for social justice, and viewed the site value tax as a way to promote a more equal distribution of land holdings and property tax burdens. It claimed that a site value system of taxation would increase equity in land distribution and correct anomalies on the property tax roll without increasing the total tax burden. This political stance was supported by several technical reports completed in the 1940s and 1950s that also recommended a switch from the capital to the site value taxation system.[21]

---

[19]Risden, "A History of Jamaica's Experience with Land Taxation based on the Site Value System," 4. The figures in the preceding paragraph are taken from the same source.

[20]Norman Manley was the father of Jamaica's present prime minister, Michael Manley.

[21]The most important of these reports were the Bloomberg (Royal) Commission of 1943, the (J.R. and Ursula) Hicks Report of 1954, and the (J.F.N.) Murray Report of 1956.

The Change Process: Administration and Behavior

After passage of The Land Valuation Act in 1956, the government created the Land Valuation Office in the Ministry of Agriculture and Lands (now the Land Valuation Department in the Ministry of Finance). The staff of 80 comprised a small nucleus of British-trained valuers headed by an Australian commissioner of valuations,[22] and a larger work force of locally-trained valuation technicians.

From 1956 to Jamaican independence in 1962, six predominantly rural parishes (St. Catherine, St. Ann, Portland, St. Mary, Trelawny, and St. Thomas) were brought under the site value system. Kingston and Montego Bay, Jamaica's two major metropolitan areas, were not included. The Land Valuation Office started with a primarily topographical 1:12,500 base map for all of Jamaica created from air photographs taken between 1949 and 1954.

The Office then conducted low-tech, low-cost field surveys in rural areas. Field staff, assisted by local "guides" (older men with a knowledge of local conditions and land ownership patterns) created "enclosure" sketches (keyed to 10,000 square meter grids and 1:12,500 map sheets) of relative parcel locations, approximate sizes, and ownership claims (loosely defined), relying on offsets, estimates, and natural boundaries.

Land Valuation has since updated its urban maps through incorporation of supplementary data, such as third-party surveys and subdivision plans deposited with government authorities.[23]

Both in keeping with the government's pledge for the tax reform to be revenue neutral and omission of Jamaica's prime urban property, the first six years of property tax reform in Jamaica resulted in no dramatic increase in tax revenue. Furthermore, there was "nothing to demonstrate by way of fundamental changes in the land tenure patterns which could be attributed to the introduction of the Site Value System."[24]

Early in 1962, the PNP lost to the Jamaica Labour Party (JLP). The JLP subsequently led Jamaica into independence in August 1962, and then governed for the following ten years. The JLP's constituency is primarily wealthy conservatives and the rural poor, so not surprisingly, the shift to site value taxation slowed down considerably. One additional parish (St. Elizabeth) was brought under the new system during the next decade, and fieldwork was completed for three more parishes (Manchester, Clarendon, and Westmoreland).

---

[22]The Land Valuation Act was also written with Australian technical assistance.

[23]A detailed account of how Jamaica's fiscal cadastre was created can be found in: Risden, "A History of Jamaica's Experience with Land Taxation based on the Site Value System," 7-8.

[24]Risden, "A History of Jamaica's Experience with Land Taxation based on the Site Value System," 9.

In 1972, the PNP was returned to power with an overwhelming majority. The country was in social turmoil: there was considerable dissatisfaction with the rapid rate of urbanization, unemployment had risen from 13 to 24 percent since independence, and disparities between the rich and poor were growing.[25]

Thus, the shift to a site value system of property taxation was resuscitated, with the same rationale that initiated this reform in 1956.

However, in addition to encouraging agrarian reform and creating an updated and accurate valuation roll, a supplementary government objective was rationalization and standardization of land-related taxes. The government therefore consolidated the property tax and local rates payments into a single unimproved land tax to be applied uniformly throughout Jamaica: land taxes were converted from a combination of a national capital value/site value tax on real property and a local charge for government services to a unified national wealth tax on the unimproved value of land.

The government felt that the rates paid to parish councils were more akin to nuisance taxes rather than payments to recover the cost of providing public services. They also believed that funds could be managed more efficiently and more equitably if tax payments were collected and distributed through the Consolidated Fund. The parish councils were regarded as too weak politically and administratively to raise and disburse government resources of any consequence, and Jamaica was considered too small to warrant a significant investment in developing the institutional capacity of the parish councils.

Policy makers were also concerned that regional disparities would be reinforced if local resource mobilization and expenditures were dependent on the local property tax base, and that such decentralization would hinder comprehensive strategic planning and equitable national development.

In addition, policy makers were skeptical that the property tax could be implemented in a fair and consistent manner with uniform national standards of valuation and assessment if administration was left to each parish council.[26]

Budgetary pressures and demands for social reform made the fiscal neutrality of this stage of reform rather ambiguous. Although Minister of Finance David Coore repeatedly try to offset increased revenue from the site value tax by reducing income tax liabilities, he also decried the small amount of revenue generated by the property tax, as in his April 1973 budget presentation: ". . . [the]

[25]Risden, "A History of Jamaica's Experience with Land Taxation based on the Site Value System," 11.

[26]These arguments for converting local rates to a national property tax were made repeatedly in recent discussions with former Minister of Finance David Coore and current Chairman of the Revenue Board Canute Miller.

total of $6 million paid by way of tax on all the land in Jamaica represents less than the amount collected by way of excise duty on one item of popular consumption."[27]

Furthermore, Prime Minister Michael Manley, in his May 1973 budget presentation, stated:

> *Now, let us start with the property tax. From time immemorial, Sir, in modern economic planning income tax has always been the method of achieving not only revenue but what we call income redistribution, that is the process by which you create equality in a society by making the better-off provide the funds for the development of the country. That is how you work towards a society of equality and justice. As everybody knows, people in Jamaica and elsewhere have found a thousand ways to get around income tax. . . .*
>
> *Therefore property tax is quite deliberately intended as an instrument of social policy because when a person has a huge home, the money they accumulated to build that home is evidence of their capacity to pay. I don't grudge it but they must support the Public Purse in order to build the society.*

The reform effort was launched with proclamation of the new valuation rolls for the parishes of Clarendon, Manchester, and Westmoreland.[28]

The press reaction was vitriolic against both the new tax structure and the valuations themselves. Most of the criticism came from influential organizations representing the owners of large rural estates, such as the "Group of 22" from the western parishes, rather than from small- or medium-scale farmers or the urban middle classes.[29]

The government's response was two-fold: it amended The Land Taxation (Relief) Act to introduce the derating of agricultural and hotel land, and launched "Land Val '74." As the culmination of a tax reform that was initiated in 1956, the objective of "Land Val '74" was:

---

[27]It is generally believed that Minister Coore was referring to money raised from the excise duty on beer. The figure quoted is in Jamaican dollars. In 1990, the average exchange rate was J$7.18 for US$1.00; see Exchange Rates following the Table of Contents for a full listing of exchange rates since 1970.

[28]A temporary system of differential tax rates was introduced during this reform to accommodate the three property tax systems being implemented in Jamaica in 1972: in four parishes (Kingston, St. Andrew, St. James, and Hanover) the tax roll was based on 1937 self-declarations of capital value; in seven parishes (Portland, St. Thomas, St. Mary, St. Ann, Trelawny, St. Elizabeth, and St. Catherine) the improved values were as much as fifteen years out of date; and three parishes (Manchester, Clarendon, and Westmoreland) had been surveyed for current unimproved values, but were still implementing the old property tax system with old capital values.

[29]Risden, "A History of Jamaica's Experience with Land Taxation based on the Site Value System," 14.

> . . . to revalue for the first time in nearly 50 years the parishes of Kingston and St. Andrew which together contained nearly 80,000 parcels and more than half the real estate value in Jamaica as well as the parishes of Hanover and St. James . . . which similarly had not been valued since the "revaluation" of 1937. As if this was not enough the objective was also to simultaneously revise the valuations in the seven parishes originally valued on the unimproved value system but which had not been revalued on the quinquennial basis as contemplated by the law. Some 390,000 valuations had to be done in this exercise and the time set by the political directorate was 12 months.[30]

Land Valuation Division staff began a crash program, accompanied by an extensive, multi-media public information campaign built on the "Land Val '74" motto: "One Country, One System, Fair and Square for All." The above-noted targets were met in 20 months. Objections totalled eight percent of valuations, or roughly 41,000 of the half-million parcels on the valuation roll. Land taxes almost quadrupled from J$6 million in 1972 to J$23 million in 1975. About half of the total tax yield came from the parishes of Kingston and St. Andrew. More than two-thirds of the parcels (those not exceeding J$2,000 in value) generated less than eight percent of revenue, while 0.6 percent of the parcels (those above J$50,000 in value) contributed to more than half of the total tax yield.[31]

---

[30]Risden, "A History of Jamaica's Experience with Land Taxation based on the Site Value System," 15.

[31]Derived from figures presented in Risden, "A History of Jamaica's Experience with Land Taxation based on the Site Value System," 18.

THE JAMAICAN PROPERTY TAX IN PRACTICE: SYSTEM PERFORMANCE

Purpose: Revenue and Non-Revenue Objectives

Revenue Generation

Property tax revenue in Jamaica has approximately tripled over the past fifteen years, rising from J$22.6 million in fiscal year 1975/76 to J$67.3 million in fiscal year 1989/90 (see Table II-2).[32]

TABLE II-2: PROPERTY TAX REVENUE IN JAMAICA

Fiscal Year	Property Tax Receipts (millions of J$)	
	Nominal J$	*1985 J$*
1975/76	22.6	113.6
1976/77	22.8	103.2
1977/78	25.0	100.8
1978/79	25.0	80.1
1979/80	24.8	68.1
1980/81	24.2	56.3
1981/82	27.8	59.7
1982/83	32.8	64.4
1983/84	29.1	49.1
1984/85	24.4	30.5
1985/86	24.2	24.2
1986/87	33.5	28.6
1987/88	65.5	49.8
1988/89	58.9	40.5
1989/90	67.3	38.7[a]

[a]Estimated.

Sources: Risden, "A Re-Examination of the Site Value as the Base for Property Taxation in Jamaica," 6-8; and Stair, *A Position Paper on The Property Taxation System*, 7.

[32]O. St. Clare Risden, "A Re-Examination of the Site Value as the Base for Property Taxation in Jamaica," paper prepared for the Conference of the International Union for Land-Value Taxation and Free Trade, Vancouver, May 1986, 6-8; and Stair, A Position Paper on The Property Taxation System, 7.

However, if nominal property tax receipts are converted to 1985 Jamaican dollars, property tax revenue in Jamaica is now actually about one-third of the total fifteen years ago, falling from J$113.6 million in fiscal year 1975/76 to J$38.7 million in 1989/90 (see Figure II-2).[33] Failure to index property tax assessments has contributed to a significant reduction in the real value of Jamaican property tax receipts.

The role of property tax revenue in the Jamaican economy has thus declined considerably over the past fifteen years: in fiscal year 1975/76, property tax receipts totalled 3.6 percent of total tax revenue and 0.9 percent of gross domestic product, but by fiscal year 1989/90, the property tax was only 1.1 percent of total tax revenue and 0.3 percent of gross domestic product (see Table II-3).[34]

FIGURE II-2:
PROPERTY TAX REVENUE IN JAMAICA

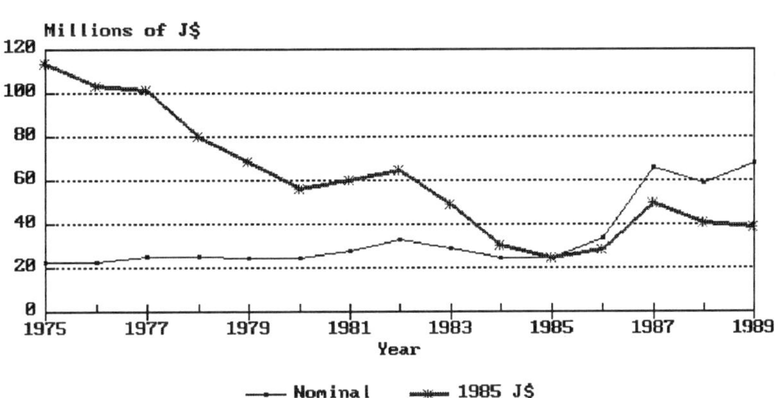

Source: Author's calculations.

[33]Gross domestic product deflators are taken from: International Monetary Fund, Bureau of Statistics, International Financial Statistics (Washington, D.C.: International Monetary Fund), monthly issues and yearbooks.

[34]Risden, "A Re-Examination of the Site Value," 6-8; Stair, A Position Paper on The Property Taxation System, 7; and International Monetary Fund, International Financial Statistics, "1990 Yearbook" (vol. 43), 438-41 and "September 1991" (vol. 44), 308-11 (Washington, D.C.: IMF, 1990 and 1991).

TABLE II-3: PROPERTY TAX REVENUE IN THE JAMAICAN ECONOMY

(millions of J$)

Fiscal Year	Property Tax Receipts	Total Tax Revenue	Share of Total Tax Revenue	Gross Domestic Product	Share of GDP
1975/76	22.6	624.4	3.6%	2,600.5	0.9%
1976/77	22.8	614.4	3.7%	2,701.6	0.8%
1977/78	25.0	639.0	3.9%	2,960.3	0.8%
1978/79	25.0	1,009.4	2.5%	3,749.4	0.7%
1979/80	24.8	1,174.7	2.1%	4,293.4	0.6%
1980/81	24.2	1,279.3	1.9%	4,773.1	0.5%
1981/82	27.8	1,501.9	1.9%	5,306.8	0.5%
1982/83	32.8	1,637.8	2.0%	5,867.1	0.6%
1983/84	29.1	1,765.2	1.6%	6,993.1	0.4%
1984/85	24.4	2,525.5	1.0%	9,355.2	0.3%
1985/86	24.2	3,130.5	0.8%	11,151.2	0.2%
1986/87	33.5	3,758.3	0.9%	13,310.1	0.3%
1987/88	65.5	4,306.9	1.5%	15,717.4	0.4%
1988/89	58.9	4,923.3	1.2%	17,471.6	0.3%
1989/90	67.3	6,275.1	1.1%	22,315.0	0.3%

Sources: Risden, "A Re-Examination of the Site Value as the Base for Property Taxation in Jamaica," 6-8; Stair, *A Position Paper on The Property Taxation System*, 7; and International Monetary Fund, *International Financial Statistics*, "1990 Yearbook" (vol. 43), 438-41 and "September 1991" (vol. 44), 308-11 (Washington, D.C.: IMF, 1990 and 1991).

Non-Revenue Objectives

Despite hopes to the contrary, the site value tax has not been an effective policy instrument for fostering social reform in Jamaica. According to the commissioner of valuations who presided over the events described above:

> The experience of the two decades from 1956 to 1976 seems to have proven that . . . fiscal measures by themselves alone are largely ineffective as a tool for fundamental agrarian reform unless such measures are applied by means of a rather steeply progressive rate of tax and to a degree of insensitivity which is not usually contemplatible in the short run given democratic political systems such as we have in Jamaica.[35]

[35]Risden, "A History of Jamaica's Experience with Land Taxation based on the Site Value System," 24.

Even if progressive property taxation could serve as a proxy for a wealth tax in pursuit of distributional objectives, it is more appropriate for aggregate property holdings than individual sites.

Land use patterns do not appear to have been influenced by the property tax in Jamaica, nor is the distribution of landholdings significantly more equitable now than it was when Jamaica achieved independence. While land prices did indeed fall during the mid-1970s, some quite dramatically, these declines are probably coincidental with "Land Val '74" rather than caused by this tax reform effort. It is more likely that land values fell in response to the steep rise in building costs and interest rates following the oil price shock of 1973/74, together with the flight of property owners during the political instability surrounding the 1976 elections and the subsequent glut of attractive property in a market of contracting demand.

Principles: Efficiency, Equity, and Sustainability

Property tax coverage is very difficult to determine in Jamaica. The valuation roll appears to be virtually comprehensive. However, equitable and remunerative coverage is seriously compromised through: the use of obsolete values; extensive relief, derating, and exemptions; low collection efficiency; and weak enforcement measures.

The 590,000-parcel valuation roll is exhaustive. It is map-based, and every parcel on the valuation roll is identified on a plan and has a unique parcel location reference number. The lack of a national legal cadastre (only about 300,000 parcels are formally registered, or about half the parcels on the valuation roll) has not prevented Land Valuation from completing its own fiscal cadastre over the past three decades.

The textual component of the valuation roll is partially automated, making it relatively easy to ascertain the distribution of property by number of parcels, total acreage, and unimproved value. Text automation has also facilitated estimatation of property tax potential (see Figure II-3).[36]

A further breakdown of these figures (see Table II-4) vividly depicts the skewed composition of the property tax in Jamaica: 75 percent of the parcels (those less than J$10,000 in value) generate 3.4 percent of gross tax assessment, while conversely, 3.1 percent of the parcels (those equal or greater than J$50,000)

[36]Land Valuation Department, "Valuation Bands Statistics," Kingston, unpublished; and author's calculations. The difference between the normalized stacked bar charts for "valuation" and "assessment" in Figure II-3 is due to progressive property tax rates.

generate 73 percent of gross tax assessment.[37] It is not possible to disaggregate these figures by sector or land use with an acceptable standard of certainty due to definitional ambiguities and data coding difficulties.

FIGURE II-3:
PROPERTY TAX COMPOSITION IN JAMAICA

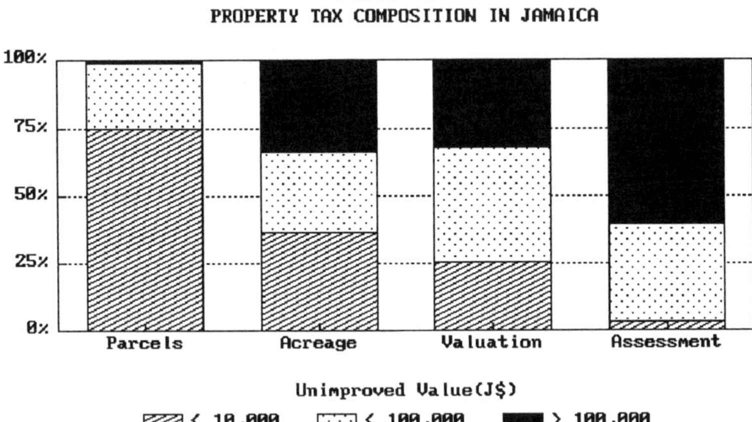

Source: Author's calculations.

[37]Land Valuation Department, "Valuation Bands Statistics," Kingston, unpublished and author's calculations.

TABLE II-4: PROPERTY TAX COMPOSITION IN JAMAICA

Unimproved 1983 Value	Total Units		Total Area		Total 1983 Valuation		Pre-Relief Tax Assessment	
(J$)	(parcels)	(%)	(acres)	(%)	(thousands of J$)	(%)	(J$)	(%)
< 6,000	328,928	55.9%	676,937	25.1%	1,031,822	14.2%	1,644,640	1.6%
< 10,000	112,352	19.1%	306,455	11.4%	806,394	11.1%	1,884,581	1.8%
< 16,000	74,425	12.6%	236,528	8.8%	900,051	12.4%	5,686,144	5.6%
< 25,000	25,514	4.3%	149,150	5.5%	480,830	6.6%	4,715,001	4.6%
< 50,000	29,311	5.0%	208,826	7.7%	986,841	13.6%	13,654,79	13.4%
< 100,000	11,334	1.9%	207,912	7.7%	733,151	10.1%	12,727,338	12.5%
< 500,000	6,010	1.0%	431,169	16.0%	1,074,189	14.8%	25,719,841	25.2%
<1,000,000	547	0.1%	139,380	5.2%	368,185	5.1%	10,453,408	10.2%
≥ 1,000,000	350	0.1%	339,396	12.6%	868,503	12.0%	25,676,200	25.1%
TOTAL	588,771	100%	2,695,753	100%	7,249,966	100%	102,161,947	100%

Sources: Land Valuation Department, "Valuation Bands Statistics," Kingston, unpublished; and author's calculations.

The quality of this once-comprehensive valuation roll has been seriously degraded by relatively infrequent revaluations: the current valuation roll and above-noted data are based on 1983 values (effective in fiscal year 1986/87). The previous revaluation was in 1974. The next revaluation is scheduled to take place in 1991, effective in 1992.[38] For example, a sample of residential properties was recently surveyed to study the effects of revaluation using 1991 market data. Unless tax rates were lowered, increases in the unimproved value of single-unit residential lots

[38] According to Commissioner of Land Valuations Elizabeth Stair, the use of private valuers during the 1983 revaluation greatly reduced the objections rate when compared with the 1974 revaluation, from approximately 8 percent to 1 percent of all parcels valued.

would range from 250 percent to 525 percent, with a concomitant tax increase (using 1986/87 tax rates) of between 545 percent and 1,470 percent. The unimproved value of most townhouse lots would more than double applying current tax rates, with tax liabilities roughly tripling (see Table II-5).[39]

TABLE II-5: SAMPLE RESIDENTIAL LAND VALUE INCREASES IN JAMAICA

Location	Total Lots or Units	Typical Parcel Size	Typical Unimproved 1983 Value	Property Tax Using 1986/87 Tax Rates	Estimated Unimproved 1991 Value		Property Tax Using 1986/87 Tax Rates	
	(#)	(sq.ft.)	(J$)	(J$)	(J$)	(▲)	(J$)	(▲)
SINGLE UNIT								
Harbour View	1,844	3,500	10,000	45.0	35,000	250%	492.5	994%
Mona Heights	780	7,000	30,000	392.5	175,000	483%	4,167.5	962%
Hope Pastures	415	11,000	40,000	592.5	200,000	400%	4,917.5	730%
Cherry Gardens	508	11,000	90,000	1,692.5	400,000	344%	10,917.5	545%
Billy Dunn	204	36,000	100,000	1,917.5	450,000	350%	12,417.5	548%
Trafalgar Park	146	11,000	40,000	592.5	250,000	525%	6,417.5	983%
Havendale	960	11,800	45,000	692.5	200,000	344%	4,917.5	610%
Norbrook	438	10,000	90,000	1,692.5	400,000	344%	10,917.5	545%
Independence City	570	2,700	8,000	25.0	30,000	275%	392.5	1,470%
TOWNHOUSES								
Haining Mews	47	1,500	22,000	240.0	50,000	127%	792.5	230%
Gallery	46	1,000	20,000	205.0	50,000	150%	792.5	287%
Oakwood	63	1,130	20,000	205.0	40,000	100%	592.5	189%
Ravinia Mews	52	1,500	22,000	240.0	45,000	105%	692.5	189%
Devon Square	29	1,580	25,000	292.5	55,000	120%	905.0	209%

Sources: Stair, *A Position Paper on The Property Taxation System*, 4a; Land Valuation Department, unpublished statistics; and author's calculations.

Information on assessment and collection is not currently available in a form useful to senior managers and policy makers. The tax roll is partially automated, but is not coded in a way that facilitates analysis as to tax revenue

[39]Stair, A Position Paper on The Property Tax System, 4a; Land Valuation Department, unpublished statistics; and author's calculations. The percentage increases in tax liabilities are greater than the percentage increases in unimproved values because of progressive property tax rates.

foregone due to relief, derating, and exemptions. The payment system is predominantly manual, and records are not compiled regarding collection rates and enforcement measures. Consolidated statements of property tax receipts do not present comparisons of tax revenue with tax liabilities, nor are current payments and arrear payments disaggregated in tax revenue reports.

However, informed estimates are not encouraging. In 1977, the Commissioner of Valuations calculated the revenue loss resulting from agricultural and hotel derating, discretionary and statutory reliefs, and non-taxable properties at 50 percent of net property tax liability .[40] A 1985 study placed the loss at approximately 42 percent, distributed as follows: agricultural derating, 30 percent; hotel derating, 2 percent; exempt properties, 7 percent; and relief, 3 percent.[41]

The same sources estimate collection efficiency (current revenue as a percent of current billings) to be about 60 percent.[42] The current Commissioner of Land Valuations concurs.[43] If so, this implies that approximately one-third of all property tax receipts are now arrear payments.[44] All those interviewed, including wealthy taxpayers, agreed that voluntary compliance was highest among rural subsistence farmers. The most common explanation is as follows:

> Land in the Jamaican situation is not regarded by the broad mass of people as being merely a source of wealth. There are emotions mixed with land tenure. It is the lifelong ambition of most of the dispossessed poor to own their own plot, however small it may be, for land ownership to their mind confers the status of being somebody in a community. It might also be mentioned that in recent colonial times before "universal adult sufferage [sic]" a period which I can personally remember as a child growing up on

---

[40]O. St. Clare Risden, An Analysis of Alternative Strategies for the Period 1977 to the Decade of the 1980s (Kingston: Land Valuation Office, April 1977), Schedule B.

[41]Holland and Follain, The Property Tax in Jamaica, 22.

[42]Risden, An Analysis of Alternative Strategies, Schedule B; Holland and Follain, The Property Tax in Jamaica, 26.

[43]Stair, A Position Paper on The Property Tax System, 7.

[44]This figure is calculated as follows: the total value of the tax roll before relief, derating, and exemptions is estimated to be J$102.2 million; the revenue loss resulting from agricultural and hotel derating, discretionary and statutory reliefs, and non-taxable properties is estimated to be 42 percent of property tax liability, or J$30.2 million, reducing total net tax collectable to J$72.0; the collection rate is estimated at about 60 percent, or J$43.2; and property tax receipts in 1989/90 (the most recent figure) total J$67.3, which leaves 36 percent of collections (the J$24.1 difference) attributable to arrears payments.

rural Jamaica, land-owning status by virtue of conferring the liability to pay taxes also conferred the right to vote.[45]

It is not easy to calculate the cost of property tax administration. The government estimates current administrative costs at about 11 percent of revenue, or J$13 per parcel; approximately J$114 in revenue is generated per parcel (see Table II-6). However, these calculations have two important shortcomings: expenses of the Land Valuation Department include those incurred for services unrelated to the property tax, while collection costs of the Inland Revenue Department have not been compiled at all.[46]

Enforcement difficulties begin with uncertainty over the quality of collection data. The posting of tax payments in the tax roll is a tedious manual process. Such postings are often slow and inaccurate, raising considerable debate about the precision of delinquency lists generated from these data.[47] Enforcement problems are compounded by a combination of: the relatively low priority of property tax collections for Inland Revenue given resource constraints, the small size of the average property tax bill, and other responsibilities; the lengthy and cumbersome enforcement procedures as interpreted in practice; and the lack of incentives for revenue field officers to pursue enforcement measures aggressively.[48]

In the words of a recent study of tax reform in Jamaica, "it is clear from our review that the property tax gets higher marks on grounds of principle than with respect to practice."[49]

---

[45]Risden, "A History of Jamaica's Experience with Land Taxation based on the Site Value System," 1.

[46]Stair, A Position Paper on The Property Tax System, 8.

[47]Holland and Follain, The Property Tax in Jamaica, 24-5.

[48]The following examples were given during interviews with officials of the Revenue Board, the Department of Inland Revenue, and the Constant Spring Revenue Services Center in Kingston:
1) Although a levy warrant or demand notice can be delivered to anyone connected with the property in question, the higher the stakes, the more inaccessible and combative the taxpayer. 2) If goods are distrained, transport and storage are a logistical headache. 3) Issuing a summons to attend court necessitates not only locating the person named in the summons, but also serving the summons no earlier than three days prior to the scheduled court session, between 6:00 a.m. and 6:00 p.m., for a J$0.25 incentive payment. 4) The process for lodging a caveat is a bureaucratic nightmare, and it has not been practical to dispose of real property according to procedures outlined in the Quit Rents Act. 5) The entire enforcement process is pursued largely at the discretion of field supervisors, which can be confusing and demoralizing for revenue field officers.

[49]Holland and Follain, The Property Tax in Jamaica, 105.

TABLE II-6: PROPERTY TAX ADMINISTRATION COSTS IN JAMAICA

Item	1985/86	1986/87	1987/88	1988/89	1989/90
1. Property Tax Receipts (in millions)	J$24.2	J$33.5	J$65.5	J$58.9	J$67.3
2. Approximate Number of Parcels	550,000	590,000	590,000	590,000	590,000
3. Revenue per arcel	J$44	J$57	J$111	J$100	J$114
4. Annual Budget of Land Valuation Department (in millions)	J$4.0	J$5.5	J$5.6	J$7.3	J$7.7
5. Cost per Parcel	J$7	J$9	J$9	J$12	J$13
6. Annual Budget ÷ Property Tax Receipts	16%	16%	9%	12%	11%

Sources: Stair, *A Position Paper on The Property Taxation System*, 8; and author's calculations.

3

PHILIPPINES CASE STUDY

The hole and the patch should be commensurate.

Thomas Jefferson,
Letter to James Madison, 1787

PHILIPPINE PROPERTY TAX IN PERSPECTIVE: CASE STUDY SNAPSHOT

Government officials have been striving to improve property taxation in the Philippines since 1972, with considerable external financial and technical assistance. Philippine reformers have been clear and consistent in their rationale for devoting substantial resources to property tax reform: development of local government capacity to generate adequate revenue for the sustained provision of community facilities and services responsive to local needs.

Philippine reformers have felt that poor property tax performance has been due to weak field implementation rather than faulty system design, especially local governments' failure to maintain complete, accurate, and current property valuation rolls. Accordingly, reformers have concentrated their efforts on increasing the coverage and improving the quality of valuation rolls via comprehensive tax mapping and simplified mass appraisal activities.

Property tax reform thus conceived has been relatively well implemented in the Philippines. Local government officials have developed and refined inexpensive, low-technology procedures for producing a credible fiscal cadastre through cost-effective tax mapping and mass appraisal techniques. Furthermore, approximately half of the nation's local governments have compiled relatively complete, current, and credible valuation rolls.

Unfortunately, the basic design of the Philippines' property tax system is not sound and the principal constraint to revenue generation is not insufficient and low quality property-related data: system design should be greatly simplified and reform efforts should encompass all subsystems of field implementation. A narrow and primarily technical focus has resulted in temporarily improved tax rolls that can neither be maintained nor translated into substantial revenue gains. Most increases in property tax receipts during the past two decades should be attributed to activities that would have been conducted with or without concurrent property tax reform projects: periodic application of new unit cost tables to property already on the tax rolls, as well as periodic reclassification of this same property. The following case study will examine the premises, execution, and results of property tax reform in the Philippines.

THE PHILIPPINE PROPERTY TAX IN LAW: SYSTEM DESIGN

Tax Base

According to Presidential Decree No. 464 (PD 464) of 1974, "there shall be levied, assessed and collected in the province, cities and municipalities an annual *ad valorem tax* on real property, such as land, buildings, machinery and other improvements affixed or attached to real property not hereinafter specifically exempted."[1]

However, once property is classified as taxable, only a portion of its current market value (as defined in Section C below) is subject to the property tax through utilization of fractional assessment levels. Furthermore, property is classified for assessment purposes "on the basis of its actual use regardless of where located and whoever uses it."[2] Classes of real property for assessment purposes are residential, agricultural, commercial, industrial, mineral, and "special."[3] Each property class is

---

[1]Presidential Decree No. 464, Chapter IV, Section 38. According to Presidential Decree No. 464, Chapter IV, Section 40 (as amended by PD 939, PD 1383, and PD 1621), exemptions from the property tax include: 1) real property owned by the national government or its political subdivisions, or by any government-owned corporation exempted by its charter, unless used by a taxable person; 2) non-profit cemeteries or burial grounds; 3) land, buildings, and improvements used exclusively for religious or charitable purposes; 4) land acquired from the public domain and converted to dairying or livestock production, for five years following conversion; 5) machinery of a pioneer and preferred industry as certified by the Board of Investments, for the first three years of operation; 6) perennial trees and plants of economic value, except where the land upon which they grow is planted principally to such growth; 7) real property in any one city or municipality belonging to a single owner, with an aggregate value of P1,000 or less; and 8) real property exempt under other laws, for example, new investments in tourism-oriented industries (PD 535), subsidized housing to employees of tax-exempt corporations and partnerships (PD 745), and foreign embassies (international convention).

[2]Presidential Decree No. 464, Chapter II, Section 19.

[3]Presidential Decree No. 464, Chapter II, Section 18. "Special" is defined as "all lands, buildings and other improvements thereon, actually, directly and exclusively used for educational, cultural, recreational or scientific purposes, as well as hospitals not owned and operated by the government or by any of its instrumentalities . . ."

assigned an assessment ratio,[4] determined by current land use, as well as by the current use and market value of buildings, machinery, and other improvements. Assessment ratios range from 15 to 50 percent for land, and from 15 to 80 percent for improvements (see Table III-1).

TABLE III-1: PHILIPPINE PROPERTY TAX ASSESSMENT RATIOS

LAND

Land Use	**Assessment Ratio**
Special Class	15%
Residential	30%
Agricultural	40%
Commercial	50%
Industrial	50%
Mineral	50%

BUILDINGS AND OTHER IMPROVEMENTS

Market Value	**Assessment Ratio**			
	Special Class	*Residential*	*Agricultural*	*Commercial/ Industrial*
≤P 30,000	15%	15%	40%	50%
>P 30,000 but ≤P 50,000	15%	20%	45%	55%
>P 50,000 but ≤P 75,000	15%	25%	50%	60%
>P 75,000 but ≤P125,000	15%	35%	55%	65%
>P125,000 but ≤P175,000	15%	45%	60%	70%
>P175,000 but ≤P250,000	15%	55%	65%	75%
>P250,000 but ≤P350,000	15%	65%	70%	80%
>P350,000 but ≤P500,000	15%	75%	75%	80%
>P500,000	15%	80%	80%	80%

---

[4] In Presidential Decree 464, Chapter I, Section 3, the assessment ratio is referred to as the "assessment level," and is defined as "the percentage applied to the market value to determine the taxable or assessed value of the property."

MACHINERIES

Machinery Use	Assessment Ratio
Special Class	15%
Agricultural	60%
Residential	70%
Commercial	80%
Industrial	80%

Source: Presidential Decree No. 464, Chapter II, Section 20 (as amended by PD 1383 and PD 1621).

Tax Rate

According to PD 464, "the provincial, city or municipal board or council shall fix a uniform rate of real property tax applicable to their respective localities . . . "[5] Tax rates may range from one-half percent to one percent for municipalities (including the provincial portion) and from one-half percent to two percent for cities (see Table III-2). A mandatory additional one percent tax on real property is levied in all jurisdictions, with proceeds earmarked for the Special Education Fund (SEF) created under Republic Act No. 5447. A supplementary five percent tax on idle lands is also mandated. Local governments and the national government may impose a special betterment levy not to exceed 60 percent of the cost of infrastructure improvements.[6]

TABLE III-2: PHILIPPINE PROPERTY TAX RATES

BASIC TAX

Local Government Unit	Minimum	Maximum
Municipality	0.25%	0.50%
Province	0.25%	0.50%
Combined Rate	0.50%	1.00%
City	0.50%	2.00%

---

[5]Presidential Decree 464, Chapter IV, Section 39.

[6]Presidential Decree No. 464, Chapter V, Sections 47 and 55.

ADDITIONAL LEVIES

Type	Rate
Special Education Fund	1.00%
Idle Lands	5.00%
Infrastructure Improvement	Total ≤ 60% of Cost of Improvements

Source: Presidential Decree No. 464, Chapter IV, Section 39; Chapter V, Section 41 (as amended by PED 1621); and Chapter V, Sections 42-44 (as amended by PD 1446).

Valuation

The provincial or city assessor must prepare and maintain an assessment roll of all real property (taxable or exempt) located within the province or city; property should be listed and valued in the name of the owner or administrator, or anyone having a legal interest in the property.[7] Discovery of property is based on owner declaration, which must be filed with the appropriate assessor once every three years, or within 60 days after acquiring or improving property.[8]

If these provisions are not met, the provincial or city assessor has the authority to declare real property in the name of the defaulting owner (or against an unknown owner if not identified). In addition, failure to file a taxpayer declaration, or the filing of a false declaration is punishable by a fine of up to P1,000 and/or up to one year imprisonment.[9]

According to PD 464, "all real property, whether taxable or exempt, shall be appraised at the current and fair market value prevailing in the locality where the property is situated."[10] In accordance with the general provision of PD 464 which requires real property to be assessed "on the basis of a uniform standard of value

[7]Presidential Decree No. 464, Chapter II, Section 8.

[8]Presidential Decree No. 464, Chapter II, Sections 6 and 6-A (as amended by PD 1383 and PD 1621).

[9]Presidential Decree 464, Chapter II, Section 7 and Chapter XI, Section 104 (as amended by PD 1383).

[10]Presidential Decree 464, Chapter II, Section 5. According to Presidential Decree No. 464, Chapter I, Section 3, market value is defined as "the highest price estimated in terms of money which the property will buy if exposed for sale in the open market allowing a reasonable time to find a purchaser who buys with knowledge of all the uses to which it is adapted and for which it is capable for being used." "Market value" is alternatively defined as "the price at which a willing seller would sell and a willing buyer would buy, neither being under abnormal pressure."

within each local political subdivision,"[11] the Department of Finance has issued a series of regulations to enable implementation of a standardized mass appraisal system. The mass appraisal process begins with the preparation of provincial and city unit cost tables (in peso per square meter)[12] for each class (property use) and grade (property quality) of real property based on a sample of market transactions. Descriptive information of property, obtained from tax declarations or field inspections, is then used to assign land and improvements to specific classes and grades, after which the total area of land and improvements is each multiplied by the appropriate square meter value to determine total property value.[13]

Provincial and city assessors must make a general revision of all real property assessments in their jurisdictions every three years to reflect changes in property value and characteristics. Assessors may undertake general revaluations more frequently, at the direction or with the approval of the secretary of finance, if significant changes in property values so warrant.[14] The president has the power to postpone the effective date of revised assessments. General revaluations entail the preparation of new unit cost tables, as well as reinspection of properties to verify ownership and to confirm physical characteristics used in appraisal.[15] Any property owner who is not satisfied with an assessor's valuation may appeal within 60 days to the board of assessment appeals of the province or city in which the property is located. The local board of assessment appeals must decide the appeal within 120 days. If either the property owner or assessor is not satisfied with the decision, the disputing party may appeal to the Central Board of Assessment Appeals within 30 days. This Board must decide the appeal within 12 months, and its decision is final. All property tax assessments must be paid in full pending the outcome of an assessment appeal, without prejudice to subsequent adjustment.[16]

---

[11]Presidential Decree 464, Chapter I, Section 2.

[12]The formal Philippine terminology for what is generally referred to a unit cost table is a "schedule of market values."

[13]The unit cost of urban land is determined primarily by location, while the unit cost of rural land is determined primarily by the land's productivity. The unit cost of buildings is determined primarily by construction materials. The current market value of machinery is either the original cost for newly acquired machinery, or the depreciated replacement or reproduction cost of older machinery.

[14]Property transfers, land development or subdivision, and major improvements may be reflected in the tax rolls as they occur, without waiting for the next general revaluation.

[15]Presidential Decree 464, Chapter II, Section 21 (as amended by PD 1621); and William Dillinger, Urban Property Tax Reform: The Case of the Philippines' Real Property Tax Administration Project, Report INU-16 (Washington, D.C.: World Bank, May 1988), 4.

[16]Presidential Decree No. 464, Chapter III, Sections 30 -37.

Collection

According to PD 464, "the collection of the real property tax and all penalties pertaining thereto, and the enforcement of the remedies provided for in this Code or any applicable laws, shall be the responsibility of the treasurer of the province, city or municipality where the property is situated."[17]

Collection procedures begin with the submission of an assessment roll by the end of December each year from the provincial or city assessor to the provincial, city, or municipal treasurer. However, treasurers are not required to produce and transmit tax bills informing taxpayers of their individual property tax liabilities, unless specifically requested by the secretary of finance. Instead, they have until the end of January to post a general notice of payment dates at local government offices and in a prominent place in each barangay (local community), publish this notice in a newspaper, and have the notice announced by a public crier.[18]

Property taxes are paid to the local government treasurer, usually in the municipal office. However, in highly urbanized areas, collection agents are sometimes used, while in rural areas barangay officials often help with tax collections. There are also occasional conduit arrangements ("local tie-ups") with banks for payment of the property tax, usually linked to financing or for large estates. The taxpayer has the option either to pay all tax liabilities by the end of March, or to pay in four equal installments over the year without incurring additional charges.[19]

The taxpayer is also entitled to a discount (currently ten percent) on the tax due if the basic property tax and the additional SEF levy (or any quarterly installment thereof) is paid in full within the prescribed payment period. Disputed taxes must be paid pending resolution of the dispute, with the contended amount annotated "paid under protest."[20]

Basic property tax receipts, including delinquent taxes and penalties, are divided as follows (see Figure III-1): for municipalities, 10 percent is distributed to the barangay, with the remainder split equally between the municipality and the province; and for cities, 10 percent is distributed to the barangay, with the remainder allocated to the city.

---

[17]Presidential Decree No. 464, Chapter VI, Section 57.

[18]Presidential Decree No. 464, Chapter VI, Section 59.

[19]Presidential Decree 464, Chapter VI, Section 60 and discussions with Department of Finance officials. Payment schedules for local or national government betterment levies are determined by special ordinance.

[20]Presidential Decree 464, Chapter VI, Section 61 and discussions with Department of Finance officials.

City and municipal shares of property tax receipts accrue entirely to their respective general funds. One-fourth of the provincial share is earmarked for its road and bridge fund, and the remaining three-fourths accrues to its general fund.[21] Special Education Fund receipts accrue entirely to the respective municipality or city, with all proceeds earmarked for education.[22] Receipts from the additional tax on idle private lands accrue to the respective general fund of the province, city, and municipality where the property is located.[23]

FIGURE III-1:
DISTRIBUTION OF PHILIPPINE PROPERTY TAX

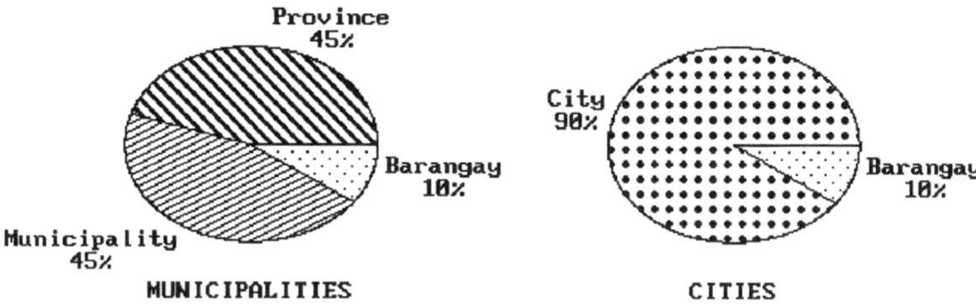

Source: Author's calculations.

Upon expiration of the property tax payment period, the provincial or city treasurers are required to post a notice specifying the date upon which the tax became delinquent, along with penalties for non-payment.[24] The taxpayer is subject to a fine of two percent of the delinquent tax for each month of delinquency, to a maximum total penalty of twenty-four percent of the delinquent tax. Outstanding

---

[21]Presidential Decree No. 464, Chapter VII, Sections 86 and 87 (as amended by PD 1230).

[22]Republic of the Philippines, Department of Finance, Bureau of Local Government Finance, Local Finance Window VI (Iloilo City: Bureau of Local Government Finance, Region VI, 1990), unnumbered.

[23]Presidential Decree No. 464, Chapter VII, Section 87.

[24]Presidential Decree No. 464, Chapter VI, Section 65. This notice is to be posted at local government offices and in a prominent place in each barangay, published in a newspaper once a week for three consecutive weeks, and announced by a public crier for at least three market days.

property tax arrears, including penalties, also accumulate as liens on title.[25] The taxpayer is also subject to the following enforcement measures, described as "remedies cumulative, simultaneous and unconditional": distraint and sale of personal property; public auction of the delinquent real property; and civil action in court. If the property itself is sold to recover tax arrears, the delinquent taxpayer has one year to redeem the property, by paying all taxes and penalties due, together with the cost of the sale and interest at 20 percent of the purchase price.[26]

Administration

The Department of Finance is given primary responsibility for administration of the property tax, including:

- development of a comprehensive system of real property appraisal that will ensure fair and realistic property valuations for taxation purposes;
- establishment of uniform assessment methods and procedures that will equalize property values in each local political subdivision;
- assurance that the property tax is just, uniform, and equitable; and
- promotion of local government tax assessment and collection efficiency, as well as optimal local government revenue utilization.

To achieve these objectives, the secretary of finance "shall exercise direct executive supervision over all assessment and treasury officials and personnel in the local governments." Thus, even though the salaries of local government assessors and treasurers are paid from local government funds, these officials are under the administrative jurisdiction of the Department of Finance. Assessors who either willfully fail to assess, through gross negligence underassess, or intentionally omit from assessment or tax rolls any taxable real property is subject to a fine of up to P1,000 and/or up to one year of imprisonment. The same penalties apply to treasurers who willfully fail to collect the property tax. Other officers required to

[25]Presidential Decree No. 464, Chapter VI, Sections 56 and 66. The property tax lien "shall be superior to all other liens, mortgages, encumbrances of any kind whatsoever; shall be enforceable against the property whether in the possession of the delinquent or any subsequent owner or possessor, and shall be removable only by the payment of delinquent taxes and penalties."

[26]Presidential Decree No. 464, Chapter VI, Sections 67 -78.

assist in administration of the property tax who willfully fail to discharge their duties are subject to a fine of up to P500 and/or imprisonment of up to six months.[27]

THE PHILIPPINE PROPERTY TAX IN TRANSITION: SYSTEM REFORM

The Change Process: Policy

The principal objectives of improving real property taxation in the Philippines were clearly articulated by President Ferdinand Marcos in 1974 when he issued a new real property tax code:

> WHEREAS, this country cannot progress steadily if its local governments are not potent political subdivisions contributing their proportionate share to national progress;
>
> WHEREAS, the past decade saw the passage of the Local Autonomy Act, the Barrio Charter, the Decentralization Act and other pieces of legislation intended to make local governments financially self-reliant and stable;
>
> WHEREAS, it is very apparent that in spite of all these laws, local governments still find difficulty in providing adequate funds with which to underwrite basic and essential public services within their respective areas of responsibility;
>
> WHEREAS, studies show that one of the main reasons behind this is the failure of local governments to fully tap the income potentialities of the real property tax;
>
> WHEREAS, to remedy the situation, there is an urgent and compelling need to upgrade assessment services by updating assessment techniques, procedures and practices and thereby bring about equitable distribution of the realty tax burden among real property owners throughout the country;
>
> NOW, THEREFORE, I . . . do hereby adopt, promulgate and decree . . . "The Real Property Tax Code" . . . .[28]

---

[27]Presidential Decree No. 464, Chapter I, Section 4 and Presidential Decree No. 464, Chapter XI, Section 106.

[28]Presidential Decree No. 464, Preamble.

The government of the Philippines has attempted to facilitate implementation of The Real Property Tax Code during the ensuing two decades through the Real Property Tax Administration Project (RPTA). Both the United States Agency for International Development (USAID) and the World Bank have contributed substantial resources to these efforts. In keeping with the above-noted global objectives of real property taxation in the Philippines, the RPTA project purpose is "to increase real property tax revenues to finance and support locally initiated development projects and services." If this project purpose is achieved, it should further the government's goal "to transform local governments into more financially self-reliant units responding to the needs of the people."[29]

The Change Process: Administration and Behavior

The RPTA began via a series of pilot projects from 1972 to 1978 as a component of the USAID-supported Provincial Development Action Program (PDAP). It was later upgraded to a self-standing nationwide program, and has since been implemented in four phases.[30] Extension of RPTA to a fifth phase is now under review.

Philippine policymakers have not attempted to use RPTA as a vehicle for promoting fundamental change in the system of real property taxation. In their analysis, the system's basic design is sound. However, a critical shortcoming has been incomplete and inaccurate valuation rolls because of reliance both on voluntary taxpayer self-declaration and cooperation among several often competing parties. RPTA has thus focussed primarily on increasing the coverage and improving the accuracy of valuation rolls through comprehensive tax mapping and simplified mass appraisal:

> The project's approach was to fundamentally change the system of discovery, from one based on owner-declaration to one based on government-executed inventory. Through this reform, the project aimed to

[29]"Real Property Tax Administration Project Logical Framework," included as Appendix B in: Public Administration Service, and Sycip, Gorres, Velayo & Co., Impact Evaluation of the Local Resource Management/Real Property Tax Administration (LRM/RPTA) Project (Manila: U.S. Agency for International Development, Philippine Mission, September 1990).

[30]Phase I: RPTA/MLGCD, May 1978 to December 1981, under the direction of the Ministry of Local Government and Community Development (MLGCD); Phase II: RPTA/MOF, January 1982 to May 1983, under the direction of the MOF; Phase III: RPTA/MDP, 1984 to 1991, also under the direction of the MOF, but as part of the larger World Bank-supported First and Second Municipal Development Projects (MDP); and Phase IV: RPTA/LRM, July 1988 to August 1991, again under the direction of the MOF, but as part of the larger USAID-supported Local Resource Management Project (LRM).

compile in each jurisdiction a comprehensive inventory of all land parcels, incorporating missing parcels and eliminating duplicate claims, and an accurate measurement of all land and building characteristics, to be used in valuation.[31]

Although the details of project implementation have varied from phase to phase, RPTA essentially has been executed via a series of contracts between the central government and local government units (LGUs)[32] for a cost-sharing arrangement whereby local resources are supplemented by national financial, commodity, and technical assistance. RPTA field work usually has been undertaken by regular staff of the local assessor and local treasurer, augmented by temporary contractual labor and aided by project inputs such as surveying equipment, vehicles, and training materials.

RPTA typically has included three components: Tax Mapping; Tax Records Conversion; and Tax Collection.[33]

Tax Mapping is the initial stage of RPTA project implementation, and is the component to which most attention and resources have been devoted. Many government and foreign assistance officials believe Tax Mapping "represents the critical, costly and time consuming component on which the entire system is dependent. Considered as the most important output of this component, the tax map represents the foundation or base needed to build the RPTA system . . ."[34]

Tax Records Conversion comprises valuation of each real property unit (RPU)[35] and preparation of an assessment roll. This entails matching of an RPU's physical characteristics with appropriate base values and adjustment factors to establish market value. Tax Records Conversion also includes preparation of a

---

[31]Dillinger, The Case of the Philippines' Real Property Tax Administration Project, 6-7.

[32]The Philippines is divided into 75 provinces and 60 cities. The provinces are further divided into 1,533 municipalities. In this discussion, "local government" refers to provinces, municipalities, and cities; "local government unit" refers only to cities and municipalities.

[33]The following discussion summarizes much more detailed descriptions of RPTA field activities in: Real Property Tax Administration (RPTA) Regional Project Management Office, Terminal Report: LRM-RPTA Project Phase III, *Region VI* (Iloilo City: RPTA Regional Project Management Office, August 1991), 11; and Dillinger, The Case of the Philippines' Real Property Tax Administration Project, 8-10.

[34]RPTA Regional Project Management Office, Terminal Report, 11. Tax Mapping is further divided into the three steps of pre-field preparation, actual field operations, and post-field tie-up.

[35]During most of RPTA implementation, one parcel of real property could comprise up to four real property units: land, plants and trees, improvements, and machinery.

notice of assessment for all properties (Part A of the Real Property Tax Order of Payment, or RPTOP).[36]

Tax Collection is under the supervision of the local treasurer, unlike Tax Mapping and Tax Records Conversion, which are directed by the local assessor. This stage includes preparation of current year property tax bills (Part B of the RPTOP), tax campaigns, tax payment, and enforcement.[37]

RPTA has been implemented in a wide variety of political and economic environments, ranging from martial law (1972 to 1981) to the "people power" revolution (1986), as well as from periods of relative economic stability and modest growth to intermittent "oil price shocks," especially in 1973 and 1978. In addition, "peace and order" conditions have not been conducive to administrative reform in several regions of the country, especially where the Moro National Liberation Front (MNLF) is waging a struggle for an autonomous Muslim state (Mindanao and the Sulu Islands) and locations where the New Peoples' Army (NPA) guerilla operations are most active (Negros, northern Luzon, eastern Samar, and southern Palawan).

Another exogenous factor affecting RPTA implementation has been the Comprehensive Agrarian Reform Program (CARP) whereby land has been transferred from large landholders to tenants. In addition to poor records of the reformed properties, there were few incentives either for previous owners to pay the tax on behalf of their former tenants or for the new owners to accept their taxpaying responsibilities:

> . . . some previous owners were delinquent in payment of property taxes at the time of reform. Large landowners have known since 1972 that it was only a matter of time before some of their lands would be confiscated. Under the statutes, owners could receive payments for their land from the Land Bank upon showing proof of payment of all real property taxes on their holdings through October 1972. Such a system could only lead to delinquency after 1972.
>
> Several aspects of the land reform system make it unlikely to expect a significant amount of compliance from tenants, too. First, there has been a great deal of uncertainty associated with the land reform process. . . . Second, the provision that tenants cannot transfer the land to anyone other than heirs or the government makes ownership of these properties unlike

[36]The assessment roll is used by the assessor as an index to tax maps and tax declarations, and by the treasurer as a control for tax collection records. It lists all properties by PIN, and summarizes property information, including the assessed value of land and improvements.

[37]This stage also includes updating of the real property tax account register (RPTAR) based on the new assessment roll.

> that of other taxed assets . . . Third, many tenants were not aware that their rental payments since 1972 would, in fact, be counted as payment toward the purchase of the land. Fourth, there may have been a lack of understanding concerning legal responsibilities associated with property ownership . . . Fifth, there may have been an ability-to-pay problem . . . [38]

RPTA implementors also encountered four administrative and financial constraints caused by the design of RPTA itself: ill-advised organizational placement within the central government; inadequate and untimely financial support to participating LGUs; weak reporting and management information systems; and overcentralized management and supervision.[39]

Despite these difficulties, the total investment in RPTA has been substantial, estimated at approximately $35.7 million:

- $8.9 million in Phases I and II (excluding the PDAP pilot projects);[40]

- $16.0 million in Phase III ($5.0 million and $11.0 million from the RPTA component of the First and Second Municipal Development Projects, respectively);[41] and

- $10.8 million in Phase IV.[42]

- RPTA has been implemented in approximately 827 LGUs, or roughly half of the 1,593 LGUs in the Philippines, over the past two decades:

---

[38]Roy Bahl and Barbara D. Miller, eds., Local Government Finance in the Third World: A Case Study of the Philippines (New York: Praeger Publishers, 1983), 52-3. Similar concerns are voiced in: Public Administration Service and SGV & Co., Impact Evaluation of the LRM/RPTA Project, ii.

[39]Detailed discussions of these problems can be found in: Daniel Holland, Michael Wasylenko, and Roy Bahl, The Real Property Tax Administration Project, Metropolitan Studies Program Monograph no. 9 (Syracuse: Syracuse University, October 1980), 29-45; Dillinger, The Case of the Philippines' Real Property Tax Administration Project, 11-15; and Public Administration Service and SGV & Co., Impact Evaluation of the LRM/RPTA Project, 4-10.

[40]Dillinger, The Case of the Philippines' Real Property Tax Administration Project, 21.

[41]The World Bank, East Asia and Pacific Projects Department, Urban and Water Supply Division, Staff Appraisal Report: Philippines Municipal Development Project, Report No. 5027-PH (Washington, D.C.: The World Bank, May 10, 1984), v; and The World Bank, Asia Regional Office, Country Department II, Infrastructure Division, Staff Appraisal Report: Second Municipal Development Project, Report No. 7873-PH (Washington, D.C.: The World Bank, November 17, 1989), ii.

[42]From the "Basic Project Identification Data" sheet contained (unnumbered) in: Public Administration Service and SGV & Co., Impact Evaluation of the LRM/RPTA Project.

- 571 LGUs in Phases I and II (nationwide);[43]
- 72 LGUs in Phase III (nationwide);[44] and
- 184 LGUs in Phase IV (in Regions V and VI).[45]

In addition to extensive geographic coverage, RPTA has certainly achieved one of its principal objectives, the generation of more complete and accurate fiscal cadastres:

> From a technical standpoint, RPTA illustrates the successful application of low cost mapping and assessment techniques. In a typical jurisdiction, RPTA began with only two sources of property information: long-outdated base maps . . . and the incomplete and inaccurate declarations of current property-tax payers. From this starting point, RPTA was able to produce comprehensive parcellary maps, and individual, objectively derived, property assessments, at an average cost of about US$2.50 per land parcel. This was made possible by the adoption of minimum standards for mapping and assessment. In preparing the parcellary maps, no attempt was made to demarcate legal boundaries or to adjudicate title. Mapping standards were instead adopted to the specific requirements of a fiscal cadastre: to account for all land in the jurisdiction, to delineate parcels sufficiently to permit subsequent identification, and to obtain the square footage data needed for assessment. Assessments themselves were derived using a simple mass appraisal technique, in which a small number of measurable property characteristics are used as the basis for calculating relative value.[46]

RPTA's impact on assessment values and tax revenue have been much less encouraging, as discussed in the following section. The current estimated cost of

[43]Dillinger, The Case of the Philippines' Real Property Tax Administration Project, 11. This figure includes the LGUs which participated in PDAP pilot projects.

[44]The World Bank, Asia Regional Office, Country Department II, Infrastructure Division, Staff Appraisal Report: Third Municipal Development Project, draft, Annex 2.

[45]Public Administration Service and SGV & Co., Impact Evaluation of the LRM/RPTA Project, 2.

[46]Dillinger, The Case of the Philippines' Real Property Tax Administration Project, iv.

extending RPTA to all remaining LGUs in the Philippines is approximately $38 million.[47]

THE PHILIPPINE PROPERTY TAX IN PRACTICE: SYSTEM PERFORMANCE

Purpose: Revenue and Non-Revenue Objectives

Revenue Generation

Nominal property tax revenue in the Philippines has increased at a compounded annual rate of nearly 20 percent over the past two decades, rising 24-fold from P178 million in 1972 to P4.3 billion in 1990 (see Table III-3)[48]. If nominal property tax receipts are converted to 1985 pesos, the compounded annual rate of increase is 5 percent over the past two decades, with total revenue rising 2.4 times from P1.2 billion in 1972 to P2.9 billion in 1990. Furthermore, after a relatively steady rise in tax receipts from 1972 to 1983, revenue fell during the mid-1980s and did not return to 1983 levels until 1989 (see Figure III-2).[49]

The role of property tax revenue in the Philippine national economy has remained relatively constant over the past two decades. Property tax revenue's share of total revenue has ranged from a 1987 low of 2.3 percent to a high in 1983 of 3.4 percent. Property tax revenue as a share of gross domestic product has remained constant at between 0.3 and 0.4 percent (see Table III-4).[50]

---

[47]Public Administration Service and SGV & Co., Impact Evaluation of the LRM/RPTA Project, ii.

[48]Department of Finance, Bureau of Local Government, "Consolidated Income and Expenditures of LGU's: Calendar Years 1972 - 1990" (Manila: Bureau of Local Government, March 1991), unnumbered.

[49]Gross national product deflators are taken from: International Monetary Fund, Bureau of Statistics, International Financial Statistics (Washington, D.C.: International Monetary Fund), monthly issues and yearbooks.

[50]Department of Finance, Bureau of Local Government, "Consolidated Income and Expenditures of LGU's: Calendar Years 1972 - 1990"; and International Monetary Fund, International Financial Statistics, "1990 Yearbook" (vol. 43), 584-89 and "September 1991" (vol. 44), 432-35 (Washington, D.C.: IMF, 1990 and 1991).

FIGURE III-2:
PROPERTY TAX REVENUE IN THE PHILIPPINES

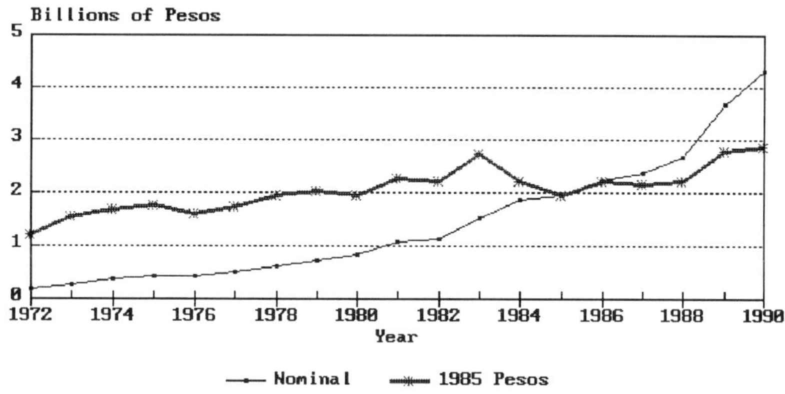

Source: Author's calculations.

TABLE III-3: PROPERTY TAX REVENUE IN THE PHILIPPINES

Year	Property Tax Receipts (millions of pesos)	
	Nominal Pesos	*1985 Pesos*
1972	178	1,211
1973	270	1,552
1974	385	1,696
1975	429	1,744
1976	431	1,602
1977	504	1,744
1978	615	1,946
1979	738	2,027
1980	821	1,955
1981	1,068	2,292
1982	1,125	2,223
1983	1,540	2,726
1984	1,875	2,216
1985	1,951	1,951
1986	2,258	2,236
1987	2,375	2,175
1988	2,670	2,231
1989	3,678	2,780
1990	4,310	2,883[a]

[a]Estimated.

Source: Department of Finance, Bureau of Local Government, "Consolidated Income and Expenditures of LGU's: Calender Years 1972 - 1990."

TABLE III-4: PROPERTY TAX REVENUE IN THE PHILIPPINE ECONOMY

(millions of pesos)

Year	Property Tax Receipts	Total Revenue	Share of Total Revenue	Gross Domestic Product	Share of GDP
1972	178	6,950	2.6%	56,070	0.3%
1973	270	9,430	2.9%	72,320	0.4%
1974	385	11,919	3.2%	99,490	0.4%
1975	429	16,657	2.6%	114,700	0.4%
1976	431	17,895	.4%	135,270	0.3%
1977	504	19,782	2.5%	154,230	0.3%
1978	615	23,826	2.6%	177,670	0.3%
1979	738	29,095	2.5%	217,540	0.3%
1980	821	34,151	2.4%	264,650	0.3%
1981	1,068	35,478	3.0%	305,260	0.3%
1982	1,125	37,710	3.0%	340,600	0.3%
1983	1,540	45,290	3.4%	384,100	0.4%
1984	1,875	56,467	3.3%	540,470	0.3%
1985	1,951	68,577	2.8%	612,680	0.3%
1986	2,258	78,714	2.9%	627,130	0.4%
1987	2,375	101,495	2.3%	708,370	0.3%
1988	2,670	111,086	2.4%	825,850	0.3%
1989	3,678	151,079	2.4%	964,000	0.4%
1990	4,310	178,522	2.4%	,066,300	0.4%

Sources: Department of Finance, Bureau of Local Government, "Consolidated Income and Expenditures of LGU's: Calender Years 1972 - 1990"; and International Monetary Fund, *International Financial Statistics*, "1990 Yearbook" (vol. 43), 584-89 and "September 1991" (vol. 44), 432-35 (Washington, D.C.: IMF, 1990 and 1991).

However, the role of property tax revenue in Philippine local government finances has increased greatly over the past two decades. In 1972, the property tax generated 27 percent of local revenue and 13 percent of total local government resources. By 1990, the property tax share of locally-generated revenue had risen to 44 percent, while property tax receipts had increased to 26 percent of total local government income (see Table III-5 and Figure III-3).[51] This growth has occurred despite a 12-fold nominal increase in local government income as well as expenditures.[52] While most would claim that revenue adequacy has not yet been achieved, these trends are especially significant given the principal objective of the real property tax to provide local governments "adequate funds with which to underwrite basic and essential public services within their respective areas of responsibility," so local governments can become "potent political subdivisions contributing their proportionate shares to national progress."[53]

FIGURE III-3:
PHILIPPINE PROPERTY TAX IN LOCAL FINANCE

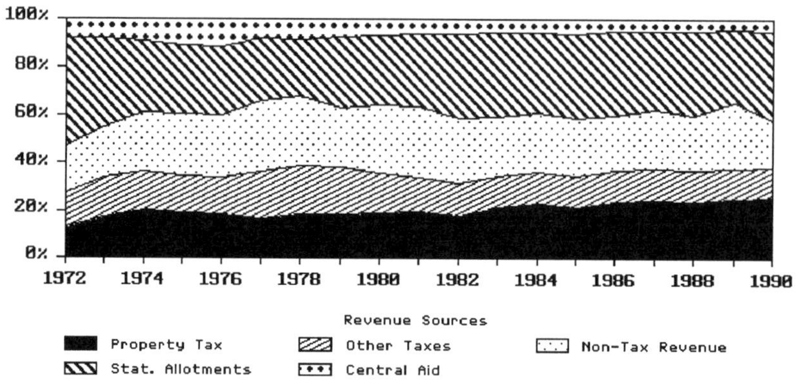

Source: Author's calculations.

---

[51]Department of Finance, Bureau of Local Government, "Consolidated Income and Expenditures of LGU's: Calendar Years 1972 - 1990."

[52]From 1972 to 1990, local government income rose from P1.4 billion to P16.6 billion, and expenditures increased from P1.3 billion to P15.4 billion (see Table III-5).

[53]Presidential Decree No. 464, Preamble.

TABLE III-5: PROPERTY TAX REVENUE IN PHILIPPINE LOCAL GOVERNMENT FINANCES

(millions of pesos)

Year	**Local Sources**				**External Sources**		**Total**	**% Prop. Tax**
	Property Tax	*Other Taxes*	*Non-Tax Revenue*	*% Prop.*	*Stat. Allot-Tax*	*Central Aid ments*		
1972	178	199	278	27%	614	110	1,379	13%
1973	270	263	337	31%	575	125	1,570	17%
1974	385	307	463	33%	554	173	1,882	20%
1975	429	346	575	32%	630	233	2,213	19%
1976	431	368	600	31%	675	260	2,334	18%
1977	504	586	890	25%	771	238	2,989	17%
1978	615	674	941	28%	774	274	3,278	19%
1979	738	799	88	29%	1,186	288	3,999	18%
1980	821	44	1,214	30%	1,238	295	4,312	19%
1981	1,068	780	1,606	31%	1,650	328	5,432	20%
1982	1,125	839	1,694	31%	2,203	354	6,215	18%
1983	1,540	953	1,752	36%	2,519	365	7,129	22%
1984	1,875	1,032	,995	38%	2,676	406	7,984	23%
1985	1,951	1,204	2,218	36%	3,205	530	9,108	21%
1986	2,258	1,266	2,182	40%	3,299	441	9,446	24%
1987	2,375	1,290	2,402	39%	3,142	452	9,661	25%
1988	2,670	1,474	2,573	40%	3,974	514	11,205	24%
1989	3,678	1,800	,014	39%	4,343	626	14,461	25%
1990	4,310	2,084	3,323	44%	6,175	740	16,632	26%

Source: Department of Finance, Bureau of Local Government, "Consolidated Income and Expenditures of LGU's: Calender Years 1972 - 1990."

Non-Revenue Objectives

The primary non-revenue objective of the real property tax is conversion of strategically located idle lands to more productive purposes through imposition of a 5 percent idle lands tax. However, this provision of the Real Property Tax Code has not yet been applied in practice.

Attempts to increase the vertical equity of property tax incidence through differential and progressive assessment levels have served mainly to encourage deliberate misclassification of property use and underestimation of property value by precisely those whose tax burden these schedules are designed to augment. Such tax evasion is sometimes undertaken at the taxpayer's volition, and sometimes it is a cooperative venture with local tax officials. In either case, the results are personally remunerative, if not revenue enhancing.[54]

Principles: Efficiency, Equity, and Sustainability

Property tax coverage is not easy to determine in the Philippines. The valuation roll appears to be relatively comprehensive, and coverage does not seem to be significantly compromised through ineffective discovery. However, the tax potential of this extensive valuation roll is not realized due to: inaccurate information on property characteristics; lack of indexing for inflation; obsolete schedules of market values; statutory limits on effective tax rates; low collection efficiency; and weak enforcement measures.

At first glance, RPTA reports might lead one to conclude that tax mapping has led to the discovery of many unlisted properties. In a sample of tax mapping results from 130 LGUs in Western Visayas and Metropolitan Manila, for example, a number of real property units rose an average of 23 percent after RPTA-sponsored tax mapping (see Table III-6).[55]

---

[54]A more detailed account of why very progressive statutory tax systems often result in highly regressive effective tax systems can be found in: Vito Tanzi, The IMF and Tax Reform, IMF Working Paper WP/90/39 (Washington, D.C.: International Monetary Fund, Fiscal Affairs Department, April 1990), 14.

[55]RPTA Regional Project Management Office, Terminal Report, 15-17; and Municipality of Muntinlupa, "Real Property Tax Administration Project, Summary of Work Accomplishment, Municipality of Muntinlupa," December 31, 1989, photocopied.

TABLE III-6: DISCOVERY OF REAL PROPERTY UNITS IN THE PHILIPPINES

Province/ City	No. of LG Us	No. of RPUs (Pre)	No. of RPUs (Post)	Increase in No. of RPUs	Percent Increase
Provinces					
Aklan	17	208,694	244,716	36,022	17%
Antique	18	168,154	206,353	38,199	23%
Capiz	16	124,055	146,023	21,968	18%
Guimaras	3	34,486	46,335	11,849	34%
Iloilo	43	406,671	456,082	49,411	12%
Negros Occid.	26	231,177	311,090	79,913	35%
Metro Manila	1	36,892	50,631	13,739	37%
Cities	6	77,458	120,682	43,224	56%
Total	**130**	**1,287,587**	**1,581,912**	**294,325**	**23%**

Note: The local government unit (LGU) from Metro Manila is the Municipality of Muntinlupa; the cities are all from Region VI (Western Visayas), and include Cadiz, Silay, Bago, Roxas, La Carlota, and San Carlos.

Sources: RPTA Regional Project Management Office, *Terminal Report*, 15-17; and Municipality of Muntinlupa, "Real Property Tax Administration Project, Summary of Work Accomplishment."

A closer look at these numbers reveals that despite the dramatic increase in real property units after tax mapping, the total number of properties on the valuation rolls did not change appreciably, and in Muntinlupa (Manila), although the number of land parcels rose 40 percent, the total area after tax mapping actually declined by 38 percent due to a municipality boundary change. The key is definitional: for much of RPTA, land and plants/trees were treated as separate real property units, so one property could comprise up to four RPUs (improvements and machinery were the other two categories). This led to a proliferation of RPUs. After Department Order 45-89 required the integration of land and plants/trees on the property record form, the increase in RPUs in the Western Visayas following tax mapping fell from 50 percent to 6 percent.[56]

Similar confusion is caused by reports regarding RPTA impact on assessed values. In the same sample of 130 LGUs from the Western Visayas and Metropolitan Manila, the assessed value of real property units doubled after RPTA (see Table III-7). However, most of this increase is not attributed to the discovery of previously unlisted properties. Instead, the rise in total assessed value is due primarily to adoption of new schedules of market values, together with reclassification of property use[57] and concomitant higher assessment ratios.[58] Similar conclusions were presented in an evaluation of earlier phases of RPTA:

> Contrary to expectations, the major source of growth in assessments is not the discovery of new parcels, but rather the revaluation of existing ones. In cities, new discoveries produced only a 4.1 percent increase in total assessments, compared to a twelve percent increase due to revaluations. In municipalities, new discoveries increased total assessments by 9 percent; revaluations increased total assessments by 42 percent.[59]

---

[56]RPTA Regional Project Management Office, Terminal Report, 15-17; and Municipality of Muntinlupa, "Real Property Tax Administration Project, Summary of Work Accomplishment." The 23 percent figure in Table III-6 combines both the "First Batch" and the "Second Batch" of participating LGUs, corresponding to before and after the issuance of Department Order 45-89.

[57]Most reclassification was due either to subdivision of agricultural land for residential use, or conversion of agricultural land to commercial or industrial use.

[58]RPTA Regional Project Management Office, Terminal Report, 17-20; Municipality of Muntinlupa, "Real Property Tax Administration Project, Summary of Work Accomplishment"; and Public Administration Service and SGV & Co., Impact Evaluation of the LRM/RPTA Project, 27.

[59]Dillinger, The Case of the Philippines' Real Property Tax Administration Project, 15.

TABLE III-7: ASSESSMENT OF REAL PROPERTY UNITS IN THE PHILIPPINES

(millions of pesos)

Province/ City	No. of LGUs	Assessed Value (Pre)	Assessed Value (Post)	Assessed Value Increase	Percent Increase
Provinces					
Aklan	17	499	2,185	1,686	338%
Antique	18	316	1,427	1,111	342%
Capiz	16	1,255	2,632	1,377	110%
Guimaras	3	221	364	143	65%
Iloilo	43	2,897	4,852	1,955	67%
Negros Occid.	26	4,434	9,145	4,711	106%
Metro Manila	1	1,956	3,436	1,480	76%
Cities	6	1,862	3,691	1,829	98%
Total	130	13,440	27,732	14,292	106%

Note: The local government unit (LGU) from Metro Manila is the Municipality of Muntinlupa; the cities are all from Region VI (Western Visayas), and include Cadiz, Silay, Bago, Roxas, La Carlota, and San Carlos.

Sources: RPTA Regional Project Management Office, *Terminal Report*, 17-20; and Municipality of Muntinlupa, "Real Property Tax Administration Project, Summary of Work Accomplishment."

Some RPTA implementors have noted that an important tax mapping objective was to remove duplications from the valuation rolls, so even a decrease in total RPUs or total assessed value could be viewed as a positive project result. Statistics have not been compiled systematically on the discovery of duplicate property listings discovered through tax mapping. However, data from Phase II of RPTA implementation suggest invalid records removed have totalled approximately 3 percent of total assessed value in cities and 10 percent of total assessed value in municipalities.[60]

Although properties usually are identified and listed on valuation rolls in some fashion, tax base coverage is decreased considerably by inaccurate information on characteristics of these properties. It appears to be common practice among taxpayers and government officials to deliberately under-report property values and fail to report changes in property condition and use, despite legal requirements to the contrary. Coverage is further eroded by the lack of a system to index values for inflation, however outdated or inaccurate these values might be, together with the constant postponement of effective dates for new market value schedules.

For instance, the peso's value in 1985 was half of its value in 1982 (see Exchange Rates following the Table of Contents), so although annual property tax revenue almost doubled during this period, the real value of property tax revenue in 1985 was actually less than it was three years earlier (see Figure III-2).

Delays in implementation of general revisions of real property assessments have occurred so often they are difficult to reconstruct. For example, the 1981 general revision's original effective date was 1982; it was postponed to 1984, delayed again until 1987, and then it took effect over a three-year period.[61] Implementation was further complicated by a general amnesty on property tax arrears from July 1987 to March 1988.

The effects of undervaluation, inflation, and postponed general revisions are compounded by statutory limits on effective tax rates. Nominal tax rates are reasonably high, with a maximum combined rate of 2 percent for municipalities and provinces and 3 percent for cities (including the SEF levy). Fractional assessment levels, however, drive these rates much lower.[62] For example, a 30 percent assessment ratio for all residential land and 15 percent ratio for a low-value residential building pushes the effective rates in municipalities down to 0.6 percent and 0.3 percent, respectively. The effects can be quite dramatic: the 1989 assessed

[60]Dillinger, The Case of the Philippines' Real Property Tax Administration Project, 15-16.

[61]40 percent in 1987, 30 percent in 1988, and 30 percent in 1989.

[62]An extensive demonstration of the effects of understated property values and fractional assessment rates is presented in: Public Administration Service and SGV & Co., Impact Evaluation of the LRM/RPTA Project, 41.

value of all property in the Western Visayas is only one-third of the estimated total market value (see Figure III-4).[63]

Coverage is decreased further by poor collection performance. Although collection efficiency (current revenue as a percent of current billings) is difficult to determine because of lack of credible and comparable billing and collection statistics, as well as considerable variation among different local government units, it appears that tax collections have averaged 50 to 60 percent of current billings and between 20 and 30 percent of total collectibles (including arrears as well as current billings) over the past decade.[64]

The introduction of collection targets in 1989 further obfuscates the calculation of collection efficiency. Recovery of tax arrears is even more difficult to determine because of the carryover of cumulative arrears that are often not collectible. For example, Western Visayas officials calculated "collection efficiency" as 88 percent in 1989.

This figure compares tax collected with the tax collection target; this target was only 35 percent of total collectibles in 1989, so tax revenue as a percent of *collectibles* was actually only 30 percent (see Figure III-5). Likewise, in 1990, "collection efficiency" exceeded 100 percent in Western Visayas, but was only 40 percent of total tax collectibles.[65]

---

[63]Republic of the Philippines, Department of Finance, Bureau of Local Government Finance, Local Finance Window VI (Iloilo City: Bureau of Local Government Finance, Region VI, 1990), unnumbered.

[64]Dillinger, The Case of the Philippines' Real Property Tax Administration Project, 19-20; Public Administration Service and SGV & Co., Impact Evaluation of the LRM/RPTA Project, Table 12; RPTA Regional Project Management Office, , Local Finance Window VI, unnumbered; and The World Bank, Staff Appraisal Report: Second Municipal Terminal Report, 10; Bureau of Local Government Finance Development Project, 53. Collection rates have not varied significantly between the basic property tax and the SEF levy.

[65]RPTA Regional Project Management Office, Terminal Report, 10; and Bureau of Local Government Finance, Local Finance Window VI, unnumbered. Similar examples are presented in: Public Administration Service and SGV & Co., Impact Evaluation of the LRM/RPTA Project, 28-30.

FIGURE III-4:
COMPOSITION OF VALUE IN WESTERN VISAYAS

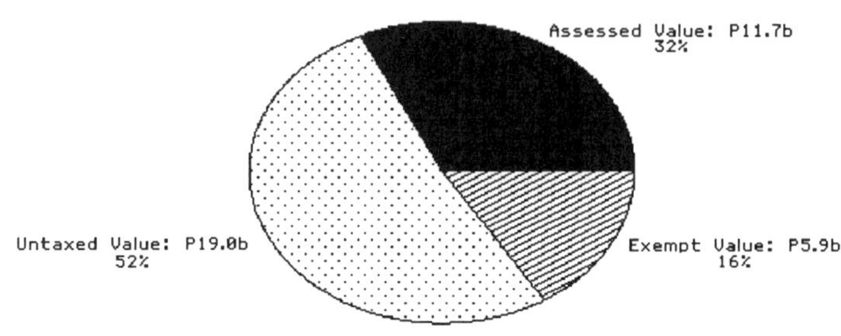

1989 TOTAL MARKET VALUE

Source: Author's calculations.

FIGURE III-5:
COLLECTION TARGETS IN WESTERN VISAYAS

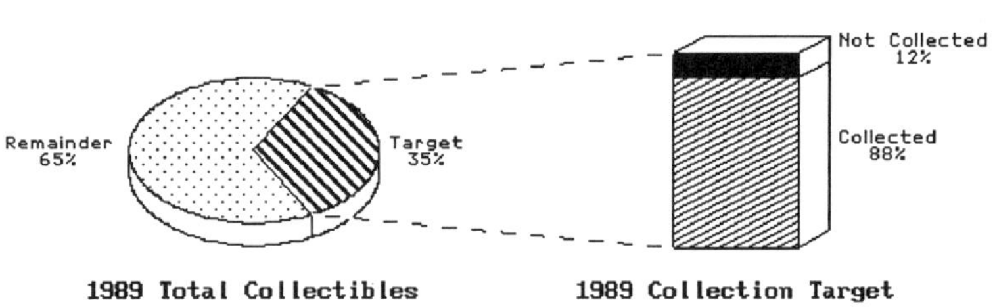

Source: Author's calculations.

FIGURE III-6:
CUMULATIVE ARREARS IN WESTERN VISAYAS

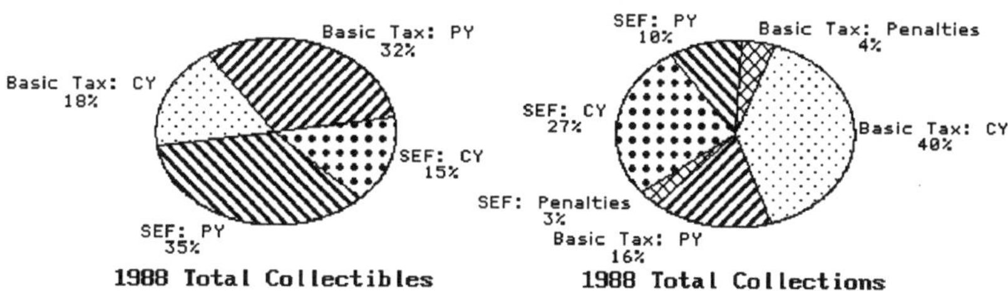

PY = Previous Years CY = Current Year

Source: Author's calculations.

Inclusion of uncollectible cumulative arrears does indeed distort collection performance in a negative and unfair way. A more accurate reflection of collection efficiency could be achieved simply by separating current from past liabilities in billing and collection statistics, so that "collection targets" are in fact one hundred percent of current billings. Progress on collection of arrears could then be monitored independently to determine the best allocation of scarce administrative resources. For example, in Western Visayas, arrears accounted for two-thirds of total collectibles in 1988 (see Figure III-6). Although 47 percent of current tax liabilities were collected, only 9 percent of arrears were collected, so local officials are faced with a dilemma: if they report "collection efficiency" as total collections versus total collectibles, the 22 percent rate understates their success in collecting current tax liabilities; if they report collections as a percent of their collection target, the 88 percent figure overstates "collection efficiency" as traditionally defined.[66]

Regarding the impact of RPTA on collection efficiency, the results of Phase II are not encouraging:

> To the extent the data permits any conclusion, it appears that RPTA's expected impact on collection do not occur. In the 76 projects providing data, collection efficiency ***dropped*** in the first post RPTA year; from an average of 56 percent pre-RPTA, to an average of 50 percent post-RPTA. Total collections (on current account) increased by only 1.1 percent, despite an increase in valid assessments of 37.5 percent; and an increase in collectibles (as reported by treasurers) of 13.6 percent.[67]

The results from Phase IV of RPTA are mixed. Collections from 1989 through 1991 in Region VI (Western Visayas) were an average of 57 percent more than 1988 collections each year. This increase is about twice the national average increase for 1989 and 1990 (see Table III-3).[68] How much of Region VI's revenue performance should be attributed to RPTA is unclear, given that: the same project package has yet to produce comparable results in Region V (the other participant in Phase IV of RPTA);[69] and Department of Finance officials generally acknowledge Western Visayas as among the best managed of its regional offices during this period, primarily because of the leadership and administrative skills of the newly-appointed regional director, especially in his aggressive application of new national schedules of market values.

Aggregate figures are not readily available to calculate the cost of property tax administration. However, it is possible to look at indicative administrative costs and returns for RPTA implementation. An evaluation of Phases I and II of RPTA concluded that for Phase II, the project cost per land parcel was approximately P40 (in 1984 prices), the 1.1 percent increase in actual collections equalled about P0.30 per parcel, and therefore:

> At this rate, a local government would have to wait 140 years to recover (without interest) the costs of the project. If pre-RPTA collection performance could, however, be sustained on post-RPTA assessments, the financial return would improve considerably. The 37 percent increase in valid ***assessments*** in Phase II represents an average increase of about P2000 per land parcel. At an average tax rate of 2.5 percent, this would yield an increase in tax liability of about P50 per land parcel. Assuming a

---

[67]Dillinger, The Case of the Philippines' Real Property Tax Administration Project, 19.

[68]Nationwide 1991 figures are not yet available.

[69]Public Administration Service and SGV & Co., Impact Evaluation of the LRM/RPTA Project, Tables 1 and 4.

sustained collection rate of 50 percent, actual tax revenues would increase by P25 per land parcel per year, an amount sufficient to cover the full cost of RPTA in slightly less than two years.[70]

Data from Phase IV of RPTA are much more encouraging. In Western Visayas, the regional project cost per RPU was P63 for the 56 LGUs that implemented all three project components, and P39 for the 73 LGUs that implemented only Records Conversion and Tax Collection (Tax Mapping was implemented earlier with other resources).[71] The post-project increase in assessed value for these 129 LGUs was P12.8 billion, or P8,100 per RPU (see Tables III-6 and III-7). At an average tax rate of 2 percent and a 50 percent collection rate for current tax liabilities, this increased assessment would generate P80 per RPU, enough to recover the project investment per RPU in less than a year. Globally, RPTA Phase IV implementation in Region VI cost P77 million over three years (July 1988 through August 1991), or 10 percent of total collections in Western Visayas from 1989 through 1991.[72] Again, using the P12.8 billion increase in assessments, and the above-noted assumptions of an average tax rate of 2 percent and a 50 percent collection rate, these assessments should generate approximately P128 million more in revenue a year, or enough to recover the regional project cost in less than one year.

Finally, wide and equitable coverage has been greatly reduced because of reluctance to invoke sanctions in response to low levels of voluntary taxpayer compliance: arrears appear generally to be inversely related to property value, with the wealthiest real estate owners the least willing to comply. These enforcement difficulties are primarily administrative and political, however, as the statutory provisions for enforcement measures are both extensive and explicit.

Enforcement problems begin with the great difficulty local treasurers have in generating a reliable delinquency list. The entire payment system is manual, cumbersome, and prone to both undetected bookkeeping errors and considerable time lags. However, even if enforcement proceedings are begun, it is an administrative nightmare to execute the milder sanctions and a political nightmare to apply the harsher sanctions. Consequently, while the theory of RPTA is to increase both revenue and equity by improving the quality and coverage of the

[70] Dillinger, The Case of the Philippines' Real Property Tax Administration Project, 22.

[71] RPTA Regional Project Management Office, *Terminal Report*, 38-40.

[72] RPTA Regional Project Management Office, Terminal Report, 38-40.

valuation roll, "RPTA now succeeds only in shifting the point of evasion from assessment to collections."[73]

[73]Dillinger, The Case of the Philippines' Real Property Tax Administration Project, 22.

4

CHILE CASE STUDY

There is one difference between a tax collector and a taxidermist - the taxidermist leaves the hide.

Mortimer Caplan, Director,
Bureau of Internal Revenue,
Time, February 1, 1963

THE CHILEAN PROPERTY TAX IN PERSPECTIVE: CASE STUDY SNAPSHOT

Chilean government officials have devoted considerable effort and resources over the past two decades to improving the efficiency and equity of property taxation. The drive to improve property taxation in Chile commenced with promulgation of a new property tax law in 1969, and continued through the next 18 years with further statutory, information systems, and administrative reform. These efforts culminated in the 1987 mandatory ten-year general revaluation of non-agricultural real estate, at which time government officials tried to fine-tune an already relatively efficient and equitable property tax system.

The first half of this exercise, normalization (the updating of property-related data) went quite well, characterized by administrative innovation and taxpayer cooperation. However, the second half of these reform activities, the general revaluation itself (determination and application of new land and building fiscal values) is now stalled indefinitely.

This is due primarily to the well-meant but ill-conceived attempt of reformers to keep their efforts revenue neutral following a decade of dramatic increases in property values. Rather than enhance equity, this policy has in fact greatly contracted the country's effective tax base, and thus led to great taxpayer resentment because of popularly perceived inequities. The political lesson is clear. Little gratitude should be expected either by those effectively outside of the tax system (property owners who were exempt before, and remain exempt after the general revaluation), or by those who benefit from the results of the general revaluation (taxpayers whose tax liabilities fall). In contrast, the vociferous discontent of those relatively few property owners hit with large tax increases and left paying most of the tax can be powerful enough to block completion of reform.

In short, property tax reform in Chile has been a well-executed effort to achieve a worthy objective stymied by well-intentioned but self-defeating constraints.

THE CHILEAN PROPERTY TAX IN LAW: SYSTEM DESIGN

Tax Base

According to Law No. 17.235 of December 24, 1969, real estate in Chile is divided into two categories for property taxation: agricultural and non-agricultural. These categories are defined by property use rather than location.[1] Annex No.1 to Law 17.235 presents an extensive list of full and partial exemptions to the property tax. These exemptions are both specific and general, and are expressed in terms of percent of property tax liability.[2]

Property tax legislation also prescribes universal individual exemptions to establish minimum taxation thresholds. These exemptions are periodically revised to reflect price changes. Current exemptions are P4.8 million for non-agricultural residential property and P770,000 for agricultural property.[3] Sometimes both a percentage exemption and a flat exemption apply to a specific property, in which case only the most favorable exemption is to be used.[4]

---

[1]Law No. 17.235, Article 1. Formally, this law is referred to as *La Ley sobre Impuesto Territorial*, and real estate is classified as *Bienes Raíces Agrícolas* and *Bienes Raíces no Agrícolas*. Agricultural real estate is that which is used or potentially used predominantly for primary agricultural production, including animal husbandry, aquaculture, and forestry. Assessment excludes property value primarily attributed to improvements such as: irrigation and drainage systems; artificial dryland pastures; anti-erosion and other environmental protection measures; bridges; and roads. Non-agricultural real estate comprises property used for purposes other than agriculture. Machinery is excluded from the real property tax base, however, as are mining buildings, equipment, and production.

[2]*Cuadro Anexo No. 1: Nómina de exenciones totales o parciales del impuesto territorial.* Annex No. 1 to Law No. 17.235 is exceedingly detailed and complex. The list of exemptions is 22 single-spaced pages, and is accompanied by 198 explanatory notes. Full exemption is provided for real estate of the national government; local governments; non-profit foundations; non-profit educational, cultural, religious and medical institutions; cemeteries; and diplomatic missions. Partial exemptions range from 20 to 75 percent, the most prevalent being for hotels, motels, hostels, and boarding houses; property of agrarian reform participants; artificially-created forests; and selected property in the provinces of Arica, Chiloé, Aysén, and Magallanes.

[3]Although the convention in Chile is to use the "$" prefix for figures in pesos, "P" will be used to indicate pesos in this text to avoid confusion with the U.S. dollar. In 1990, the average exchange rate was P305.06 for US$1.00; see Exchange Rates following the Table of Contents for a full listing of exchange rates since 1970.

[4]Marco Montes, "Introduction to the Chile Case Study," in *International Conference on Property Taxation and Its Inter-action with Land Policy: Resource Manual*, vol. 2 (Cambridge, Mass.: Lincoln Institute of Land Policy, September 1991), 671.

Tax Rate

According to Law No. 17.235 (as amended), the tax rate is 20 per mil, or 2 percent, per annum. The same tax rate applies to all real property in Chile, regardless of location or use. This tax rate is applied to total taxable value, defined as the sum of the property's land and building fiscal value, less exemptions. In addition, a 30 percent tax assessment surcharge is applied to all real estate, except residential property less than or equal to P8.8 million.[5]

Valuation

Real estate valuation in Chile is done on a mass appraisal basis for property taxation, using standard unit costs for land and buildings and then applying a series of adjustment coefficients to these base values to determine "fiscal value" (see Figure IV-1). Fiscal value is formula-derived for taxation purposes, and thus, approximates but is not synonymous with market value.[6]

Agricultural land is divided into twelve classes of current or potential use based on 1960 aerophotography. The focus on actual or potential productivity is essential as the tax on agricultural land serves as a proxy income tax for farmers, who are not subject to the national income tax.[7]

Each class of agricultural land is assigned a base value per hectare, by location, which is then adjusted slightly to accommodate special conditions or regulations, if warranted.[8]

---

[5]Law No. 17.235, Article 15, as amended by Law No. 18.591, Article 20. The residential property exemption is as of June 1991. Most tax-related exemptions in Chile are adjusted regularly for inflation, so what might occasionally appear as inconsistencies in this chapter are inflation-indexed nominal figures for different points in time.

[6]Although market prices are an important component of fiscal value calculations, fiscal values tend to be about 80 percent of market value, because the government: tries to simplify and standardize property valuation by focussing on dominant property attributes that are principal determinants of market value and disregarding property characteristics that marginally affect value; groups similar properties into categories rather than employing an unbroken continuum of values; and prefers to aim below market value to provide itself with a reasonable margin of error.

[7]Four classes of irrigated or irrigable land and eight classes of dry land; the dry land is further broken down into four classes of dry but arable land, and four classes of dry and non-arable land. "Tabla de Clasificación de los Suelos Agrícolas Según Capacidad Potencial de Uso Actual - Fijada por Decreto Supremo No. 208, de 26 de Enero de 1964" (D.O. de 27 de Febrero de 1965).

[8]The latest (1979) revaluation decree for agricultural land, along with corresponding per hectare prices and adjustment factors (in July 1990 pesos) can be found in: Servicio de Impuestos Internos, *Boletin*, n.s. 441

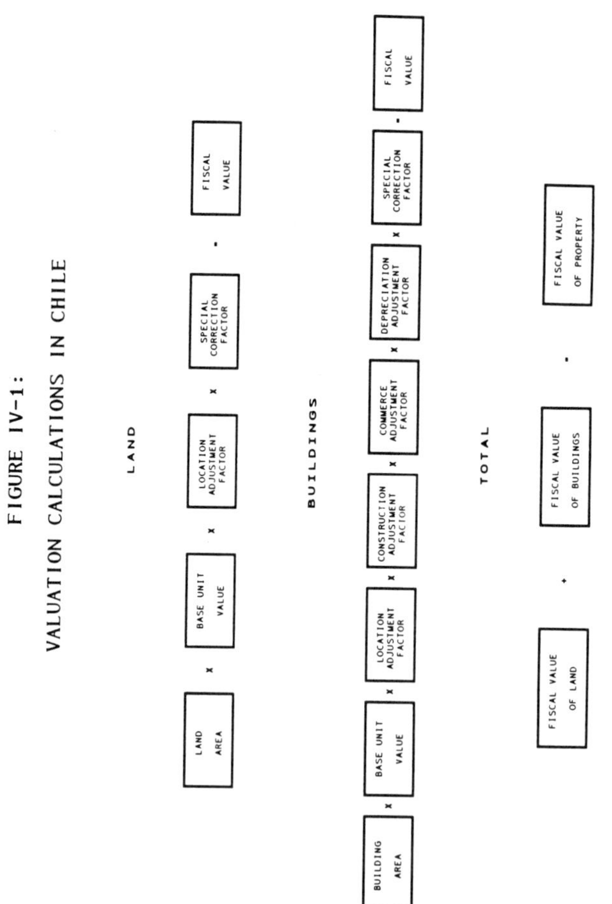

(Agosto 1990), 27.888-27.902. General procedures and data requirements for valuation of agricultural property are outlined in: Law No. 17.235, Article 4.

For non-agricultural land, municipal land value maps are prepared, and each parcel is assigned to a homogeneous urban zone (ZCS, *zona características similares*), or an area of the city with common land characteristics and similar land values. In many cases, these zones are broken down further into microzones for greater precision. As with agricultural land, a base unit price is assigned to each ZCS, and then multiplied by adjustment and correction factors as appropriate.

Buildings, whether on agricultural or non-agricultural land, are grouped into six general classes and thirty-three sub-classes based on construction type. Concurrently, buildings are classified in terms of quality and condition of construction. Matrixes are then prepared combining construction type and quality, and detailing unit values for each category of building listed (see Table IV-1). These base unit values are then multiplied by various adjustment factors to accommodate differences in location, special construction features, degree of commercialization, and age.[9]

Land and building values for both agricultural and non-agricultural property are supposed to be revised every five to ten years,[10] with semi-annual indexing for inflation in the interim.[11]

Valuations can also be modified between general revaluations to correct clerical, calculation, or classification errors; add omissions; and reflect significant value changes due to construction, rehabilitation, demolition, natural disaster, public works, or altered use.[12] Property discovery and property changes are based on the principle of self-declaration, with selective verification and audit by the government. Valuations are undertaken by the Internal Tax Service (SII, *Servicio de Impuestos Internos*).[13]

---

[9]The latest (1990) revaluation decree for non-agricultural property, along with corresponding unit prices and adjustment factors (in July 1990 pesos) can be found in: Servicio de Impuestos Internos, *Boletin*, n.s. 441 (Agosto 1990), 27.875-27.886. General procedures and data requirements for valuation of non-agricultural property are outlined in: Law No. 17.235, Article 4.

[10]Law No. 17.235, Article 3.

[11]Law Decree No. 2.325, Article 1. Property tax values are adjusted automatically every semester based on the consumer price index. The last general revaluation for agricultural land was in 1979 (effective in 1980). The 1990 revaluation has been postponed until 1991 (effective 1992). The last general revaluation for non-agricultural land was implemented in 1990, but its effective date has been postponed until 1993.

[12]Law No. 17.235, Articles 28-37.

[13]Montes, "Introduction to the Chile Case Study," 671-72. Valuations can be appealed to the regional director of SII under whose territorial jurisdiction the property is located. Further objections can be taken to the Special Appeals Court on Property Valuation, and finally, to the Supreme Court.

TABLE IV-1: VALUATION CATEGORIES FOR NON-AGRICULTURAL REAL ESTATE IN CHILE

CONSTRUCTION CLASSES

Construction Type		Structure Type		Code
1.	Traditional	Steel		A
		Concrete		B
		Masonry		C
		Stone		D
		Wood		E
		Adobe		F
2.	Prefabricated	Metal		G
		Wood		H
		Wood/Type A Roof		J
		Plates or Panels		K
3.	Large Structures (*Galpones*)	**Vertical**	**Roof**	
		Solid Steel Rods	Solid Steel Rods	QQ
		Solid Steel Rods	Self-Supporting	QM
		Steel Frames	Solid Steel Rods	AQ
		Steel Frames	Steel Frames	AA
		Steel Frames	Self-Supporting	AM
		Poured Concrete	Solid Steel Rods	BQ
		Poured Concrete	Steel Frames	BA
		Poured Concrete	Poured Concrete	BB
		Poured Concrete	Wood	BE
		Poured Concrete	Self-Supporting	BM
		Masonry	Solid Steel Rods	CQ
		Masonry	Steel Frames	CA
		Masonry	Wood	CE
		Masonry	Self-Supporting	CM
		Wood	Wood	EE
		Adobe	Wood	FE
		Self-Supporting Sheets/Plates	Self-Supporting	MM

(Table IV-1, cont'd)

		Vertical		**Code**
4.	Silos and Similar	Metal Silos		SA
		Poured Concrete Silos		SB
	Structures	Poured Concrete Cubes		SC
5.	Complementary Works	Pavements		P
		Swimming Pools		W
6.	Other			--
Construction Type		**Quality**		**Code**
1.	Traditional and Prefabricated	Very High		1
		High		2
		Average		3
		Low		4
		Very Low		5
2.	Large Structures (*Galpones*)	High		1
		Average		2
		Low		3
3.	Complementary Works	**Quality**	**Condition**	
		Special	Good	1
		Special	Ordinary	2
		Special	Bad	3
		Normal	Good	4
		Normal	Ordinary	5
		Normal	Bad	6

Source: Servicio de Impuestos Internos, Dirección Nacional, "Tasación de los Bienes Raíces de la II Serie (no Agrícolas)," Resolución D.O. de 8-8-1990.

After SII completes its valuations for a particular locality, it compiles these valuations into a valuation roll, including valuations of exempt real estate except national property in public use, and transmits this valuation roll to the Comptroller General and the local treasurer. SII also prepares an annual taxpayer roll (*rol anual de contribuciones*), which includes property identification information, fiscal value, exemptions (if any), and tax liability. The taxpayer roll is transmitted to the Comptroller General and the provincial treasurer.[14]

Collection

SII produces four bills per year for each property with taxes due, in two batches: March and August. Each batch is CPI adjusted based on the inflation rate during the previous semester, with the increase split evenly between the current semester's two bills. The first two installments are due on April 30 and June 30, while the last two installments are due on September 30 and November 30. All corrections for previous years are issued in a third batch of bills in October, due on December 30. The Treasury Service is responsible for distributing property tax bills, usually by post in urban areas and through municipal governments in rural areas.[15]

The property tax is payable by the owner, occupant, beneficiary, renter, or possessor of the property without prejudice to claims of property title.[16] Taxpayers may pay at most commercial banks, which have a three-day float before turning property tax payments over to the Treasury.

Property tax receipts follow the universal destiny protocol of national revenue in Chile: they are paid to the Treasury, and then allocated by budget legislation. This legislation now assigns all property tax receipts to municipalities, in two parts: 40 percent is distributed to the municipality in which it was collected, and 60 percent is credited to a common municipal fund (*El Fondo Común Municipal*) for redistribution based on an income-sharing formula.[17]

The Treasury sends delinquent taxpayers an administrative collection notice (*cobranza administrativa*), usually within three months of the due date. If payment is still not received, the Treasury proceeds to send a judicial collection notice (*cobranza judicial*) one month later. The Treasury continues to pursue collection measures if the tax delinquency is not cleared, culminating in attachment, seizure, and auction of the property to settle tax liabilities.[18]

---

[14]Law No. 17.235, Articles 13-14 and 38-45.

[15]Montes, "Introduction to the Chile Case Study," 672.

[16]Law No. 17.235, Article 46.

[17]Law Decree No. 3.063, Articles 37 and 38.

[18]This summary of enforcement procedures is based on discussions with Treasury officials.

Administration

Property tax administration is split primarily between SII and the Treasury. SII is responsible for issuing technical instructions and administrative guidelines necessary for the valuation and assessment of real property.[19] SII is also responsible for several other sources of internal revenue, such as the income tax, the value-added tax, and excise taxes. The Treasury is responsible for delivery of property tax billings, collection of property tax payments, and enforcement of sanctions for property tax delinquencies, although it has delegated most of the actual cashier collection functions to Chile's banking system.[20]

THE CHILEAN PROPERTY TAX IN TRANSITION: SYSTEM REFORM

The Change Process: Policy

In accordance with Law No. 17.235, the Servicio de Impuestos Internos undertook a general revaluation of non-agricultural real estate from 1987 to 1991.[21]

According to the Minister of Finance, the principal policy objective of this general revaluation was to improve the equity and efficiency of the property tax system. Although an increase in revenue was expected, revenue enhancement was not a primary goal, and the global increase in non-agricultural real estate tax liabilities was limited to a maximum of 20 percent more than before revaluation.[22]

The Minister of Finance also stipulated that this objective could best be achieved through the full participation of the institutional beneficiaries of property tax revenue (the municipalities) and the central government body responsible for

---

[19]Law No. 17.235, Article 4. Most SII activities related to the property tax are undertaken in the Valuation and Informatics Subdirectorates. SII has only 100 professional personnel and 100 administrative support staff, although it did augment its resources with about 150 external experts during the past three years to assist it with the last general revaluation of non-agricultural property. SII is run through 13 administrative regions, in addition to its head office.

[20]A third party involved peripherally in property taxation is the National Service of Mining and Geology, which is responsible for tax revenue from mineral production.

[21]Law No. 17.235, Article 3 requires a general revaluation every five to ten years. General revaluations of non-agricultural and agricultural properties were completed in 1977 and 1980, respectively. The general revaluation of agricultural properties has been postponed indefinitely.

[22]Montes, "Introduction to the Chile Case Study," 675 and 691.

oversight of local government (the Under Secretariat for Regional and Administrative Development in the Ministry of Home Affairs).

The government decided to refrain from introducing major structural changes during the general revaluation given the great time, effort, and turmoil normally entailed in revaluations even without policy reform. Instead, the government resolved to try to improve property tax administration within the framework of existing legislation, decrees, and regulations.

Empirical data supported the government's desire to stress improved fairness and increased cost-effectiveness during the revaluation rather than revenue generation or policy reform. The government believed that the dynamics of urbanization, coupled with application of the automatic general inflation adjustment, had distorted both the absolute level and the relative distribution of fiscal values. The government also felt this was creating growing taxpayer resentment, more appeals, and decreasing rates of voluntary compliance.[23]

In addition, the property tax was quite expensive to administer. In 1985, the cost to revenue ratio was the highest of all taxes, using approximately 20 percent of SII field personnel while generating only 3.5 percent of total tax revenue. Furthermore, the SII Computer Center estimated that 40 percent of both programming maintenance and operations was dedicated to property tax administration.[24]

Although the property tax itself was not the object of policy reform, the general revaluation of non-agricultural properties took place within the context of more than a decade of comprehensive reform of tax policy and tax administration.[25]

Major policy changes included: tax code reformulation in 1974; income tax revision in 1974, complete overhaul in 1984, and marginal rates adjustments in 1988 and 1990; replacement of the sales tax with the value added tax (VAT) in 1974 and subsequent conversion of important excise taxes to surcharges on the VAT, incorporation of new property transactions into the general VAT in 1987, and reduction of the VAT rate from 20 to 16 percent in 1988; and gradual simplification of minor taxes.

Administrative reforms included: establishment of the Informatics Development Program in 1977; introduction of the computer-based Property Information System and Taxpayer Unique Account System in 1977 and the

---

[23]Montes, "Introduction to the Chile Case Study," 673-75.

[24]Montes, "Introduction to the Chile Case Study," 673; and Servicio de Impuestos Internos, unpublished statistics.

[25]Marco Montes, "Chile Case Study," Presentation at the International Conference on Property Taxation and Its Interaction with Land Policy, Cambridge, Mass., September 22-28, 1991, photocopied.

Information System for Tax Administration in 1980 (substantially expanded in 1986 and 1989); and administrative restructuring and rationalization of both SII and the Treasury Service in 1980, including a staff reduction of approximately 50 percent in each agency.

The Change Process: Administration and Behavior

The general revaluation of non-agricultural properties was divided into two distinct phases: first, the updating of property information for taxable properties, termed "normalization" and second, determination of new land and building fiscal values, designated "revaluation."

Normalization was designed to incorporate property changes not captured by SII's routine updating procedures. This was essential so that undetected new or modified properties would be comparable with "normal" properties, defined as properties with data accurately reflecting their current physical characteristics. The success of normalization therefore depended largely on taxpayer cooperation in honestly completing and promptly returning new self-declaration forms.

The purpose of revaluation was to recalculate property values for taxation purposes. Revaluation was to be conducted through a series of mass appraisal formulas that recalibrated physical property characteristics with changes in absolute and relative market prices, as reflected in updated land and building unit values and accompanying adjustment factors. Normalization thus required significant interaction with taxpayers, while revaluation relied mainly on the interpretation and application of third-party derived SII data bases.

Normalization[27]

The most important political and operational decision made during normalization was to limit the universe of participants dramatically: the government decided to include only those properties previously valued at more than P1.0 million in the

---

[26]The following discussion is based on interviews with Elizabeth Stair (Commissioner of Land Valuations), Norma Dixon (Commissioner of Inland Revenue), and Dennis Larman (Managing Director of Fiscal Services (EDP) Ltd.).

[27]The following summary of normalization activities draws heavily on conversations with SII and Treasury officials in Chile, as well as on two much more detailed written accounts: Montes, "Chile Case Study," photocopied; and Montes, "Introduction to the Chile Case Study," 676-87.

declaration process, reducing the target group by 40 percent, from 2.1 million to 1.25 million taxpayers.[28]

A second critical decision taken prior to implementation of normalization was the necessity for the government to provide both positive and negative incentives to elicit maximum public understanding and cooperation.

Positive incentives comprised a combination of facilitating administrative procedures, an extensive public information campaign, and a limited tax amnesty. Considerable effort was expended to design a tax declaration form that was both computer oriented and easy to understand, and SII took the initiative in solicitating information by completing part of this form with a property's physical description for the taxpayer to confirm or correct. The public information campaign was designed to cultivate a broad base of popular and political support, so was directed not only at taxpayers, but also at the general public as well as executive and legislative officials. The campaign utilized television, radio, and print media, and emphasized tax equity, the uses of property tax revenue, and the ease of complying with the government's call for taxpayer cooperation.[29] The government further encouraged taxpayer compliance by forfeiting its right to charge retroactively, for up to three years, the difference in property tax liabilities resulting from inaccurate property information. Instead, the taxpayer would be charged retroactively for only one year.

The primary negative incentive was the converse of this tax amnesty: reduced tax liabilities due to the intentional provision of inaccurate information would be due for the entire three years, with an additional fine of 25 percent of the tax difference. There was also a psychological threat that it would be difficult to avoid detection of misinformation because the declaration form sent to taxpayers was already partially completed with computer-generated data.

All 1.25 million declaration forms (labelled "F-28") were mailed to taxable properties above the minimum value threshold by April 1987. Only 6 percent (75,000) of the declaration forms were returned by the postal service as undeliverable. The declaration process was administered in all 323 municipalities in Chile through SII regional offices, with the assistance of local government

---

[28]Montes, "Introduction to the Chile Case Study," 677-78; conversion from 1991 U.S. dollars to nominal pesos by the author. This exclusion limit was set somewhat below the P1.8 million residential exemption that relieved 850,000 of the 2.1 non-agricultural properties of their tax liabilities to balance three competing concerns: capturing properties whose increased value might make them taxable; adapting the anticipated workload to SII's financial, administrative, and computational resources; and minimizing taxpayer inconvenience.

[29]For example, special ten-page supplements, including examples of the twenty most common situations, were inserted in the papers of the two most important newspaper chains. In addition, the SII Director, Subdirectors, and Property Tax Department Chief were frequent guests on television and radio discussion panels and news shows, and numerous press conferences and interviews were held to explain policy and procedures, and to respond to inquiries. The Minister of Finance and the SII National Director also made special presentations to the President, presidential advisors, and legislative commissions.

officials. Completed declaration forms were sent to the SII main office in Santiago for data entry and processing, which were finished by the end of June 1988.[30]

SII officials took great care to screen all new taxpayer-provided data on property characteristics to ensure that this information indeed helped to clean up rather than pollute their SII data base, and to minimize taxpayer objections and appeals caused by SII administrative error:

> Therefore a complex set of verification and validation tests were designed based on data consistency checks and logical relationships between different information items declared on the Form F-28 and the original information registered in the old database.
>
> Land area, buildings area, fiscal value and modifications on type and quality of constructions were ranged comparing pre and post normalization data and specific range acceptance criteria were set for each one. . . . if all information items on the incoming form were within acceptable ranges, the database was updated. Forms which contained unacceptable errors on any information item did not automatically update the database but generated an error message stating the type of error and the item affected.[31]

This method served two purposes: it provided an overall quality control mechanism, and it helped to distinguish data entry from data source errors.[32]

Events progressed quickly in 1989, and SII's ultimate deadline was met - 1989 bills were issued on time.[33] Taxpayer response to normalization was quite positive, as 96 percent of the targeted taxpayers participated.[34] Normalization results are discussed in Section IV below.

---

[30]Montes, "Introduction to the Chile Case Study," 679.

[31]Montes, "Introduction to the Chile Case Study," 681.

[32]A special version of Form F-28 was created, designated Form F-284, to facilitate corrections. Form F-284 presented both original SII data and new tax declaration information, and provided space for corrections by field staff. Approximately 400,000, or one-third of the completed tax declaration forms were sent back to the field for verification. Regional staff either confirmed or corrected data on returned forms, often conducting a field inspection if a desk review was inconclusive.

[33]Montes, "Introduction to the Chile Case Study," 683. All corrected declarations had been received and processed at SII headquarters by the end of January; by March 15, notices of fiscal value modification had been sent to the 767,000 taxpayers whose tax liabilities were affected by fiscal value changes; and by the end of March, 696,000 tax bills for 1989's first two installments had been sent to taxpayers.

[34]1,207,000 of the 1,257,000 F-28 declaration forms mailed by SII were completed and returned to SII.

Revaluation[35]

While normalization entailed the selective revision of SII's data base of property characteristics, concentrating resources on the top 60 percent of properties, revaluation prescribed the comprehensive recalculation of fiscal value for all non-agricultural properties on the fiscal cadastre.

The fiscal value of a property's land component is determined primarily by the unit price of land in the homogeneous urban zone in which the property is located, modified by adjustment and correction factors as appropriate. The fiscal value of a property's building component is determined mainly by the unit price corresponding to the building's construction type and quality, also modified by a variety of adjustment and correction factors as appropriate.

Thus, to complete the general revaluation, SII had to:

- redefine homogeneous urban zones throughout Chile, and determine new unit values for these zones based on actual market prices;

- establish definitions for construction types and qualities, and determine new unit values for these building classifications, also based on actual market prices;

- calculate adjustment factors for both land and buildings; and

- apply these new value tables and valuation formulas to all non-agricultural properties.

Urban zones and the price of land within these zones were determined through a combination of spatial and textual data.

Although the government acknowledged maps of some sort were required to define the urban zones, SII and the municipalities decided that rather than undertake an expensive cartographic exercise to create highly accurate maps, they would update their relatively imprecise municipal property layout maps. These maps, while not sufficient for a legal cadastre, served the needs of a fiscal cadastre well: they comprised both general display and unscaled sketches (planchettes), and depicted the property identification number (PIN), relative location, and approximate dimensions of each property. The primary objective of this exercise was to identify properties not yet on the maps, and to assign PINS to these properties.

---

[35]The following summary of revaluation activities draws heavily on conversations with SII and Treasury officials in Chile, as well as on two much more detailed written accounts: Montes, "Chile Case Study," photocopied; and Montes, "Introduction to the Chile Case Study," 687-94.

Price information was gathered through establishment of a land transactions price data bank, fed by information from classified advertisements in newspapers, real estate publications and agents, reports from banks and other financial institutions, and notary reports.

The information on property transaction prices was then combined with the municipal property layout maps to produce land value maps. In addition, to ensure nationwide price consistency, the central SII office used a multivariate model to adjust the proposed municipal land price maps.[36]

The revaluation of non-agricultural properties was completed by July 1990; the results are presented in Section IV below. Unlike the normalization exercise, these results have yet to become effective, due primarily to dramatic political changes in Chile during and after the revaluation.

In December 1989, President Pinochet was defeated by an opposition alliance, after having ruled Chile since 1973. The new "Concertation Government" took office in March 1990, and began the long and difficult transition from military dictatorship to coalition democracy.

The new government at first proceeded with plans to implement the new revaluation.[37] According to SII management and staff, public reaction seemed to be relatively passive until the largest Chilean newspaper chain initiated a vitriolic campaign against the revaluation. After a major opposition party joined in this campaign, the government decided not to risk defeat of other measures awaiting Parliament's approval, and postponed the application of new property values for a year. In April 1991, while SII and the Treasury were taking measures to accommodate this delay, the government decided to postpone adoption of the revaluation results for another two years.

Members of the present government believe that given the current debate on regional and municipal government administrative and fiscal reform, it is inappropriate to introduce new property values until Parliament determines who will have the authority to administer the property tax and how property tax revenue will be distributed in the future. Others claim that the tax administration functions of valuation, assessment, and collection have been victimized by the broad policy

---

[36]This model incorporated factors such as population (total and taxpayer), tax revenue potential (property, income, and value added taxes), development status (measured by sewage and telephone connections), and aggregate building characteristics.

[37]First, a Presidential Decree was issued in June 1990 which temporarily decreased the tax rate from 2 to 1.1 percent and raised the general residential exemption from P2.5 to P4.5 million to keep the reform relatively revenue neutral (the 30 percent assessment surcharge had already been eliminated). Then, official new land and building base prices were issued, and tax bills were printed by SII and distributed by the Treasury to the roughly 750,000 post-revaluation tax liable properties. Finally, a special notification (Form 2852) of revaluation results was sent to all 2.2 million properties, with reference copies (and accompanying tax rolls) distributed to all municipalities and Treasury provincial offices.

issues of who should bear the tax, and who should benefit from tax revenue. As one former SII official remarked, "politics won over technical competence."[38] The effect of normalization and revaluation on the equity of property tax incidence are explored further in Section

THE CHILEAN PROPERTY TAX IN PRACTICE: SYSTEM PERFORMANCE

Purpose: Revenue and Non-Revenue Objectives

Revenue Generation

Unlike many other countries, property tax revenue in Chile has grown not only in nominal but in real terms as well over the past decade (see Table IV-2 and Figure IV-2). Nominal property tax revenue grew at a compounded annual rate of 24.7 percent over the past ten years, increasing more than nine-fold from P4.4 billion to P40.0 billion.[39] Automatic semi-annual indexing to the consumer price index has resulted in the maintenance of the value of the tax base in real terms. When converted to 1985 pesos, property tax revenue has been relatively constant during most of the 1980s; the two major exceptions are the increases following the 1980 general revaluation of agricultural properties and the 1987 normalization of non-agricultural properties. Overall, property tax revenue increased 53 percent in real terms during the past decade, at a compounded annual rate of 4.3 percent.[40]

Property tax revenue's share of gross domestic product has remained at between 0.6 and 0.9 percent during the past decade. Property tax revenue now constitutes 2.7 percent of total tax revenue, having ranged from a low of 2.2 percent in 1981 to a high of 4.0 percent in 1983 (see Table IV-3). In contrast, the value added tax now generates two-thirds of all tax revenue, while income tax receipts contribute 17 percent of total tax revenue (see Figure IV-3).[41]

---

[38]Montes, "Introduction to the Chile Case Study," 694.

[39]Montes, "Chile Case Study," photocopied; conversion from 1991 U.S. dollars to pesos by the author. The dramatic increase in nominal property tax revenue is largely a function of Chile's average annual inflation rate of 20.5 percent from 1980 to 1989.

[40]Gross domestic product deflators are taken from: International Monetary Fund, Bureau of Statistics, *International Financial Statistics* (Washington, D.C.: International Monetary Fund), monthly issues and yearbooks.

[41]Montes, "Chile Case Study," photocopied (conversion from 1991 U.S. dollars to nominal pesos by the author).

TABLE IV-2: PROPERTY TAX REVENUE IN CHILE

Year	Property Tax Receipts (billions of pesos)	
	Nominal Pesos	*1985 Pesos*
1980	4.4	10.8
1981	6.8	14.8
1982	7.3	14.0
1983	9.4	14.3
1984	12.1	16.1
1985	14.5	14.5
1986	18.3	15.4
1987	22.3	15.4
1988	29.8	17.0
1989	35.1	18.3
1990	40.0	16.5

Source: Montes, "Chile Case Study," photocopied (conversion from 1991 U.S. dollars to pesos by author).

FIGURE IV-2:
PROPERTY TAX REVENUE IN CHILE

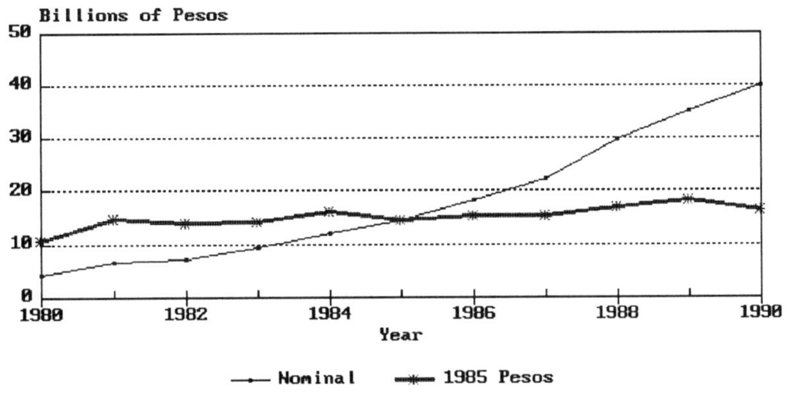

Source: Author's calculations.

TABLE IV-3: PROPERTY TAX REVENUE IN THE CHILEAN ECONOMY

(billions of pesos)

Year	Property Tax Receipts	Total Tax Revenue	Share of Total Tax Revenue	Gross Domestic Product	Share of GDP
1980	4.4	179.5	2.5%	707.0	0.6%
1981	6.8	307.5	2.2%	979.8	0.7%
1982	7.3	257.6	2.8%	921.8	0.8%
1983	9.4	234.8	4.0%	1,105.5	0.9%
1984	12.1	340.2	3.6%	1,447.1	0.8%
1985	14.5	431.2	3.4%	1,825.3	0.8%
1986	18.3	588.6	3.1%	2,437.0	0.8%
1987	22.3	734.8	3.0%	3,022.3	0.7%
1988	29.8	1,006.2	3.0%	3,940.3	0.8%
1989	35.1	1,158.4	3.0%	4,882.6	0.7%
1990	40.0	1,484.5	2.7%	6,054.6	0.7%

Sources: Montes, "Introduction to the Chile Case Study" (conversion from 1991 U.S. dollars to pesos by author).

FIGURE IV-3:
COMPOSITION OF TAX REVENUE IN CHILE

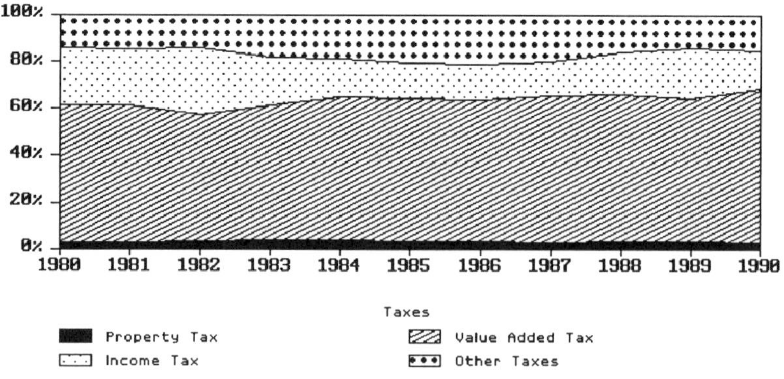

Source: Author's calculations.

Although the property tax is insignificant as a source of national revenue, it dominates local government revenue. All property tax receipts are allocated to the municipalities, where they comprise approximately half of all local own source revenue in Chile as a whole, and are commonly more than 70 percent of own source revenue in small towns (see Figure IV-4).[42]

Non-Revenue Objectives

Normalization and revaluation in Chile were implemented with self-imposed limits on revenue growth. Several adjustments were made when improvements in administrative efficiency, data and price accuracy, and tax burden equity led to unacceptable increases in total tax liabilities. Thus, technically, the property tax reform in Chile achieved its objectives of redistributing the property tax burden based on more complete, current, and tenable data without significantly increasing the total magnitude of this tax burden. However, the general revaluation has not yet been applied because in the zero-sum redistribution of the property tax burden, some tax bills increased significantly while others fell, creating the appearance of unfairness and causing some to raise objections effectively.

Principles: Efficiency, Equity, and Sustainability

The fiscal cadastre in Chile is dominated by non-agricultural properties, whether in terms of number of units or tax liability: non-agricultural real estate comprised 83 percent of all properties and 77 percent of all property tax liabilities in 1990. Furthermore, approximately two-thirds of both agricultural and non-agricultural properties are tax exempt (see Table IV-4).[43]

This fiscal cadastre appears to have virtually universal coverage, as demonstrated by the small increase in property listings during the last normalization and revaluation of non-agricultural properties: fewer than 3,000 properties were added to the 2.1 million non-agricultural properties on the valuation roll following normalization, and less than 1 percent were added after revaluation.[44]

---

[42]Discussions with SII officials in Chile; and Montes, "Chile Case Study," photocopied.

[43]Servicio de Impuestos Internos, unpublished statistics.

[44]Montes, "Chile Case Study," photocopied. The disposition of agricultural property is traditionally more stable than non-agricultural real estate, so SII rural coverage should be at least as good as its urban coverage.

TABLE IV-4: COMPOSITION OF REAL PROPERTY IN CHILE IN 1990

LAND USE			**Agricultural**		**Non-Agricultural**	
			TOTAL			
(Type)	#	%	#	%	#	%
Taxable	158,156	*35%*	749,255	*33%*	907,284	*34%*
Exempt	298,395	*65%*	1,489,581	*67%*	1,785,549	*66%*
TOTAL	456,551	*17%*	2,238,836	*83%*	2,692,833	*100%*

Source: Servicio de Impuestos Internos, unpublished statistics.

The accuracy and currency of the valuation roll were certainly improved after normalization and revaluation, which dramatically affected the distribution of the property tax burden on the revised tax roll. Normalization results support this conclusion (see Figure IV-5 and Figure IV-6).[45] These normalization results appear to have been accomplished at relatively little political or financial cost:

- Only 16,000 appeals were filed (1.3 percent of returned self-declarations).

- Normalization expenses of approximately P1.3 billion (see Figure IV-7) averaged only about P1,000 per property, roughly 5 percent of the average increase in tax liability per property and 2 percent of property tax billings in 1988.

[45]The following statistics are from: Montes, "Introduction to the Chile Case Study," 685-87: Data from 64 percent of the 1,207,000 self-declaration forms returned to SII directly affected fiscal values; approximately 70,000 more properties became exempt, when new data was coupled with a 33 percent rise in the general residential exemption to limit the increase in total tax revenue; and an even greater shift in tax burden is indicated by the much smaller pool of properties with increased rather than decreased tax liabilities, despite most properties' higher fiscal value and an overall significant increase in total tax billings. The general residential exemption was increased from P1.8 million to P2.4 million to reduce the annual property billing in 1989 by 15 percent, and thus keep total property tax liabilities constant in real terms after the 15 percent real increase in 1988.

FIGURE IV-4:
STRUCTURE OF MUNICIPAL REVENUE IN CHILE

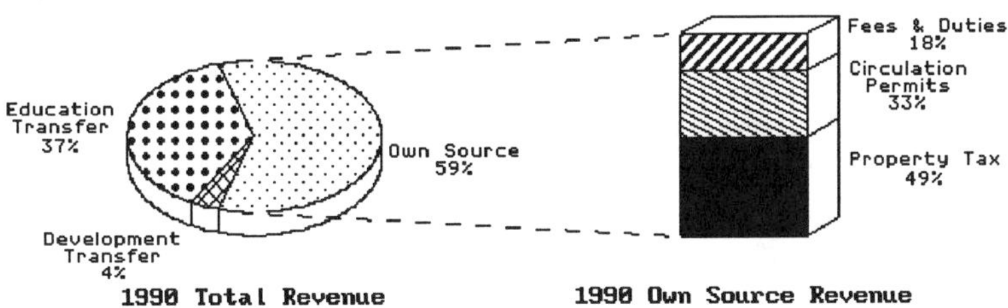

Source: Author's calculations.

FIGURE IV-5:
RESULTS OF NORMALIZATION IN CHILE

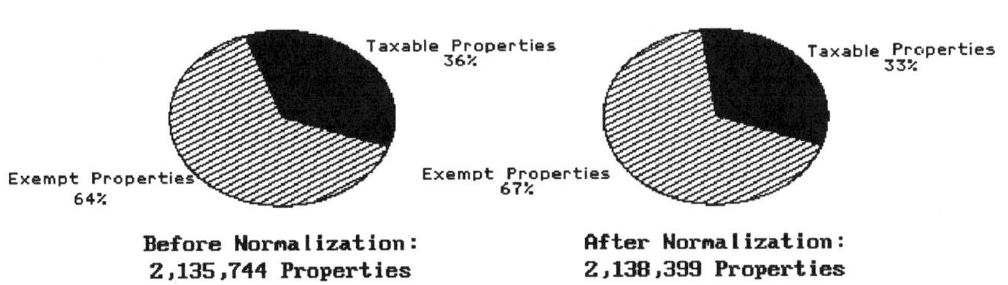

Source: Author's calculations.

FIGURE IV-6:
RESULTS OF NORMALIZATION IN CHILE

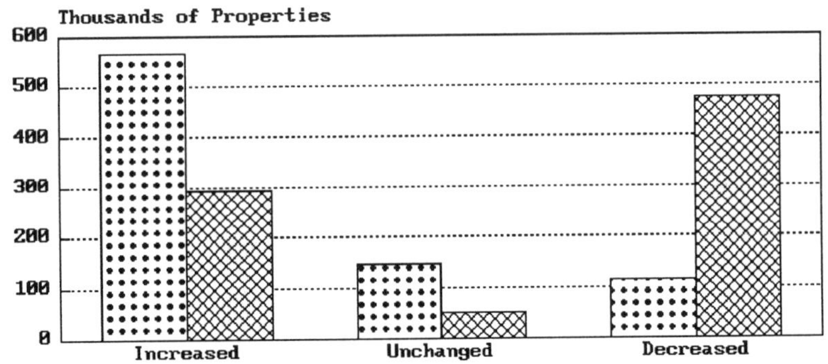

Fiscal Value Tax Liability

Source: Author's calculations.

FIGURE IV-7:
NORMALIZATION COSTS IN CHILE

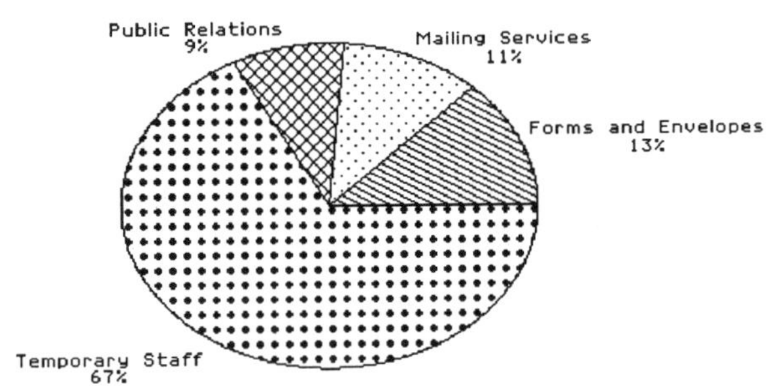

COMPOSITION OF EXPENSES

Source: Author's calculations.

Implementors of normalization believe that taxpayer resistance was minimized by providing extensive public information, increasing the general residential exemption, and allowing payment of 1988 increases in six installments as supplements to the four 1989 and first two 1990 bills.[46]

Preliminary revaluation data indicated that property values would probably double, and could even triple. To keep the reform fiscally neutral, the government eliminated the 30 percent surcharge, reduced the tax rate to 1.1 percent and increased the general residential exemption to P4.5 million (see Section III above).

The following adjusted revaluation results, although not yet applied to tax billings, reinforce the normalization effects of increased valuation roll accuracy and greater tax burden equity, with a five percent increase in revenue potential:[47]

- Two-thirds of all properties remain exempt (see Figure IV-8).

- Roughly the same number of properties have higher and lower tax liabilities, indicating a rather symmetrical redistribution of a fixed tax burden (see Figure IV-9).

FIGURE IV-8:
RESULTS OF REVALUATION IN CHILE

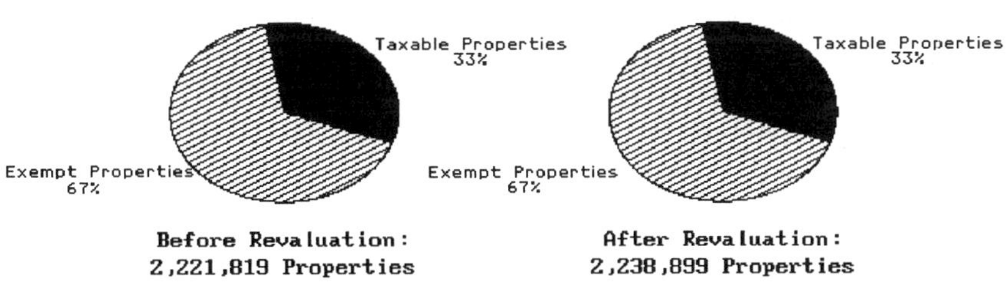

Source: Author's calculations.

---

[46]Montes, "Introduction to the Chile Case Study," 686.

[47]The following statistics are from: Montes, "Introduction to the Chile Case Study," 692.

FIGURE IV-9:
RESULTS OF REVALUATION IN CHILE

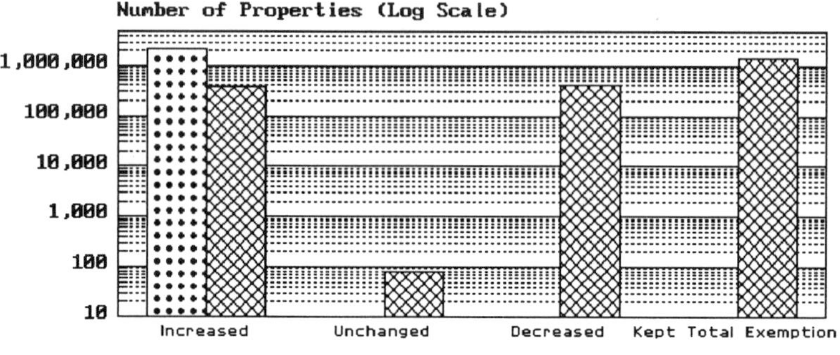

Note: All fiscal values increased.
Source: Author's calculations.

However, property tax performance is less encouraging when measured by another key indicator of coverage and equity: collection efficiency. After increasing from 58 to 69 percent in 1981, the collection rate has fluctuated between 66 and 76 percent since 1982 (see Figure IV-10).[48] These collection figures are especially puzzling. Although they are taken from official Central Bank, SII, and Treasury Service reports, they do not reflect the considerable emphasis on enforcement during the general revaluation, including the seizure and auctioning of selected delinquent properties throughout the country. Furthermore, conversations with Chilean officials reflected a common belief that on-time collection rates now varied between 80 and 85 percent, with late payments bringing this rate up to between 90 and 95 percent.

This discrepancy seems to stem from differences in the meaning of "collection efficiency," traditionally defined as current revenue compared with current billings. In the case of Chile, this should exclude late payments in the numerator and arrears in the denominator, but include both the basic tax assessment and the 30 percent assessment surcharge as current tax liabilities and receipts. It is not clear whether those quoting the higher rates exclude late payments, and whether those citing the lower rates include the 30 percent surcharge in the tax billing and collection figures.[49]

---

[48]Montes, "Introduction to the Chile Case Study," 706.

[49]For example, during discussions in Santiago in June 1991, the SII Subdirector of Studies cited the following figures for the past two years:

Year	Tax Billings	Tax Collections	Collection Rate

However, in either case, the cost of property tax administration is relatively high. In 1990, property tax expenses were 35 percent of total tax administration costs in Chile and 8 percent of property tax revenue generated (see Figure IV-11),[50] but property tax receipts comprised only 3 percent of total tax revenue (see Table IV-3 and Figure IV-3).

Perhaps the thoughts of property tax reformers in Chile are now echoing those of Ralph Waldo Emerson, who wrote in *The Conservative*: "Reform has no gratitude, no prudence, no husbandry."

FIGURE IV-10:
COLLECTION EFFICIENCY IN CHILE

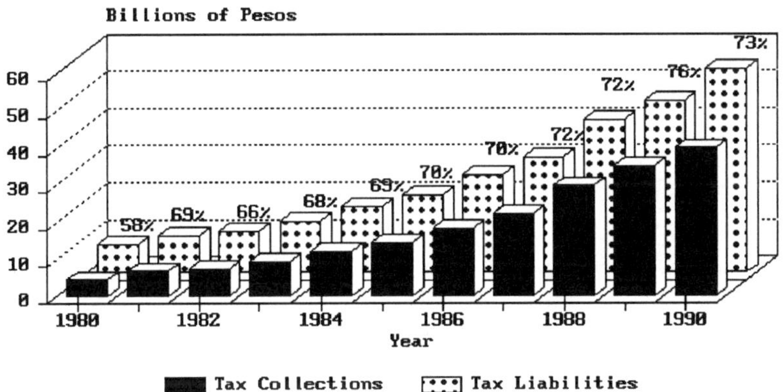

Source: Author's calculations.

1989	P53.9 billion	P49.9 billion	92.6%
1990	P59.4 billion	P55.8 billion	93.9%

However, the official sources noted earlier present the following figures for the same period (see Figure IV-10):

Year	Tax Billings	Tax Collections	Collection Rate
1989	P46.2 billion	P35.1 billion	76.0%
1990	P54.8 billion	P40.0 billion	73.0%

[50]Montes, "Chile Case Study," photocopied.

FIGURE IV-11:
1990 TAX ADMINISTRATION COSTS IN CHILE

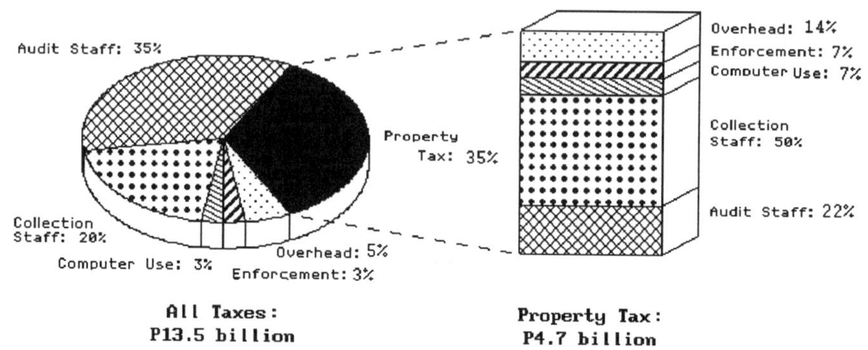

Source: Author's calculations.

5

INDONESIA CASE STUDY

The land is more dangerous than the ocean.

Ovid, *Tristia*, I, c. 10

THE INDONESIAN PROPERTY TAX IN PERSPECTIVE: CASE STUDY SNAPSHOT

Indonesian government officials have devoted the past six years to a complete overhaul of property tax policies and operations. The process is about two-thirds completed, and the results have been quite promising to date.

Property tax reform commenced with fundamental system redesign, culminating in promulgation of new legislation which took effect in 1986. Statutory reform of property taxation was the last major piece of a comprehensive tax reform effort launched in the mid-1980s, and emphasized the principles of uniformity, simplicity, and generality. This legislation consolidated seven different statutes related to the taxation of real property, switched the tax base from annual rental value to capital market value, adopted a single tax rate for all property uses in all locations for all values, and greatly curtailed exemptions.

Indonesian reformers began a property tax improvement program (PBBIP) in 1987 to facilitate implementation of this new legislation, with substantial support from the World Bank. Initially, most PBBIP resources were devoted to tax mapping and property appraisal. However, in 1989, reformers concluded that although property tax subsystems for data collection and property valuation were quite weak, the principal constraint to improving property tax efficiency, equity, and sustainability was poor collections. Indonesian reformers thus decided to make better property tax billing, payment, and enforcement procedures PBBIP's top priority.

The main product of this collection-led strategy has been SISTEP (Payment Point System), with: single-installment payment at a pre-designated bank office located near the tax object by a uniform due date; pre-printed matching bills and receipts; streamlined records and reports; and a computer-generated delinquency list with which to initiate credible enforcement proceedings. An important component of SISTEP has been utilization of positive and negative incentives for taxpayers and government officials. SISTEP has also served as a "back door" route to automation of Indonesia's 65 million object property tax roll, since the system is not feasible if traditional manual operations are maintained. Service has improved substantially and revenue has risen dramatically in areas where SISTEP has been adopted, so the government is continuing to replicate the system throughout Indonesia.

Efforts to improve property-related data activities have been less fruitful, due primarily to experimentation with inordinately expensive, complex, and confusing techniques for data collection and property valuation. Indonesian reformers are now trying to simplify these unpopular and unmaintainable procedures considerably, via field-testing of a variety of alternatives in diverse settings around the country.

THE INDONESIAN PROPERTY TAX IN LAW: SYSTEM DESIGN

Tax Base

Indonesia's property tax, PBB (*pajak bumi dan bangunan*, land and building tax), is applied to the capital market value of all land and buildings in the country except those in categories specifically exempted by the property tax law.[1]

Land is defined as Indonesia's surface area, including waterways and seas, together with the area underneath. Buildings are defined as permanent construction on land or water which yields benefits, including: roads and emplacements within building complexes; toll roads; swimming pools; expensive fencing and gardens; sports facilities; docks and piers; and pipes, receptacles, and processing facilities for oil, water, and gas.[2]

Tax liable property is referred to as the "tax object" (*obyek pajak*). Anyone responsible for clearing the property tax liability is a "tax subject" (*subyek pajak*), defined as "a person or organization that actually has a land right, and/or derives benefit from land, and/or owns, controls, and/or derives benefit from a building." If there is confusion over who should pay the tax for a particular property, the director general of tax can designate any tax subject for that property as the taxpayer.

---

[1]*Undang-Undang Republik Indonesia Nomor 12 Tahun 1985 Tentang Pajak Bumi Dan Bangunan, Pasal 2.*

[2]*Undang-Undang Nomor 12 Tahun 1985, Pasal 1;* and *Penjelasan Atas Undang-Undang Republik Indonesia Nomor 12 Tahun 1985 Tentang Pajak Bumi dan Bangunan, Pasal 1.*

Receipts documenting payment of the property tax do not constitute proof of ownership.[3]

Land and buildings not subject to the property tax are excluded via a general statutory exemption.[4] In addition, the property tax law exempts the first Rp. 2 million in building value from PBB, which has since been revised upward to Rp. 3.5 million.[5] National and local government facilities are taxable.[6]

The minister of finance is empowered to grant discretionary relief because of a natural disaster such as an earthquake, flood, landslide, fire, drought, or crop failure. The minister may also grant relief for other cases of genuine financial hardship, such as those faced by farmers in poor regions and long-time urban residents whose growth in income has not matched the rapid escalation in the value of their property.[7]

Although property tax relief has traditionally been both temporary and quite specific, the first long-term blanket relief from the property tax was recently provided for eight years for new investment in Indonesia's thirteen eastern provinces (*Indonesia Timur*).[8]

---

[3]*Undang-Undang Nomor 12 Tahun 1985, Pasal 4;* and *Penjelasan Atas Undang-Undang Nomor 12 Tahun 1985, Pasal 4.*

[4]These include property used for the public good by non-profit religious, social, health, educational, and national cultural organizations; cemeteries; natural, protected, or tourist forests; national parks; village pasturelands; national land for which private rights have not been issued; diplomatic missions; and specially-designated international organizations.

[5]In 1990, the average exchange rate was Rp. 1,842.83 for US$1.00; see Exchange Rates following the Table of Contents for a full listing of exchange rates since 1970.

[6]*Undang-Undang Nomor 12 Tahun 1985, Pasal 3;* and *Keputusan Menteri Nomor 25/KMK.04/1988 Tentang Besarnya Faktor Penyesuaian Untuk Batas Nilai Jual Bangunan Tidak Kena Pajak Bumi dan Bangunan, Pasal 1.*

[7]*Undang-Undang Nomor 12 Tahun 1985, Pasal 19;* and *Penjelasan Atas Undang-Undang Nomor 12 Tahun 1985, Pasal 19.*

[8]*Keputusan Menteri Keuangan Republik Indonesia Nomor 748/KMK.04/1990 Tentang Pengenaan Pajak Bumi dan Bangunan Bagi Investasi di Wilayah Tertentu.* This minister of finance decree provides 50 percent PBB relief for 8 years for new investment, or for an increase in prior investment of at least 30 percent, in the provinces of: West, East, South, and Central Kalimantan; North, South, Central, and Southeast Sulawesi; East and West Nusa Tenggara; East Timur; Maluku; and Irian Jaya. The decree is effective for investments made beginning January 1, 1990, in the sectors of: agriculture; plantations; livestock; fisheries; mining; forestry; industry; real estate; industrial estates; hotels; tourism; and economic infrastructure, including land, sea, and air transport.

Once land and buildings are classified as taxable, only a portion of their market value (as defined in Section C below) is subject to PBB through utilization of a fractional assessment level. The property tax law limits the "assessment value" (*NJKP, nilai jual kena pajak*) of land and buildings to no less than 20 percent and no more than 100 percent of their market value; the precise assessment level is set by government regulation (*peraturan pemerintah*) based on prevailing economic conditions.[9] The PBB assessment ratio has been 20 percent for all property in all locations since the property tax law took effect in 1986.[10]

Fixed machinery and equipment have been excluded from the tax base indefinitely due to the administrative difficulties of assessing such property.

Tax Rate

The property tax rate is a flat 0.5 percent for all land and buildings in all sectors everywhere in Indonesia.[11]

Valuation

Land and buildings are valued on the basis of their capital market value (*NJOP, nilai jual obyek pajak*): the average price obtained from normal market sales and purchases, or in the absence of market transactions, the market price of comparable property or the replacement price of new property.[12]

Tax subjects are required to declare the value and physical characteristics of their property via submission of a Tax Object Declaration Form (*SPOP, Surat Pemberitahuan Obyek Pajak*), although final determination of NJOP and tax assessment based on this value are the responsibility of property tax officials. SPOPs must be completed in a "clear, truthful, and complete" manner, signed, and returned to tax authorities within 30 days of receipt by the tax subject. Tax authorities may proceed with valuation and assessment even if a SPOP is not submitted. If the SPOP is not returned on time or is not truthful, the taxpayer may

---

[9] *Undang-Undang Nomor 12 Tahun 1985, Pasal 6;* and *Penjelasan Atas Undang-Undang Nomor 12 Tahun 1985, Pasal 6.*

[10] *Peraturan Pemerintah Republik Indonesia Nomor 46 Tahun 1985 Tentang Penetapan Besarnya Persentase Nilai Jual Kena Pajak Bumi dan Bangunan.*

[11] *Undang-Undang Nomor 12 Tahun 1985, Pasal 5.*

[12] *Undang-Undang Nomor 12 Tahun 1985, Pasal 1;* and *Penjelasan Atas Undang-Undang Nomor 12 Tahun 1985, Pasal 1.*

be served a Tax Assessment Notice (*SKP, Surat Ketetapan Pajak*), and then must pay all taxes due within 30 days, plus a 25 percent penalty.[13]

The minister of finance is required to establish NJOP standards every three years in general, and annually in rapidly developing areas.[14] This has been done by issuing ministerial decrees that provide NJOP guidance as follows:

- for urban and rural property, land is divided into 50 classes and buildings into 20 classes, with each class assigned a square meter market price and a square meter tax assessment (currently 0.1 percent of the market price);[15] and

- for plantations, forests, and mines (known as the "P3" sectors, *perkebunan/perhutanan/pertambangan*), formulas are provided which essentially use gross product as a proxy to determine capital value.[16]

The latest decree values range from Rp. 100 to Rp. 3.1 million per square meter for land, and from Rp. 50,000 to Rp. 1.2 million per square meter for buildings (see Table V-1).[17]

Property tax officials use a variety of methods to place land and buildings into one of the above-noted classes. This enables the officials to first assign a unit price, and then, when multiplied by area, to determine an NJOP; the product of the NJOP, the assessment ratio, and the tax rate is the tax assessment (see Figure V-1).

---

[13]*Undang-Undang Nomor 12 Tahun 1985, Pasal 9-10;* and *Penjelasan Atas Undang-Undang Nomor 12 Tahun 1985, Pasal 9-10.* The SKP penalty is 25 percent of the increase in tax liability when tax authority information is used instead of data from the taxpayer-submitted SPOP. In addition, according to *Undang-Undang Nomor 12 Tahun 1985, Pasal 21;* and *Penjelasan Atas Undang-Undang Nomor 12 Tahun 1985, Pasal 21*, notaries and government officials responsible for handling property transactions are required to send monthly reports to property tax officials regarding property sales, gifts, inheritances, and similar transfers.

[14]*Undang-Undang Nomor 12 Tahun 1985, Pasal 6;* and *Penjelasan Atas Undang-Undang Nomor 12 Tahun 1985, Pasal 6.*

[15]The effective statutory tax rate of 0.1 percent = the 0.5 percent nominal tax rate x the 20 percent assessment ratio.

[16]Buildings, as well as land not in active production, are valued in a traditional manner, but productive land is valued in general at 10 times the annual gross output during the prior year for mines and forests, and based on the annual harvest for plantations.

[17]*Keputusan Menteri Keuangan Republik Indonesia Nomor 1324/KMK.04/1988 Tentang Penentuan Klasifikasi dan Besarnya Nilai Jual Obyek Pajak Sebagai Dasar Pengenaan Pajak Bumi dan Bangunan.*

Once land and buildings are initially classified, they are informally revalued between formal decrees via "classification creep" (see Section IV).

Land is classified through the compilation of local land value books (*buku nilai tanah*) based primarily on information from local government officials, in which land is divided into zones of one or more village (rural areas) or by street (urban areas). Although the presentation is textual, if depicted spatially, the result would be a land value map.

Most rural buildings and low-income urban buildings are worth less than the minimal taxable level. Remaining buildings are supposed to be classified using one of three techniques: a weighted average of building components (*rata-rata bobot*) whose total score of up to one hundred points falls into one of the twenty building classes; a computer-based mass appraisal model, also based primarily on building components, but modified by a series of adjustment factors; or individual appraisal. In fact, all three systems are still being tested, refined, and compared with each other, so most field staff use a valuation shorthand: "eyeballed lookalikes" are grouped together into comparable classes.

FIGURE V-1:

ASSESSMENT CALCULATIONS IN INDONESIA

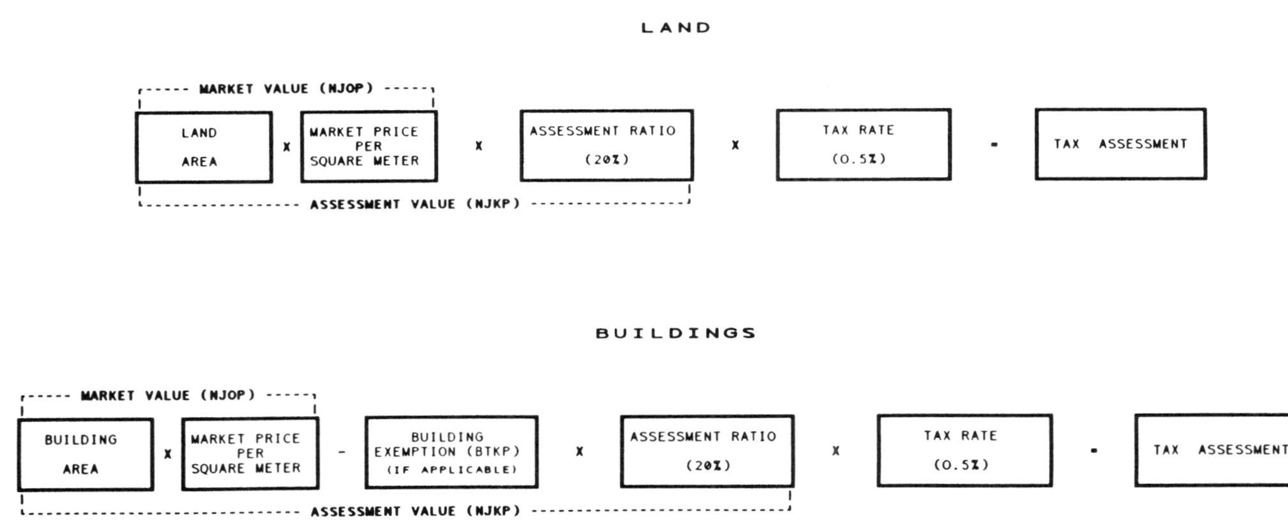

Source: Direktorat Pajak Bumi dan Bangunan.

TABLE V-1: INDONESIAN LAND AND BUILDING CLASSES

(all figures in rupiahs per square meter)

LAND

Class	Market Price Range	Designated Market Price	Tax Assessment
1	>3,000,000	3,100,000	3,100.00
2	>2,850,000 but ≤3,000,000	2,925,000	2,925.00
3	>2,708,000 but ≤2,850,000	2,779,000	2,779.00
4	>2,753,000 but ≤2,708,000	2,640,000	2,640.00
5	>2,444,000 but ≤2,753,000	2,508,000	2,508.00
6	>2,261,000 but ≤2,444,000	2,352,000	2,352.00
7	>2,091,000 but ≤2,261,000	2,176,000	2,176.00
8	>1,934,000 but ≤2,091,000	2,013,000	2,013.00
9	>1,789,000 but ≤1,934,000	1,862,000	1,862.00
10	>1,655,000 but ≤1,789,000	1,722,000	1,722.00
11	>1,490,000 but ≤1,655,000	,573,000	1,573.00
12	>1,341,000 but ≤1,490,000	1,416,000	1,416.00
13	>1,207,000 but ≤1,341,000	1,274,000	1,274.00
14	>1,086,000 but ≤1,207,000	1,147,000	1,147.00
15	> 977,000 but ≤1,086,000	1,032,000	1,032.00
16	> 855,000 but ≤ 977,000	916,000	916.00
17	> 748,000 but ≤ 855,000	802,000	802.00
18	> 655,000 but ≤ 748,000	702,000	702.00
19	> 573,000 but ≤ 655,000	614,000	614.00
20	> 501,000 but ≤ 573,000	537,000	537.00
21	> 426,000 but ≤ 501,000	464,000	464.00
22	> 362,000 but ≤ 426,000	394,000	394.00
23	> 308,000 but ≤ 362,000	335,000	335.00
24	> 262,000 but ≤ 308,000	285,000	285.00
25	> 223,000 but ≤ 262,000	243,000	243.00
26	> 178,000 but ≤ 223,000	200,000	200.00
27	> 142,000 but ≤ 178,000	160,000	160.00
28	> 114,000 but ≤ 142,000	128,000	128.00
29	> 91,000 but ≤ 114,000	103,000	103.00
30	> 73,000 but ≤ 91,000	82,000	82.00
31	> 55,000 but ≤ 73,000	64,000	64.00
32	> 41,000 but ≤ 55,000	48,000	48.00
33	> 31,000 but ≤ 41,000	36,000	36.00
34	> 23,000 but ≤ 31,000	27,000	27.00
35	> 17,000 but ≤ 23,000	20,000	20.00
36	> 12,000 but ≤ 17,000	14,000	14.00
37	> 8,400 but ≤ 12,000	10,000	10.00
38	> 5,900 but ≤ 8,400	7,150	7.15
39	> 4,100 but ≤ 5,900	5,000	5.00
40	> 2,900 but ≤ 4,100	3,500	3.50
41	> 2,000 but ≤ 2,900	2,450	2.45
42	> 1,400 but ≤ 2,000	1,700	1.70
43	> 980 but ≤ 1,400	1,200	1.20
44	> 690 but ≤ 980	840	0.84
45	> 480 but ≤ 690	590	0.59
46	> 340 but ≤ 480	410	0.41

(Table V-1, cont'd)

Class	Market Price Range	Designated Market Price	Tax Assessment
47	> 240 but ≤ 340	290	0.29
48	> 170 but ≤ 240	210	0.21
49	> 120 but ≤ 170	150	0.15
50	≤120	100	0.10

BUILDINGS

Class	Market Price Range	Designated Market Price	Tax Assessment
1	>1,034,000	1,200,000	1,200
2	> 902,000 but ≤1,034,000	968,000	968
3	> 744,000 but ≤ 902,000	823,000	823
4	> 656,000 but ≤ 744,000	700,000	700
5	> 534,000 but ≤ 656,000	595,000	595
6	> 476,000 but ≤ 534,000	505,000	505
7	> 382,000 but ≤ 476,000	429,000	429
8	> 348,000 but ≤ 382,000	365,000	365
9	> 272,000 but ≤ 348,000	310,000	310
10	> 256,000 but ≤ 272,000	264,000	264
11	> 194,000 but ≤ 256,000	225,000	225
12	> 188,000 but ≤ 194,000	191,000	191
13	> 136,000 but ≤ 188,000	162,000	161
14	> 128,000 but ≤ 136,000	132,000	132
15	> 104,000 but ≤ 128,000	116,000	116
16	> 92,000 but ≤ 104,000	98,000	98
17	> 74,000 but ≤ 92,000	83,000	83
18	> 68,000 but ≤ 74,000	71,000	71
19	> 52,000 but ≤ 68,000	60,000	60
20	≤52,000	50,000	50

Source: *Keputusan Menteri Keuangan Republik Indonesia Nomor 1324/KMK.04/1988 Tentang Penentuan Klasifikasi dan Besarnya Nilai Jual Obyek Pajak Sebagai Dasar Pengenaan Pajak Bumi Dan Bangunan.*

Collection

Property tax officials prepare Tax Assessment Notices (*SPPTs, Surat Pemberitahuan Pajak Terhutang*) once a year. Until recently, tax calendars varied both within and among jurisdictions, but efforts are now underway to standardize tax bill production, delivery, and payment periods (see Section III).

SPPTs are generally sorted by sector (rural, urban, plantation, forestry, and mining) and value (Book I through Book V) for valuation, assessment, and collection statistics.[18]

Property tax officials can distribute SPPTs themselves, send them by post, or enlist the assistance of local government officials. SPPT distribution methods vary from locality to locality, but in general, low-value bills are delivered by village (*desa*) or neighborhood (*kelurahan*) officials, while high-value bills are delivered by staff of the district or municipal revenue office (*DIPENDA, Dinas Pendapatan Daerah*).

Taxpayers have three options to address SPPT problems:

- An objection (*keberatan*) may be filed with the tax department within three months of receipt of the SPPT if the taxpayer feels a mistake has been made in the billing. A decision must be issued within twelve months; no reply is considered a positive ruling.

- An appeal (*banding*) may be filed with the tax court within three months following an objection ruling.

- A request for a tax reduction (*pengurangan*) of up to 75 percent may be filed with the tax department within 60 days of receipt of the SPPT if the taxpayer believes that paying the tax assessment is a genuine hardship. A decision must be issued within 90 days; no reply is considered a positive ruling.[19]

Taxpayers have six months to pay their bills; the filing of an objection or an appeal does not relieve the taxpayer of the obligation to pay the full tax due on time.

Until recently, SPPTs could be paid at virtually any state bank or post office branch anywhere in the country in any number of installments. Efforts are now underway to implement a Payment Point System (*SISTEP, Sistem Tempat Pembayaran*), under which taxpayers must pay at a pre-designated bank office in

---

[18]"Book" classifications are based on the following tax assessments:

Book I	:	≤ Rp. 5,000
Book II	:	> Rp. 5,000; ≤ Rp. 25,000
Book III	:	> Rp. 25,000; ≤ Rp. 100,000
Book IV	:	> Rp. 100,000; ≤ Rp. 500,000
Book V	:	> Rp. 500,000

[19]*Undang-Undang Nomor 12 Tahun 1985, Pasal 15-17;* and *Penjelasan Atas Undang-Undang Nomor 12 Tahun 1985, Pasal 15-17.*

one installment anytime within six months after receiving the SPPT (see Section III). Local government collection agents are sometimes used under both systems, especially in rural areas.

Enforcement measures for delinquent taxes are explicit: a 2 percent penalty per month for up to 24 months can be imposed through issuance of a Dunning Notice (*STP, Surat Tagihan Pajak*); and, one month after issuance of an STP, harsher sanctions may be imposed, culminating in the seizure and auction of assets to clear tax arrears (*Surat Paksa, Sita, Lelang*).[20]

Property tax receipts are considered assigned state revenue. Ten percent is paid directly to the National Treasury (*Kas Negara*) and the remaining ninety percent is divided among local governments (PEMDA, *pemerintah daerah*): 18 percent for the province, 72 percent for the district or municipality, and 10 percent for collection fees (see Figure V-2 and Table V-2).[21]

FIGURE V-2:
DISTRIBUTION OF INDONESIAN PROPERTY TAX

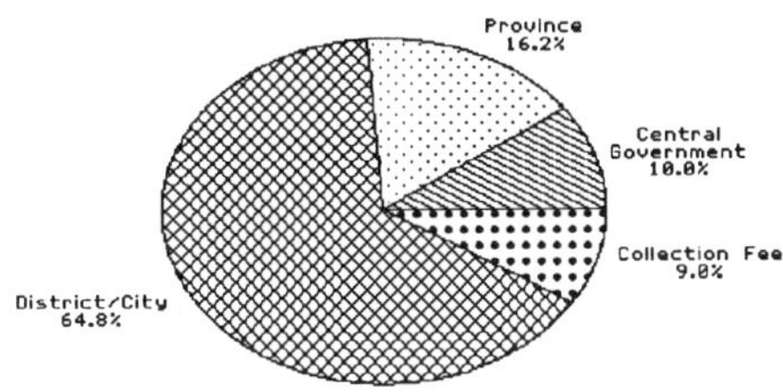

Source: Author's calculations.

[20]*Undang-Undang Nomor 12 Tahun 1985, Pasal 11-13;* and *Penjelasan Atas Undang-Undang Nomor 12 Tahun 1985, Pasal 11-13.*

[21]*Undang-Undang Nomor 12 Tahun 1985, Pasal 18;* and *Penjelasan Atas Undang-Undang Nomor 12 Tahun 1985, Pasal 18.* These collection fees are in addition to annual budget allocations for the Land and Building Tax Directorate, making the Indonesian property tax a relatively expensive tax to administer.

TABLE V-2: DIVISION OF THE PROPERTY TAX COLLECTION FEE IN INDONESIA

	PBB (General)	PBB (Operations)	PEMDA (All Levels)
SECTOR			
Rural	15%	---	85%
Urban			
Jakarta, Bandung, Medan, Semarang Surabaya, and Ujung Pandang	,35%	20%	45%
Other Cities	15%	--	85%
Plantation	30%	40%	30%
Forestry and Mining	25%	50%	25%

Note: PBB refers to the Land and Building Tax Directorate (*Direktorat Pajak Bumi dan Bangunan*); PEMDA is a general term for local government (*pemerintah daerah*).

Source: Keputusan Menteri Keuangan Republik Indonesia Nomor 665/KMK.09/1989.

Administration

Property tax administration is the responsibility of the Ministry of Finance's Directorate of Land and Building Tax (*Direktorat PBB*), in the Directorate General of Tax. Policy is set in Jakarta, and implementation is delegated to 108 field offices throughout Indonesia's 27 provinces and approximately 300 districts and municipalities. PBB has about 5,400 employees, 15 percent of whom have college degrees.[23]

Although PBB is now installing microcomputers in its field offices, it still relies heavily on the Ministry of Finance's central and regional computer facilities (BAPEKSTA/KPDR), as well as private contractors for data entry, processing, storage, and output services. PBB has begun contracting out the cashier and

---

[22]The following discussion is based on interviews with Elizabeth Stair (Commissioner of Land Valuations), Norma Dixon (Commissioner of Inland Revenue), and Dennis Larman (Managing Director of Fiscal Services (EDP) Ltd.).

[23]Karsono Surjowibowo, "*Kebijaksanaan Pajak Bumi dan Bangunan, Aspek Administrasi dan Manajemen Operasional Bagi Hasil Pajak,*" 10, photocopied.

accounting functions of tax collection to state banks, to improve taxpayer services and enable PBB to devote more resources to data, valuation, and enforcement activities.

PBB works quite closely with the Ministry of Home Affairs, especially the Directorate General for Government Administration and Local Autonomy (PUOD) in Jakarta and local government officials in the field, as these are the primary institutional beneficiaries of the property tax.

THE INDONESIAN PROPERTY TAX IN TRANSITION: SYSTEM REFORM

The Change Process: Policy

On December 27, 1985, the Government of Indonesia enacted a Land and Building Tax (PBB, *Pajak Bumi dan Bangunan*), effective January 1, 1986. The goal of this new legislation was to maximize the equitable generation of local property tax revenue. PBB Law No. 12/1985[25] emphasized the principles of uniformity, simplicity, and generality:[26]

- PBB replaced seven different statutes related to the taxation of real property, including the dominant Regional Development Contribution of 1965 (IPEDA, *Iuran Pembangunan Daerah*), the widely-evaded Net Wealth Tax of 1932 (*Pajak Kekayaan*), and the non-trivial Household Tax of 1908 (*Pajak Rumah Tangga*).[27]

---

[24]The following discussion is based on interviews with Elizabeth Stair (Commissioner of Land Valuations), Norma Dixon (Commissioner of Inland Revenue), and Dennis Larman (Managing Director of Fiscal Services (EDP) Ltd.).

[25]*Undang-Undang Republik Indonesia Nomor 12 Tahun 1985 Tentang Pajak Bumi dan Bangunan.*

[26]A detailed comparison of the old and new property tax systems in Indonesia can be found in: Roy Kelly, *Property Taxation in Indonesia: An Analysis of the New Property Tax Law of 1986*, Development Discussion Paper No. 271 (Cambridge, Mass.: Harvard Institute for International Development, July, 1988).

[27]Other land-based statutes retracted include: *Verponding* Law of 1923 (a property tax on Europeans and Eurasians registered as individual landowners according to Western law) and *Verponding* Law of 1928 (a similar tax on Indonesians with property title); *Pajak Hasil Bumi* of 1959 (an agricultural income tax based on farm yield); and *Pajak Jalan* of 1942 (a road tax).

- The tax base was switched from annual rental value to capital market value; the assessment ratio was to begin at 20 percent of market value, and gradually increase to 100 percent of market value.[28]

- A single tax rate of 0.5 percent was to be applied uniformly to all property uses in all locations for all values, rather than to differentiate by property sector, site, or size.[29]

- Exemptions were greatly curtailed, being confined to traditional general exclusions, as well as limited and temporary discretionary exemptions.[30]

- Priority was placed on rectifying absolute rather than relative impoverishment, so a building exemption was established which effectively eliminated virtually all rural and low-income urban housing from the property tax base.[31]

PBB Law No. 12/1985 was promulgated in the context of comprehensive tax reform initiated in the mid-1980s, and the features of the new property tax statute were consistent with the nature of early income tax and value added tax reforms:[32]

- An initial emphasis on revenue neutrality, with a gradual shift to revenue enhancement.

---

[28]IPEDA essentially was levied as follows: for agricultural property, at 5 percent of the value of net annual production (or annual rental value of unproductive land); for urban property, at .18 percent of capital value (formally, 5 percent of rental value - rental value was defined as 6 percent of assessed value, which in turn was defined as 60 percent of capital value).

[29]For example, under IPEDA, residential land was given a 50 percent concession over commercial land; transmigration sites were typically exempted; and progressive tax rates were introduced in 1979, tied to the size of landholdings.

[30]The IPEDA director had the authority to determine special exemptions. This invited a considerable number of discretionary exclusions, including all government land and buildings, as well as some state enterprises.

[31]IPEDA also excluded most rural and low-income urban dwellings by exempting housing valued at less than Rp. 14,000 per square meter. IPEDA and PBB building exemptions have facilitated property tax administration by allowing the use of simple mass appraisal techniques for essentially a land tax on low-value real estate. However, an unintended effect of building exemptions has been increased tax regressivity due to the tendency of wealthy real estate owners to artificially split their property into multiple small units in order to claim multiple building exemptions for one building complex.

[32]A discussion of the entire reform package can be found in: Malcolm Gillis, "Comprehensive Tax Reform: The Indonesian Experience, 1981-1988," in *Tax Reform in Developing Countries,* ed. Malcolm Gillis, 79-114 (Durham: Duke University Press, 1989).

- Distribution neutrality, except for the exemption of the very poor to ensure that those in absolute poverty would not be hurt by tax reform.

- Economic neutrality, rather than using the tax system to try to guide private consumption, investment, and employment decisions.

- Priority on upgrading tax administration and facilitating taxpayer compliance, including code simplification, operations automation, and procedural streamlining and depersonalization.

The Government of Indonesia launched a PBB Improvement Program (PBBIP) in 1987 to facilitate implementation of PBB Law No. 12/1985. Roughly 10 percent of the World Bank-financed $270 million Urban Sector Loan was committed in support of PBBIP, totalling $25.6 million.[33]

Initially, most attention and resources were devoted to improving property valuation.[34] For example, 98 percent of the PBBIP component of the Urban Sector Loan was allocated to valuation activities, with an emphasis on appraisal of expensive urban property and overseas valuation training.[35] Although there was a "PBB Action Plan B" to improve tax management and administration, these activities were also seen primarily as increasing coverage through better identification, registration, and assessment procedures. The need to improve collection and enforcement systems was acknowledged, but only in general terms, unaccompanied by a specific strategy or significant resources.[36] PBBIP emphasis

---

[33]World Bank, East Asia and Pacific Projects Department, Urban and Water Supply Division, *Staff Appraisal Report: Indonesia Urban Sector Loan*, Report No. 6598-IND (Washington, D.C.: World Bank, April 23, 1987), ii and 80.

[34]World Bank, *Staff Appraisal Report: Indonesia Urban Sector Loan*, 76-80.

[35]According to PBB Action Plan A, 10,000 top-value properties in the cities of Jakarta, Bandung and Medan were to be individually valued by foreign valuation firms or organizations, in conjunction with counterpart local firms. Concurrently, a further 50,000 properties in Jakarta were to be valued by semi-individual methods by 90 PBB valuers under the direction of 10 expatriate individual valuers. In addition, the program was to offer three-year scholarships for professional valuation degrees at overseas universities, as well as three-month valuation courses at the Malaysian Government's National Institute of Valuation.

[36]World Bank, *Staff Appraisal Report: Indonesia Urban Sector Loan*, 78-9.

on property registration and valuation was also reflected in complementary PBB Directorate activities during PBBIP implementatation.[37]

However, the government revised substantially PBBIP strategy in terms of policy priorities and management imperatives after the initial phase of PBBIP implementation prompted a reanalysis of principal constraints to property taxation (see Figure V-3). Although it was evident that problems abounded for data collection and processing operations, as well as valuation and assessment activities, government officials decided that the most urgent problems and immediate constraints to increased revenue and improved equity were poor collections. The government thus decided it would attempt to bill and collect current tax liabilities in a more efficient and fair manner, including the application of enforcement measures to recover tax delinquencies, before focussing on improving the quality and quantity of the data that generated these tax assessments:

> *The first conclusion* was that priority should be placed on *increasing the collection ratio.* It was recognized that the ultimate objective of the property tax was to collect revenue. Property information and valuation were seen as *intermediate outputs* to guarantee equity in the allocation of the property tax burden while revenue collection was seen as the *final output* for the property tax system.
>
> *The second conclusion* was that secondary priority should be taken to *increase the coverage ratio* as this would have a greater revenue impact (at a lower political cost) than improvements in the valuation ratio. . . .
>
> *The third conclusion* was that work on improving the valuation ratio should be focused on improving the existing *Buku Nilai Tanah* (Land Value Book) and the classification system for buildings, on developing a computer-assisted valuation system, and on developing a valuation approach for the unique highest value properties. . . .
>
> *The fourth conclusion* was that priority must be placed on improving both property tax policy development and property tax administration in Indonesia.[38]

---

[37]Direktorat Pajak Bumi dan Bangunan. For example, the World Bank and Asian Development Bank allocated approximately $8.9 million from several irrigation loans from 1987 to 1991 to support PBB data and valuation activities in rural areas, consisting mainly of the mapping and reclassification of irrigated land. In addition, the Government of Indonesia allocated $18.3 million in central and local government project funds from 1986 to 1991 for PBB data and valuation activities.

[38]Harvard Institute for International Development, Indonesia Property Tax Project, *Advisory Assistance on Property Tax Administration: Indonesia's Collection-Led Implementation Strategy for Property Tax Reform - Final Report* (Jakarta: HIID, December 1990), i. Emphasis in the original.

FIGURE V-3:

STRATEGY FORMULATION IN INDONESIA

ACTIVITY	PROBLEM	RESPONSE
DATA COLLECTION AND PROCESSING	* Tax Roll Omissions. * Inaccurate, Incomplete, and Outdated Information Regarding Property Size, Characteristics, and Market Value. * Manual Records Management for 35 Million Taxpayers and 65 Million Tax Objects.	* Program for Data Collection and Processing, Including Design and Automation of a Property Information Management System (PIMS). * New Computer-Coded Property Declaration Form (SPOP), Which Facilitates Internal Validation and External Verification. * Use of State Electric Company (PLN) Data for Spotting Omissions and Inaccuracies.
ENFORCEMENT	* Never Tried for Failure to Report or Misreporting Property Tax Information.	* Desk Reviews, Field Audits, and Issuance of Surat Ketetapan Pajak (SKP).
VALUATION AND ASSESSMENT	* Low Appraised Values Relative to Market Values. * Manipulation of Land and Building Classification. * Wide Dispersion of Effective Tax Rates. * Inequitable Distribution of Tax Burden.	* Improvement of Land Value Book (Buku Nilai Tanah). * Simplification and Testing of Building Scoring System (Nilai Rata-Rate Bobot). * Indexing of Values. * Research and Design of Computer Assisted Valuation (CAV) Systems.
COLLECTIONS	* Fradulent Bills and Receipts. * Pocketed Payments. * Multiple Payment Points, Payments, Due Dates, and Collection Institutions. * Voluminous Paperwork. * Inaccurate/Incomplete Reports, Records, and Accounts. * Approximately 60% Collection Efficiency. * No Delinquency List.	* Introduction of Payment Point System (SISTEP): - Tax Payment at Pre-Designated Bank Branches or Sub-Units. - Uniform Due Date. - No Installment Payments. - Pre-Printed Matching Bills and Receipts. - Streamlined Records and Reports, With Emphasis on Negative List. - Computer-Generated Delinquency List.
ENFORCEMENT	* Difficult to Apply Penalties for Non-Payment of Property Tax.	* Automatic Imposition of 2% per Month Penalty and Issuance of Surat Tagihan Pajak (STP), Followed By Selective Issuance of Surat Paksa (SP), and Property Seizure/Auction.

Source: Author's formulation.

This new approach was referred to as a "collection-led" strategy of property tax reform. The government complemented its priority on collections with several measures to maximize immediate impact while minimize risk of failure: concentration on high value urban properties; preliminary field testing of reforms in a pilot project; further fine-tuning of reforms through phased replication; and sustained emphasis on simple, standard, and uniform policies and procedures throughout Indonesia.

The Change Process: Administration and Behavior

In early 1989, the PBB Directorate (*Direktorat Pajak Bumi dan Bangunan*) formulated a pilot project with the following two principal aims:

> *First*, new or revised systems and procedures for key activities relating to administration of the property tax were to be tested under actual field conditions, and modified as necessary before replication throughout Indonesia.
>
> *Second*, the pilot project would provide the opportunity to observe the functioning of all aspects of PBB administration closely, at one location over an extended period, as well as to collect data for monitoring tax collections, coverage, valuation accuracy, and tax delinquency.[39]

Tangerang District (*Kabupaten Tangerang*) was selected as the pilot project location, because:

- Tangerang is a diversified area that is fairly typical in its mix of properties, in terms of value, sectoral designation, and property use;[40] and
- Tangerang's proximity to Jakarta would permit continuous monitoring at reasonable cost.[41]

---

[39]Harvard Institute for International Development, Indonesia Property Tax Project, *Advisory Assistance on Property Tax Administration: Tangerang Pilot Project - Final Report*, 2 vols. (Jakarta: HIID, April 1990), i.

[40]There are approximately 450,000 taxpayers and 600,000 tax objects in Tangerang. Although Tangerang is primarily rural, it is also part of the Jakarta greater metropolitan area (Jabotabek), and consequently receives a significant part of the urban overspill from DKI Jakarta, with new housing and commercial development, as well as major industrial expansion, taking place throughout the district. Like most jurisdictions in Indonesia, a small percentage of the properties in Tangerang constitute a disproportionate share of the district's tax base: roughly 0.5 percent of the properties, almost all in urban areas, account for about 40 percent of total billings (excluding the international airport and a major toll road).

The Director General of Taxation approved the Tangerang Pilot Project (TPP) on March 18, 1989[42] for implementation during fiscal year 1989/90.[43]

Although collection activities in Tangerang were given top priority during TPP, the pilot project actually commenced with property information activities (*pendataan*) in April 1989 due to the first nation-wide implementation of the mandatory three-year general revaluation:

> The pendataan exercise afforded an opportunity to test the newly designed, modular, computer-compatible SPOP [property declaration] form on which property information and other spatial information such as the PLN (electrical company) control number, the telephone number, and building registration numbers were recorded as appropriate. The pendataan strategy also involved an exercise to link the PLN electricity data base with PBB data for Book IV and V properties in order to facilitate identification of unregistered or misrecorded high-value properties. Use of the PLN information to audit and update PBB information was successfully tested in January 1990.[44]

The Minister of Finance officially launched the Payment Point System (SISTEP, *Sistem Tempat Pembayaran*) in Tangerang in June 1989. Key features of SISTEP are:

- Payment at a pre-designated bank branch or sub-unit located near the tax object.
- Payment in one installment.
- A uniform due date.
- Re-printed matching bills and receipts.

---

[41]Tangerang lies on Jakarta's western border.

[42]DJP Kep-13/PJ.7/1989.

[43]April 1, 1989 through March 31, 1990.

[44]HIID, *Indonesia's Collection-Led Implementation Strategy for Property Tax Reform - Final Report*, iii.

- Streamlined records and reports, with an emphasis on monitoring delinquencies.

- A computer-generated delinquency list.

SISTEP logistics are quite demanding, because application of a uniform due date necessitates distribution of all tax bills to taxpayers and all tax receipts to banks within a relatively short period.[45]

In fact, SISTEP has been an effective "back door" mechanism for establishing the foundation of PBB's automated Property Information Management System: by computerizing the heart of property tax administration, the tax roll and accompanying tax payment information, PBB has created the core of an automated system to which other modules can later be added, such as property characteristics or property valuation.

SISTEP implementation also requires considerable initiative and close teamwork. During the pilot project, the Tangerang PBB Service Office (KPPBB Tangerang) took the lead, but worked very closely with the BRI (Bank Rakyat Indonesia), the receiving bank in Tangerang, as well as with DIPENDA Tkt. II (Dinas Pendapatan Daerah), the District Revenue Service.

Another critical element of SISTEP is considerable attention to public information and training. KPPBB Tangerang therefore conducted an intensive, multi-media campaign during the six-month payment period, and organized special orientation meetings with subdistrict and village chiefs. Special training sessions were also held for bank staff. In addition, senior officials provided sustained, high-profile support for efforts in Tangerang.

SISTEP entails fundamental behavioral change by both taxpayers and tax officials, so SISTEP's success thus far is due primarily to a combination of positive and negative institutional and individual incentives that have been able to elicit desired responses from key participants.

For example, although SISTEP is a potential challenge to tax and local government officials because it turns cashier and accounting functions over to the banks and thereby eliminates many opportunities for corruption, the banks have three very strong incentives to manage PBB accounts carefully and honestly: maintainance of their professional credibility and good public reputation; adequate remuneration for services rendered, in terms of a mutually acceptable float period; and a contract with the Tax Directorate General to compensate PBB in cash for the

[45]In Tangerang, the tax due date was December 31, 1989; if taxpayers were not to be deprived of their six-month payment period, all 450,000 bills and 450,000 receipts had to be prepared and distributed by the end of June. This was accomplished during a three-month period through a crash data conversion program from a manual to a computer system by the Ministry of Finance computer center (BAPEKSTA), together with a heavy reliance on local government officials for distribution of bills to taxpayers.

value of any property tax receipts not properly accounted for, i.e. missing, lost, or destroyed.

SISTEP also provides taxpayers with strong incentives to comply: service is greatly improved by exploiting the extensive network and commercial efficiency of Indonesia's banking system; especially in urban areas, taxpayers can pay their taxes directly at bank branches or subunits rather than via often corrupt tax collectors, so they are more confident the funds will actually be used for their intended purpose; and SISTEP automation enables PBB to generate a reliable delinquency list and undertake follow-up enforcement measures, thereby making taxpayers accountable for their actions.

Finally, SISTEP offers tax and local government officials effective incentives to cooperate: institutionally, improved taxpayer service and a credible threat that sanctions will be imposed for noncompliance are a potent combination to improve collections, while personally, greater collections also means more income from collection fees; tax disbursements to local government are more frequent and predictable under SISTEP, facilitating local government planning and administration; and while fraud and corruption are always possible, SISTEP internal controls and external validation make the effort much more demanding, and the risk of getting caught significantly higher than under the traditional payment system.

After SISTEP had been running for almost six months in Tangerang, PBB officials tried one last effort to encourage voluntary compliance during the last week in December, before the penalty period was to begin in January. KPPBB Tangerang sent computer-generated Final Warning Letters (*Surat Pemberitahuan*) to taxpayers responsible for Book IV and V properties who had not yet paid their tax liabilities.

A delinquency list was compiled at the end of January 1990 for Book IV and V properties still with outstanding tax liabilities, data were re-verified, and Dunning Notices (STPs, *Surat Tagihan Pajak*) were issued for all confirmed unpaid bills. KPPBB Tangerang has proceeded to apply enforcement measures for Book IV and V unpaid 1989/90 tax liabilities, including Warning Notices (*Surat Tegoran*) and Final Notices (*Surat Paksa*), and is now finalizing preparations for selective seizure (*sita*) and auctioning (*lelang*) of property.

Enforcement measures for low value (Book I, II, and III) properties in Tangerang have been implemented somewhat differently than those for high value (Book IV and V) properties:

> Although the delinquency rate for low value properties was about 40 percent, PBB officials decided it would be more cost-effective and socially responsible to issue STPs selectively, given the volume of tax objects, the

> relatively small amount of average tax liability for these properties, and these properties' predominantly rural nature.
>
> Thus, sample Book I, II, and III properties, mostly of relatively high value, were selected from 63 desa (villages) distributed throughout Tangerang's 19 kecamatan (subdistricts). An average of 3 desa were selected from each kecamatan, and 20 to 25 properties were selected from each desa. In total, 1,180 STPs were issued for Book I, II, and III properties, or 0.3 percent of the 444,212 Book I, II, and III properties on the Tangerang tax roll. . . . The response to these STPs is not yet known.[46]

Preliminary evaluation of SISTEP led to replication of the system to twelve new municipalities and districts during fiscal year 1990/91.[47]

SISTEP is now being further replicated in sixty more municipalities and districts during fiscal year 1991/92, split almost equally between locations on Java and locations on the outer islands (see Table V-3). After second stage replication, SISTEP would thus only cover one-fourth of all of Indonesia's municipalities and districts, but would cover over one-third of all tax objects and almost two-thirds of all tax liabilities (see Figure V-4).[48] Expansion criteria again stressed cost-effectiveness, realism, and balance.[49] SISTEP results to date are discussed in Section IV below.

An interim strategy was developed in Tangerang for upgrading the PBB Directorate's existing valuation system while awaiting completion and testing of the new mass valuation model being developed as part of the World Bank-assisted valuation activities described earlier:

---

[46]HIID, *Tangerang Pilot Project - Final Report*, iv.

[47]First stage replication included the following nine municipalities (*kotamadya*) and three districts (*kabupaten*): *on Java*, West Jakarta City, Bandung City, Cirebon City and District, Semarang City, Kendal District, and Surabaya City; *off Java*, Medan City, Palembang City, Balikpapan City, Pasir District, and Ujung Pandang City. Criteria for expansion included: high revenue potential for maximum return on minimum investment; relatively high-caliber personnel and effective field administration to ensure sufficient implementation capacity, together with feasible logistics and a critical mass of tax objects to facilitate cost-effective supervision; fully or partially automated electronic data processing of PBB records to allow computer-assisted tax administration; and reasonable working relationships with other local institutions to promote inter-agency cooperation.

[48]As of June 1990, there were 296 Indonesian cities and districts, approximately 50 million total rural and urban tax objects, and a total rural and urban tax assessment of Rp. 292 billion.

[49]Criteria included: relatively high urban and rural tax potential, with a workload proportionate to the expected increase in revenue; proximity to first stage replication municipalities and districts, sufficient field management capability, and adequate regional and central supervisory capacity; symmetrical regional distribution to facilitate future expansion and sustainability.

The proposed upgraded PBB mass valuation methodology was based on three fundamental principles governing valuation systems designed for property taxation purposes: *simplicity*, *equity*, and *cost effectiveness*.

The recommended improvements entailed two principal components: land and buildings. *Land* was to be valued using an updated, internally consistent "buku nilai tanah [land value book]," while *buildings* were to be valued using a simplified, externally verifiable "bobot [weighted average of building components]" system.[50]

Policy and institutional reforms have also been undertaken during PBBIP implementation:

- Preparation for reallocation of the central government's share of PBB revenue to village (rural) and community (urban) level governments.
- Partial rationalization of the collection fee system between the PBB Directorate and local government, and among different levels of local government.
- Indefinite postponement of the land transfer tax.
- Exclusion of machinery and equipment from the property tax base.
- Complete reorganization of the Directorate General of Tax.
- Preliminary development of a computer-based, integrated, textual and spatial Property Information Management System (PIMS).

---

[50]HIID, *Tangerang Pilot Project - Final Report*, v.

TABLE V-3: SECOND-STAGE REPLICATION OF THE PAYMENT POINT SYSTEM IN INDONESIA

Location	City or District	Total Tax Assessment	Total Tax Objects	Computer-Entered Tax Objects	Un-Entered Objects
	(#)	(Rp.b)	(000s)	(000s)	(%)
Java	35	93.4	11,429	2,803	75%
Sumatra	12	10.1	787	239	70%
Sulawesi	5	5.7	910	137	85%
Kalimantan	5	4.2	337	207	39%
Other Islands	3	5.0	311	44	86%
Total	60	118.4	13,774	3,430	75%

Note: All figures are for rural and urban properties only, as of June 1990.
Source: Direktorat Pajak Bumi dan Bangunan.

FIGURE V-4:
PAYMENT POINT SYSTEM COVERAGE
IN INDONESIA

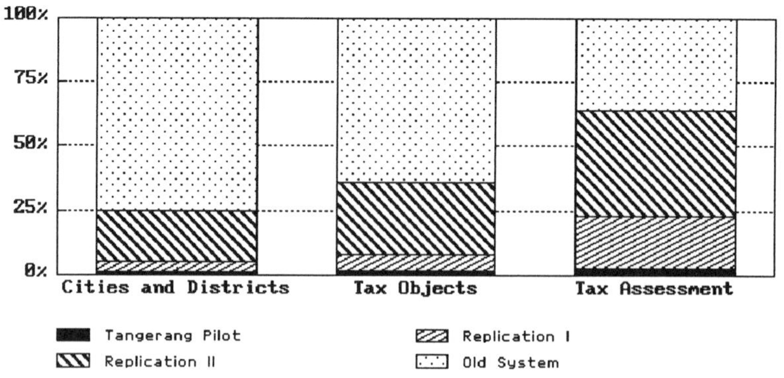

Source: Author's calculations.

THE INDONESIAN PROPERTY TAX IN PRACTICE: SYSTEM PERFORMANCE

Purpose: Revenue and Non-Revenue Objectives

Revenue Generation

Nominal property tax revenue in Indonesia has increased at a compounded annual rate of nearly 25 percent over the past two decades, rising 100-fold from Rp. 7.9 billion in 1970 to Rp. 771 billion in 1991 (see Table V-4).[51]

When nominal property tax receipts are converted to 1985 rupiahs, the compounded annual rate of increase drops to nine percent over the past two decades, with total revenue rising six times from Rp. 85 billion in 1979 to Rp. 503 billion in 1991 (see Figure V-5).[52]

Until 1986, the relatively slow but steady increase in nominal property tax revenue maintained the real value of property tax receipts. Since tax reform, however, receipts have more than tripled in nominal terms and increased 139 percent in constant (1985) rupiahs. The dramatic increase since 1989 is due primarily to the first PBB general revaluation and concomitant use of new land and building unit value tables.

These aggregate data do not reveal a significant change in the composition of property tax revenue over the past two decades. In 1970, three-fourths of all property tax receipts came from rural properties; by 1991, the rural sector share had fallen to 15 percent, while the mining sector had risen from a negligible 6 percent share in 1970 to constitute roughly half of all PBB revenue twenty years later. During the same period, the urban sector share more than doubled, increasing from 10 percent in 1970 to 22 percent in 1991 (see Figure V-6).[53]

Thus, even though revenue from rural and urban properties increased at a compounded annual rate of almost 20 percent in nominal terms and nearly 5 percent in constant rupiahs over the past two decades, rising from Rp. 7 billion in

---

[51]Direktorat Pajak Bumi dan Bangunan.

[52]Gross domestic product deflators are taken from: International Monetary Fund, Bureau of Statistics, *International Financial Statistics* (Washington, D.C.: International Monetary Fund), monthly issues and yearbooks.

[53]Direktorat Pajak Bumi dan Bangunan.

1970 to Rp. 286 billion in 1991 (see Figure V-7), the growth in P3 sector revenue[54] far outpaced these traditional sources of property tax receipts: P3 revenue increased at a compounded annual rate of 33 percent in nominal terms and nearly 17 percent in constant rupiahs over the past two decades, rising from just over Rp. 1 billion in 1970 to more than Rp. 485 billion in 1991.[55]

TABLE V-4: PROPERTY TAX REVENUE IN INDONESIA

Fiscal Year	Property Tax Receipts (billions of rupiahs)	
	Nominal Rp.	*1985 Rp.*
1969/70	7.9	84.9
1970/71	9.9	103.1
1971/72	11.9	109.2
1972/73	15.1	104.1
1973/74	19.9	93.0
1974/75	29.0	120.8
1975/76	35.8	130.2
1976/77	42.6	137.0
1977/78	53.3	154.5
1978/79	64.0	140.0
1979/80	74.3	125.9
1980/81	90.6	129.6
1981/82	95.6	130.1
1982/83	105.1	119.8
1983/84	137.6	144.8
1984/85	166.6	166.6
1985/86	154.8	155.0
1986/87	244.1	210.8
1987/88	316.0	257.5
1988/89	367.8	270.6
1989/90	615.0	430.4
1990/91	771.0	502.9[a]

[a]Estimated.
Source: Direktorat Pajak Bumi dan Bangunan.

[54]"P3" refers to the plantation, forestry, and mining sectors.

[55]Direktorat Pajak Bumi dan Bangunan.

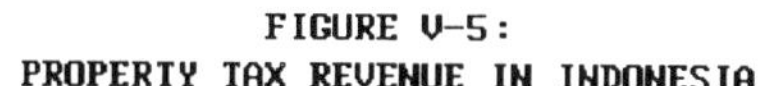

FIGURE V-5:
PROPERTY TAX REVENUE IN INDONESIA

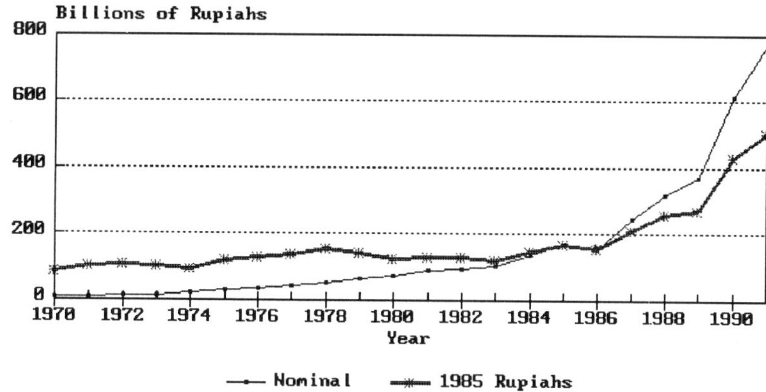

Source: Author's calculations.

FIGURE V-6:
SECTORAL COMPOSITION OF PROPERTY TAX
REVENUE IN INDONESIA

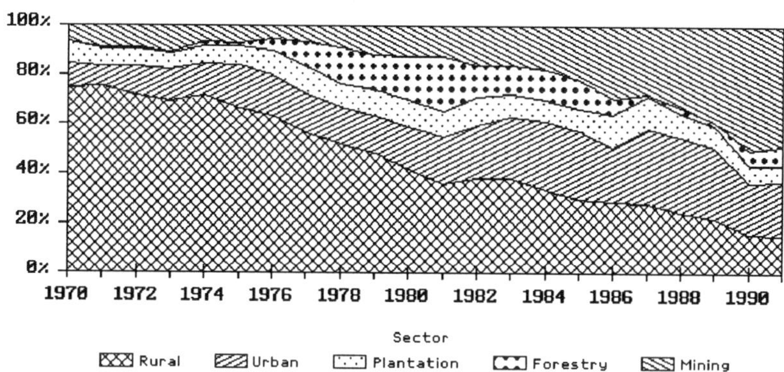

Source: Author's calculations.

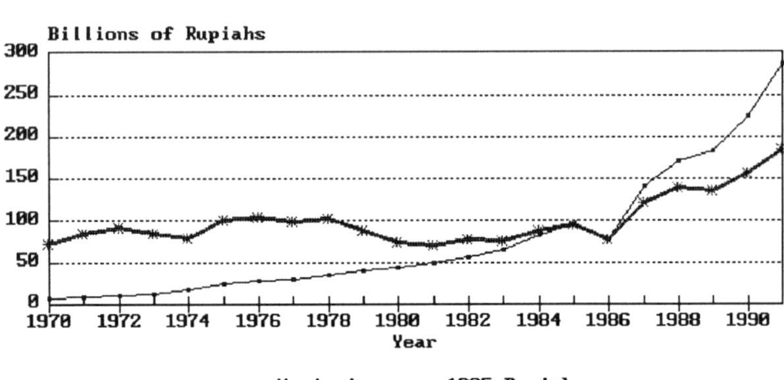

Source: Author's calculations.

As PBBIP was but one component of comprehensive tax reform, it is interesting to note the size and composition of national tax revenue in relation to the Indonesian economy, and property tax receipts within this larger context.

Total domestic tax receipts as a percentage of gross domestic product have more than doubled from 1967 to 1987, rising from 7.1 to 15.5 percent. Most of this increase has come from tax receipts on oil and LNG exports; the rise in non-oil and LNG domestic tax receipts as a percentage of gross domestic product was much smaller, increasing from 6.2 percent in 1967 to 8.4 percent in 1987 (see Table V-5).[56]

The property tax share of total tax revenue has more than doubled between 1983 and 1990, but is still insignificant, rising from 0.9 to 2.5 percent. Even if oil and LNG revenue is not included, the property tax share of total tax revenue has remained quite small from 1983 to 1990, increasing from 2.7 to 3.7 percent. In addition to oil and LNG revenue, the dominant national taxes are now the value added tax and the income tax (see Figure V-8).[57]

---

[56]Malcolm Gillis, "Episodes in Indonesian Economic Growth," in *World Economic Growth*, ed. Arnold C. Harberger (San Francisco: Institute for Contemporary Studies, 1984), table 3 for years 1967-79; Ministry of Finance unpublished statistics for years 1980-87. Both cited in Malcolm Gillis, "Comprehensive Tax Reform: The Indonesian Experience, 1981-1988," *in Tax Reform in Developing Countries*, ed. Malcolm Gillis (Durham: Duke University Press, 1989), table 4.1.

[57]Departemen Keuangan; and Gillis, "The Indonesian Experience, 1981-1988," table 4.3. 1990 figures are estimates.

TABLE V-5: TAX REVENUE IN THE INDONESIAN ECONOMY

Year	Non-Oil Domestic Tax Receipts as a Percentage of GDP[a] [1]	Tax Receipts on Oil and LNG Exports as a Percentage of GDP [2]	Total Domestic Tax Receipts as a Percentage of GDP [3/*1* + *2*]
1967	6.2	0.9	7.1
1968	6.0	1.2	7.2
1969	7.3	1.7	9.0
1970	8.3	2.0	10.3
1971	8.7	3.0	11.7
1972	8.7	4.3	13.0
1973	9.2	5.1	14.3
1974	7.4	9.0	16.4
1975	7.9	9.8	17.7
1976	8.4	10.4	18.8
1977	8.4	10.2	18.6
1978	8.8	10.2	19.0
1979	7.9	13.7	21.6
1980	7.2	15.8	23.0
1981	6.1	15.0	21.1
1982	6.8	12.2	19.0
1983	6.7	14.1	20.8
1984	6.1	14.6	20.7
1985	8.0	11.8	19.8
1986	9.1	5.2	14.3
1987[b]	8.4	7.1	15.5

[a]Non-oil tax revenue includes surpluses from domestic oil operations in 1986 and 1987: 1986 = Rp. 977 billion; 1987 = Rp. 114 billion. [b]All 1987 figures are estimates.

Sources: Gillis, "Episodes in Indonesian Economic Growth," in *World Economic Growth*, table 3 for years 1967-79; Ministry of Finance unpublished statistics for years 1980-87. Both cited in Gillis, "Comprehensive Tax Reform: The Indonesian Experience, 1981-1988," in *Tax Reform in Developing Countries*, table 4.1.

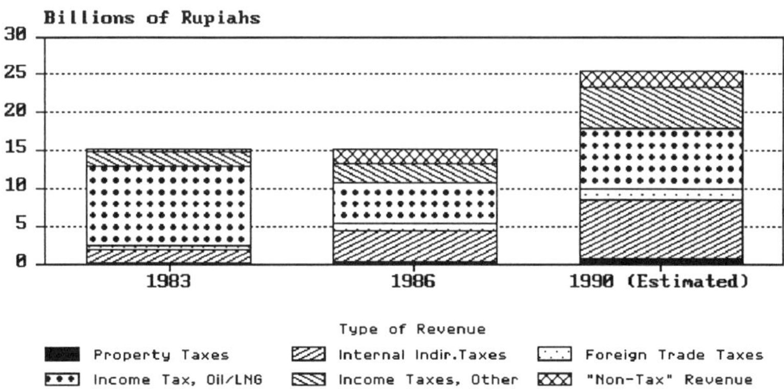

Source: Author's calculations.

In contrast to its share of national tax revenue, the property tax is a major component of local government income. In fiscal year 1987/88, property tax receipts constituted 6 percent of provincial revenue and 12 percent of district and municipal revenue; if central grants are excluded, the share of property tax receipts rises to 17 percent and 31 percent, respectively (see Figure V-9).[58]

Non-Revenue Objectives

In general, PBB officials have concentrated on increasing property tax receipts; non-revenue objectives have been handled through the expenditure side of the budget. The only significant deviation from this practice has been the tax holiday for new investment in Eastern Indonesia, which has succeeded in accomplishing little more than reducing already poor local governments' main source of discretionary revenue.

Relief for low-value property improvements has been augmented by increasing the building exemption from Rp. 2 million to Rp. 3.5 million, while horizontal and vertical equity have been enhanced by improved tax roll accuracy and completeness, and greater valuation precision and consistency.

An unintentional byproduct of property taxation in Indonesia has been the quasi-legal use of paid PBB bills as evidence of land and building ownership.

[58]Karsono Surjowibowo, "The Property Tax in Indonesia," paper prepared for the Municipal Finance Seminar, Cipanas, December 1990, 3.

Although the property tax law is quite explicit in stating that receipts documenting payment of the property tax do not constitute proof of ownership,[59] lack of a comprehensive legal cadastre has left many residents with few alternatives. However, documenting PBB payments has diverted a considerable amount of PBB Directorate field staff time from the principal task of administering the property tax, and has encouraged substantial informal payments for services rendered - no fees may be charged for preparation of *riwayat tanah*, or land histories.

Finally, although a blanket tax liability threshold has been proposed several times, government officials have rejected such a policy. While they acknowledge that it is not revenue enhancing to include so many low value properties in the PBB system, these officials believe that such a broad tax base serves other important purposes: it helps in the nation-building process by encouraging a spirit of *gotong-royong* (mutual help and community solidarity), and instills among the citizenry a taxpaying responsibility essential for long-term development.

Principles: Efficiency, Equity, and Sustainability

There is a common perception among government officials and donor agency staff that a major deficiency of property taxation in Indonesian is a deficient information base.

For example, Indonesia's total taxable land area is often compared with total hectares actually taxed, with the conclusion that rural and urban coverage is only 60 percent, while P3 coverage is less than 30 percent (see Figure V-10).[60]

This belief is also reflected in the tremendous amount spent on property data and valuation activities, totalling $27.2 million and $18.1 million, respectively (see Tables V-6 and V-7).[61]

Although the unit cost for data activities is relatively low (roughly $2 per object), much of the property covered is low-value rural land that generates even

---

[59]*Penjelasan Atas Undang-Undang Nomor 12 Tahun 1985, Pasal 4, Ayat (1).*

[60]Surjowibowo, "*Kebijaksanaan Pajak Bumi dan Bangunan,*" 11.

[61]Surjowibowo, "*Kebijaksanaan Pajak Bumi dan Bangunan,*" 12; and International Land Information Services, *Pajak Bumi dan Bangunan Improvement Plan (PBBIP) Advisory Assistance for Property Valuation: Completion Report on Contracts 1164, 1264, 1547 and 144* (Jakarta: ILIS, May 1991), 8-15 and 23-31.

less in annual tax revenue. The valuation costs might also appear moderate at between $44 and $772 per object, but again, the urban property valued seldom generates a comparable amount of annual tax revenue.

In fact, the highly skewed distribution of property, especially in urban areas where most of the property tax base lies, when coupled with the very low effective tax rate, raises doubts about the advisability of such substantial investments in data and valuation activities: the tax assessment of two-thirds of Indonesia's urban property is less than Rp. 5,000 and constitutes 7 percent of total urban assessed value; conversely, the tax assessment of 0.3 percent of urban property is greater than Rp. 500,000, and constitutes 47 percent of total urban assessed value. These doubts are reinforced by the observation that both data and valuation activities are generally restricted to the current tax roll, so identification of new tax objects or discovery of gross mislistings is minimal.[62]

---

[62]World Bank, *Staff Appraisal Report: Indonesia Urban Sector Loan*, 81.

TABLE V-6: PROPERTY DATA ACTIVITIES IN INDONESIA

Fiscal Year	Cost (Rp.b)	Area[c] (Ha.th)	Parcels (1000s)	Increased Billing (Rp.b)	Change (Percent)
Domestic	*Funds*[a]				
1986/87	0.7	93	123	1.5	80%
1987/88	1.5	625	834	2.9	62%
1988/89	1.8	438	584	2.1	32%
1989/90	8.3	4,340	5,787	11.7	60%
1990/91	20.5	14,769	n.a.	n.a.	n.a.
Subtotal	32.8	20,265	7,328	1 8.2	58%
External	*Funds*[b]				
1987/88	4.6	610	2,685	10.0	97%
1988/89	2.9	206	1,165	3.5	47%
1989/90	2.3	251	1,308	3.7	34%
1990/91	5.6	474	n.a.	n.a.	n.a.
Subtotal	15.4	1,541	5,158	17.2	59%
All Funds					
1986/87	0.7	93	123	1.5	80%
1987/88	6.1	1,235	3,519	12.9	86%
1988/89	4.7	644	1,749	5.6	40%
1989/90	10.6	4,591	7,095	15.4	51%
1990/91	26.1	15,243	n.a.	n.a.	n.a.
Total	48.2	21,806	12,486	35.4	57%

[a] APBN/DIK; Biaya Operasional; APBD/DIPDA; INPRES.

[b] World Bank; Asian Development Bank.

[c] Rural and urban for domestic funds; rural only for external funds.

Sources: Surjowibowo, *"Kebijaksanaan Pajak Bumi dan Bangunan,"* 12; and author's calculations.

TABLE V-7: PROPERTY VALUATION ACTIVITIES IN INDONESIA

City	Top Value Properties			High Value Properties			Computer Assisted Valuation		
	Objects (#)	Cost ($m)	Cost/ Object ($)	Objects (#)	Cost ($m)	Cost/ Object ($)	Objects (#)	Cost ($m)	Cost/ Object ($)
Jakarta	7,443	5.33	716	51,027	6.06	119	52,580	2.23	42
Medan	1,380	1.48	1,072	------	----	---	10,613	0.48	45
Bandung	1,490	1.15	772	------	----	---	12,222	0.46	38
Surabaya	-----	----	---	------	----	---	13,446	0.70	52
Badung (Bali)	-----	----	---	------	----	---	3,168	0.20	63
Total	10,313	7.96	772	51,027	6.06	119	92,029	4.07	44

Source: ILIS, *Completion Report on Contracts 1164, 1264, 1547 and 144*, 8-15 and 23-31.

In contrast to its share of national tax revenue, the property tax is a major component of local government income. In fiscal year 1987/88, property tax receipts constituted 6 percent of provincial revenue and 12 percent of district and municipal revenue; if central grants are excluded, the share of property tax receipts rises to 17 percent and 31 percent, respectively (see Figure V-9).[63]

Furthermore, the claims of increased tax assessments resulting from these data and valuation activities is spurious. Although assessments have indeed risen, this has been true in both project and non-project areas, due primarily to "classification creep" between general revaluations, as well as the first general revaluation itself in 1989: land unit prices increased 15-fold on average, and as much as 3,100 percent in the mid-value classes (Classes 26 through 29), while building unit prices doubled for most classes (see Figure V-11).[64]

---

[63]Karsono Surjowibowo, "The Property Tax in Indonesia," paper prepared for the Municipal Finance Seminar, Cipanas, December 1990, 3.

[64]These increases are based on a comparison of unit values for land and buildings according to *Keputusan Menteri Keuangan Republik Indonesia Nomor 1003/KMK.04/1985* (effective in 1986) and *Keputusan Menteri Keuangan Republik Indonesia Nomor 1324/KMK.04/1988* (effective in 1989). Despite the dramatic rise in unit values, the top end of the scale is still well below market prices of prime urban property. The non-uniform increases in land and building unit prices, when coupled with a relatively uniform bumping up to higher value classes, however, makes a compelling case for the periodic general indexation of property values to prevent the tendency for excessive and arbitrary reclassification.

FIGURE V-9:
INDONESIAN PROPERTY TAX IN LOCAL FINANCE
(FISCAL YEAR 1987/88)

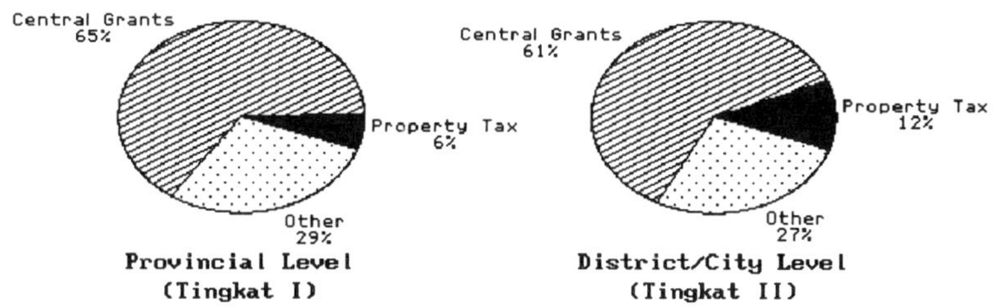

Source: Author's calculations.

FIGURE V-10:
PROPERTY TAX COVERAGE IN INDONESIA
(LAND COMPONENT)

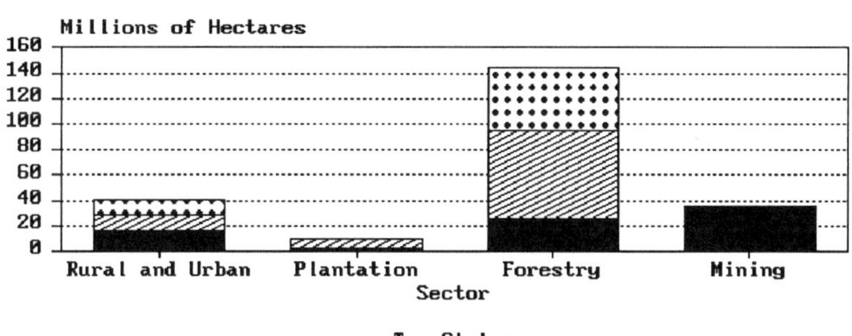

Tax Status

Already Taxed Liable But Untaxed Tax Exempt

Note: Mining Total Area Unknown.

Source: Author's calculations.

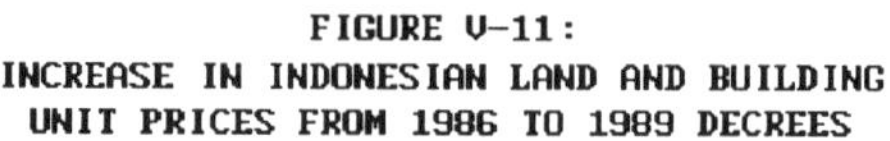
FIGURE V-11:
INCREASE IN INDONESIAN LAND AND BUILDING
UNIT PRICES FROM 1986 TO 1989 DECREES

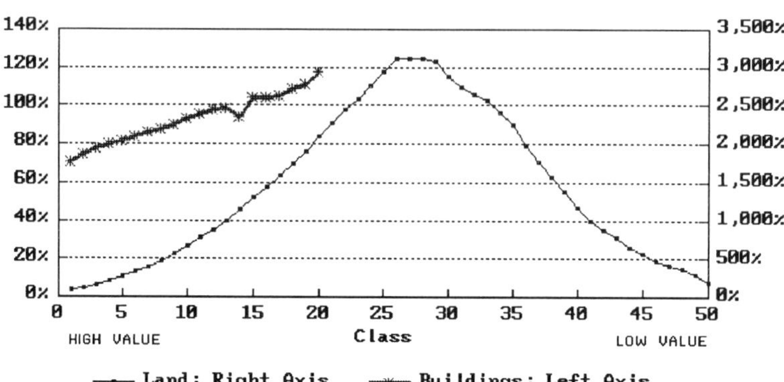

Source: Author's calculations.

For example, rural and urban property assessments increased anywhere from 8.1 percent in Irian Jaya to 55.6 percent in Southeast Sulawesi between 1989 and 1990, with an average increase of 19.1 percent (see Table V-8).[60] Perhaps coincidentally, the increase in values for the 41,383 benchmark valuation properties in Jakarta between 1988 and 1989 was also 19.1 percent.[61] In fact, PBBIP's overall revenue target, a doubling of the 1985/86 property tax revenue by 1988/89, was achieved a year ahead of schedule, well before most of the data and valuation activities affected property tax billings.[62]

---

[60]Direktorat Pajak Bumi dan Bangunan.

[61] ILIS, *Completion Report on Contracts 1164, 1264, 1547 and 144*, 35.

[62]This explicit revenue target is taken from: World Bank, *Staff Appraisal Report: Indonesia Urban Sector Loan*, 11.

TABLE V-8: RURAL AND URBAN PROPERTY ASSESSMENTS IN INDONESIA

Province	1989 (Rp.b)	1990 (Rp.b)	Change (Rp.b)	Change (%)
1. D.I. Aceh	2.55	3.44	0.89	34.9%
2. North Sumatra	17.43	24.05	6.62	38.0%
3. West Sumatra	4.36	5.68	1.32	30.3%
4. Riau	3.99	5.49	1.50	37.6%
5. Jambi	1.86	2.11	0.25	13.4%
6. South Sumatra	7.18	7.80	0.62	8.6%
7. Bengkulu	0.85	0.99	0.14	16.5%
8. Lampung	7.42	9.03	1.61	21.7%
9. D.K.I. Jakarta	59.02	67.76	8.74	14.8%
10. West Java	60.94	70.12	9.18	15.1%
11. Central Java	29.16	36.83	7.67	26.3%
12. D.I. Yogyakarta	3.93	4.69	0.76	19.3%
13. East Java	48.99	55.77	6.78	13.8%
14. West Kalimantan	2.38	2.75	0.37	15.5%
15. Central Kalimantan	0.97	1.08	0.11	11.3%
16. South Kalimantan	1.93	2.25	0.32	16.6%
17. East Kalimantan	3.87	4.60	0.73	18.9%
18. South Sulawesi	13.46	16.65	3.19	23.7%
19. Southeast Sulawesi	0.90	1.40	0.50	55.6%
20. North Sulawesi	5.14	5.65	0.51	9.9%
21. Central Sulawesi	2.93	3.23	0.30	10.2%
22. Bali	5.14	7.08	1.94	37.7%
23. West Nusa Tenggara	3.87	4.83	0.96	24.8%
24. East Nusa Tenggara	2.92	3.77	0.85	29.1%
25. East Timor	0.23	0.29	0.06	26.1%
26. Maluku	2.20	2.49	0.29	13.2%
27. Irian Jaya	0.86	0.93	0.07	8.1%
Total	294.48	350.76	56.28	19.1%

Source: Data from Direktorat Pajak Bumi dan Bangunan; compilation and adjustments by the author.

There is also considerable debate about the quality of new computer-generated valuations in terms of comparable assessment for similar properties and consistent relative differences for dissimilar tax objects, as well as the capacity of the PBB Directorate to provide data necessary to sustain the model and the ability of tax officials and taxpayers to understand how computer-assisted tax assessments were derived:

> *The valuation models must be simplified and then tested against valuation standards. This will ensure that the model predicts market value accurately, can be explained to the taxpayer and can be constructed with minimum data needs.*[65]

An alternative hypothesis for the major deficiency in property tax coverage is deliberate omissions or gross misrepresentations on the valuation roll, together with poor collections and negligible enforcement: a 0.1 percent effective tax rate, even at current market values, allows considerable room for data and valuation error before significantly affecting property tax liabilities. However, non-reporting and mis-reporting, or non-payment and under-payment, especially if skewed to high-value urban properties, would have a much more dramatic impact on coverage and equity.

When PBBIP was first conceived, rural and urban collection rates throughout Indonesia were about 60 percent of current assessments,[66] and there appeared to be an inverse correlation between property value and taxpayer compliance.[67] Collection rates have improved dramatically since then, even when compared with current assessments rather than annual collection targets: rural and urban collection efficiency averaged 80 percent nationally and 87 percent on Java and Bali in fiscal year 1990/91 (see Table V-9 and Figure V-12).[68] Most PBB Directorate staff and local government officials now believe this progress is due primarily to SISTEP implementation, so a brief review of SISTEP results might be revealing.

---

[65]Joseph K. Eckert, "Evaluation of the CAV to Date and Recommendations for Simplification and Implementation," Memorandum PBB/91/DPRT/365, June 28, 1991, photocopied. A more positive view of the computer-assisted valuation model is presented by one of the model's developers in: Robert Faber, "Simulation of Real Market Value: An Experience," in *International Conference on Property Taxation and Its Interaction with Land Policy: Resource Manual*, vol. 1, 358-77 (Cambridge, Mass.: Lincoln Institute of Land Policy, September 1991).

[66]World Bank, *Staff Appraisal Report: Indonesia Urban Sector Loan*, 79.

[67]Field interviews with staff of the PBB Directorate and local government officials.

[68]Direktorat Pajak Bumi dan Bangunan.

TABLE V-9: FISCAL YEAR 1990/91 COLLECTION RATES FOR RURAL AND URBAN PROPERTIES IN INDONESIA[a]

Province	Total Assmts.	Collect. Targets	Targets/ Assmts.	Colls.	Colls./ Targets	Colls./ Assmts.
	(Rp.b) [1]	(Rp.b) [2]	(%) [3] (2/1)	(Rp.b) [4]	(%) [5] (4/2)	(%) [6] (4/1)
1. D.I. Aceh	3.44	2.63	76.5%	1.86	70.7%	54.1%
2. North Sumatra	24.05	20.55	85.4%	14.96	72.8%	62.2%
3. West Sumatra	5.68	3.68	64.8%	3.93	106.8%	69.2%
4. Riau	5.49	5.89	107.3%	3.22	54.7%	58.7%
5. Jambi	2.11	2.10	99.5%	1.44	68.6%	68.2%
6. South Sumatra	7.80	7.41	95.0%	4.42	59.6%	56.7%
7. Bengkulu	0.99	1.09	110.1%	0.60	55.0%	60.6%
8. Lampung	9.03	7.19	79.6%	7.06	98.2%	78.2%
9. D.K.I. Jakarta	67.76	73.62	108.6%	57.61	78.3%	85.0%
10. West Java	70.12	56.41	80.4%	57.50	101.9%	82.0%
11. Central Java	36.83	28.81	78.2%	32.05	111.2%	87.0%
12. D.I. Yogyakarta	4.69	4.18	89.1%	4.20	100.5%	89.6%
13. East Java	55.77	49.51	88.8%	52.95	106.9%	94.9%
14. West Kalimantan	2.75	2.90	105.5%	1.74	60.0%	63.3%
15. Central Kalimantan	1.08	1.50	138.9%	0.51	34.0%	47.2%
16. South Kalimantan	2.25	2.91	129.3%	1.56	53.6%	69.3%
17. East Kalimantan	4.60	4.03	87.6%	3.93	97.5%	85.4%
18. South Sulawesi	16.65	14.48	87.0%	9.14	63.1%	54.9%
19. Southeast Sulawesi	1.40	0.97	9.3%	0.51	52.6%	36.4%
20. North Sulawesi	5.65	4.91	86.9%	3.99	81.3%	70.6%
21. Central Sulawesi	3.23	2.58	79.9%	1.80	69.8%	55.7%
22. Bali	7.08	4.87	68.8%	5.78	118.7%	81.6%
23. West Nusa Tenggara	4.83	3.20	66.3%	3.24	101.3%	67.1%
24. East Nusa Tenggara	3.77	2.96	78.5%	2.91	98.3%	77.2%
25. East Timor	0.29	0.28	96.6%	0.13	46.4%	44.8%
26. Maluku	2.49	2.75	110.4%	1.30	47.3%	52.2%
27. Irian Jaya	0.93	1.01	108.6	0.81	80.2%	87.1%
Total	350.76	312.42	89.1%	279.15	89.4%	79.6%

[1] Total Assessments
[2] Collection Targets
[3] Ratio of Targets to Assessments
[4] Collections
[5] Ratio of Collections to Targets
[6] Ratio of Collections to Assessments

Source: Data from Direktorat Pajak Bumi dan Bangunan; calculations by the author.

FIGURE V-12:
REGIONAL COMPARISONS IN INDONESIA
IN FISCAL YEAR 1990/91

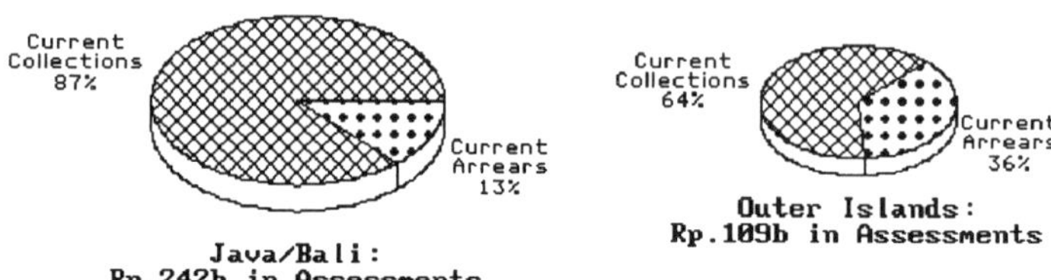

Note: Rural and urban sectors only.

Source: Author's calculations.

During the first year of SISTEP implementation, PBB collections in Tangerang totalled Rp. 8.2 billion, almost twice the previous year's receipts of Rp. 4.2 billion (see Figure V-13).

FIGURE V-13:
FY 1989/90 COLLECTIONS IN TANGERANG

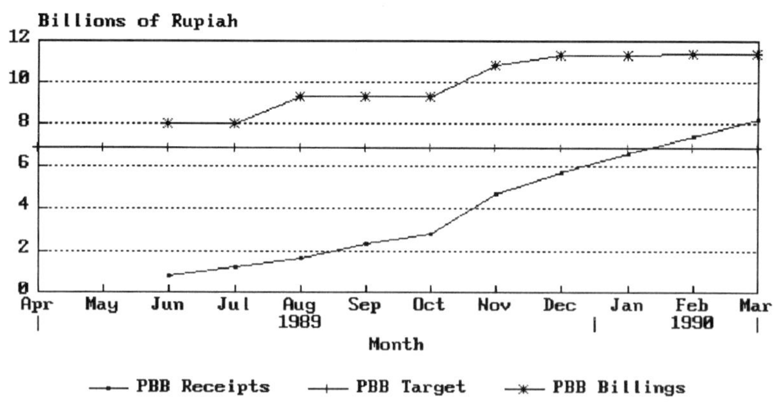

Source: Author's calculations.

Although PBB collections roughly doubled as a whole in fiscal year 1989/90, most of PBB's increased national revenue came from the P3 sectors, which comprise a handful of tax objects, mostly institutional, and thus, are only marginally affected by introduction of SISTEP. If urban and rural collections in Tangerang are compared with PBB's performance elsewhere in Indonesia for the same sectors, the results are quite different (see Figure V-14):

> Tangerang's urban and rural receipts increased 82 percent, while the increase in urban and rural collections elsewhere averaged one-fourth of Tangerang's growth. For example, urban and rural receipts on Java as a whole increased only 23 percent, and the increase for all of Indonesia was only 22 percent. . . .[69]

Despite this impressive revenue increase, Tangerang's collections still amounted to just 73 percent of total billings of Rp. 11.3 billion, which also doubled in 1989/90. The Tangerang collection rate thus remained virtually the same as the previous year (see Figure V-13). KPPBB Tangerang staff calculated that, after allowing for undelivered tax bills, there was still a potential Rp. 700 million to Rp. 1 billion in foregone revenue from Book IV and V properties alone.[70]

The generation of a reliable delinquency list after the December 31, 1989 uniform tax due date enabled KPPBB Tangerang to experiment with systematic enforcement measures to try to recover these tax arrears.

The results of the Final Warning Letter (*Surat Pemberitahuan*) sent to Book IV and V properties were encouraging (see Figure V-15):

> During the first week of January 1990, one week after despatch of the warning letters, the number of delinquent tax payers for high value properties dropped by nearly 20 percent, and the amount of collections received during that week alone amounted to 22 percent of the total tax collected during the previous six months. . . .[71]

---

[69]HIID, *Tangerang Pilot Project - Final Report*, 13.

[70]HIID, *Tangerang Pilot Project - Final Report*, 13.

[71]HIID, *Tangerang Pilot Project - Final Report*, 13.

The results of the Dunning Notices (STPs, *Surat Tagihan Pajak*) were less impressive: only 6 percent of remaining Book IV and V delinquencies were paid (see Figure V-16).

KPPBB Tangerang thus proceeded with enforcement measures, still concentrating on high-value urban properties. These proceedings culminated in October 1991, with seizure of the assets of a wood pressing company in Tangerang to recover property tax arrears of Rp. 3.3 million. The confiscation was done in a high-profile manner, receiving wide coverage in the mass media.

FIGURE V-14:
FY 1989/90 URBAN AND RURAL RECEIPTS
IN INDONESIA

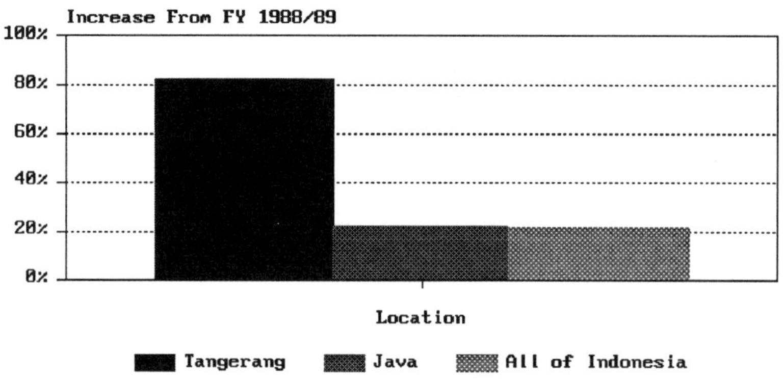

Source: Author's calculations.

FIGURE V-15:
RESULTS OF BOOK IV/V FINAL WARNING
IN TANGERANG

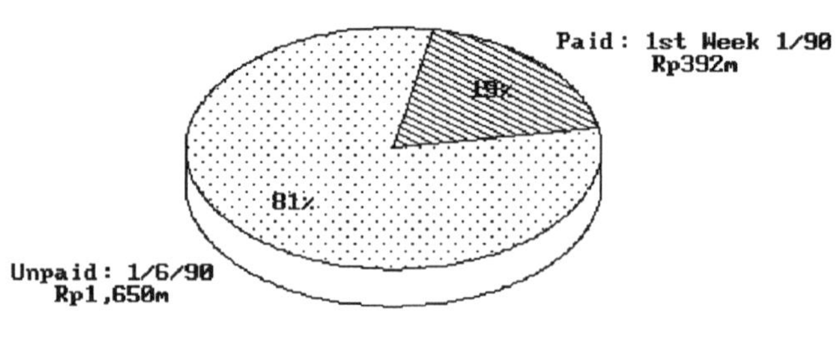

Source: Author's calculations.

FIGURE V-16:
RESULTS OF BOOK IV/V STPs
IN TANGERANG

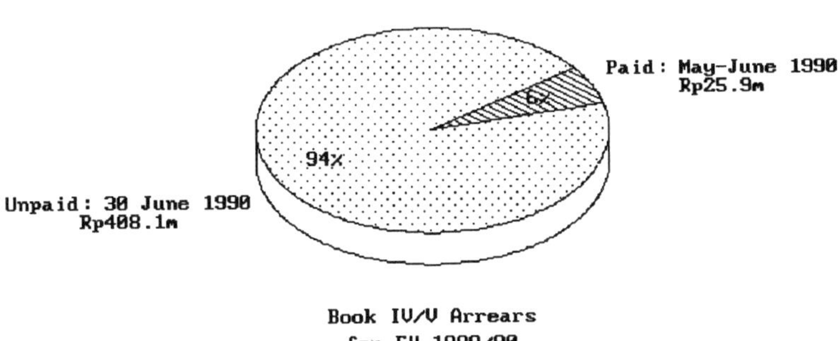

Source: Author's calculations.

During the month of January 1990, an interim evaluation of the Tangerang Pilot Project was conducted. In addition to determining the status and appropriateness of the collection-led reform strategy, this evaluation examined the use of PLN data as a proxy for high-value property by designing and testing a "PBB Compliance Monitoring Program."

The evaluation concluded that implementation of the payment point system in Tangerang had been successful to date, but ultimate success depended on enforcement follow-through. The evaluation also found that "while the first order of business was to implement the collections procedures and move to enforcement, it is now important to devote some attention to increasing the number of tax objects on the rolls . . . and improving the quality of data on tax objects."[72]

During the evaluation, a sample of 201 PLN accounts with installed capacity greater than 10,000 VA was drawn and studied to determine the usefulness of PLN data in achieving PBB objectives, with the following results (see Figure V-17):

---

[72]Karl E. Case, *Interim Evaluation of the Tangerang Pilot Project and Report on Compliance Monitoring Program*, Jakarta, January 1990, 3-5, photocopied.

- 190 properties were identified, of which 157 were located on the tax roll (82 percent of objects and 94 percent of value); and

- one-third of the 157 properties located on the tax roll were delinquent.[73]

A field audit master list was compiled using criteria that compared installed capacity with building area and tax assessment (see Figure V-18), with the following results:

- 28 of the most striking anomalies were visited;

- on average, reported land area was 15 percent less than actual land area, reported building area was 49 percent less than actual building area, and tax bills were 41 percent too low (see Figure V-19).[74]

The evaluation concluded that PLN data was indeed valuable to PBB officials:

> The use of PLN data for Pendataan purposes . . . shows great promise and seems to provide a cost effective way to update the tax rolls, but it also presents a number of difficulties. Specifically, PLN data should be used to: (1) discover high value (Book IV and Book V) properties not already on the tax rolls, (2) target KPPBB resources on specific properties for field audit of PBB data used for valuation, (3) enroll newly developed properties recently receiving PLN hookup, and (4) provide random properties for Compliance Monitoring Teams sent periodically from the Central Office of PBB.[75]

These recommendations reflect the long-term objective of SISTEP not only to increase taxpayer voluntary compliance, but also to relieve PBB field personnel of cashier and accounting functions so they can improve tax roll coverage and quality in a timely and cost-effective manner. The PLN experiment is especially intriguing because it is replicable throughout the urban areas of Indonesia with minimum lead time and at a negligible cost.[76]

---

[73]Case, *Interim Evaluation of the Tangerang Pilot Project*, 16.

[74]Case, *Interim Evaluation of the Tangerang Pilot Project*, 6.

[75]Case, *Interim Evaluation of the Tangerang Pilot Project*, 7.

[76]For example: field investigations were conducted in one week, primarily by relatively unskilled local staff, using readily available PBB and PLN data; both the PLN data base and PBB tax rolls (under SISTEP) are computerized in standard formats on accessible and compatible media throughout Indonesia; and for

FIGURE V-17:
DISTRIBUTION OF EVALUATION SAMPLE
IN TANGERANG

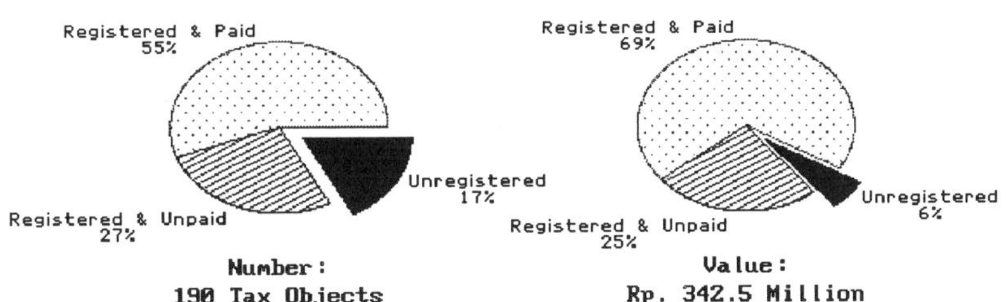

Source: Author's calculations.

FIGURE V-18:
FIELD AUDIT CRITERIA IN TANGERANG

Installed Capacity		Building Area		Total Tax
> 400,000 VA	*but*	< 5,000 Sq. Meters		
> 100,000 VA	*but*	< 2,000 Sq. Meters		
> 100,000 VA			*but*	< Rp.1,000,000
> 60,000 VA	*but*	< 1,000 Sq. Meters		
> 60,000 VA			*but*	< Rp. 600,000
> 10,000 VA	*but*	< 100 Sq. Meters		
> 10,000 VA			*but*	< Rp. 200,000

Source: Author's calculations.

---

modest honoraria, PLN meter readers can continue to help tax officials utilize textual and spatial data to locate property tax objects in the field.

FIGURE V-19:
FIELD AUDIT RESULTS IN TANGERANG

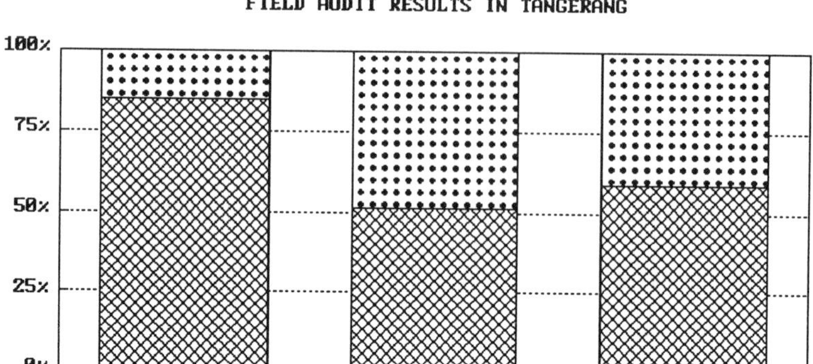

Source: Author's calculations.

Tangerang performance continued to improve during fiscal year 1990/91, and substantial progress was made in the twelve SISTEP cities and districts of first-stage replication: billings increased 15 percent (Rp. 10.2 billion); receipts increased 41 percent (Rp. 17.9 billion); and collection efficiency rose 23 percent (from 65 to 79 percent).[77]

Enforcement measures are also proceeding, albeit unevenly, in SISTEP areas, given Tangerang's success with continued enforcement: its collection rate rose to 84 percent in 1990/91. Perhaps Edmund Burke was correct when he wrote, in his treatise *On American Taxation*, "To tax and to please, no more than to love and to be wise, is not given to men."

[77]Direktorat Pajak Bumi dan Bangunan.

6

SYNTHESIS

The Thurians ordained that whosoever would go about to abolish an old law, or establish a new one, should present himself with a halter around his neck, to the end that, if his proposal were not approved, he might be hanged at once.

Michel de Montaigne,
Essays, I, 1580

OVERVIEW

This synthesis is presented in two parts: first, a cross-country analysis of property taxation in Jamaica, the Philippines, Chile, and Indonesia; and second, general guidelines for property taxation in developing countries. The cross-country analysis highlights similarities and differences in property tax systems, reform efforts, and results in the four case study countries. These empirically derived lessons are then paired with the findings of the literature review presented earlier, and placed within the context of the study's conceptual framework. The product is a set of guidelines on what the property tax can and cannot do well in developing countries, and how best to utilize property taxation to attain objectives for which it is most suited.

CROSS-COUNTRY ANALYSIS

Comparison of Property Tax Systems in Case Study Countries

Formally, property taxation in the case study countries has more differences than similarities. However, in the translation of policies to practice, these statutory contrasts are overshadowed by common environmental conditions, administrative practices, and human behavior. Thus, operationally, property tax systems in Jamaica, the Philippines, Chile, and Indonesia are more like each other than ever consciously intended by their respective designers (see Table VI-1).

TABLE VI-1: COMPARISON OF PROPERTY TAX SYSTEMS IN CASE STUDY COUNTRIES

Characteristic	Jamaica	Philippines	Chile	Indonesia
1. Tax Base	Capital Market Value of Unimproved Land (Site Value)	Capital Market Value of Land, Buildings, and Machinery	Capital Fiscal Value of Land and Buildings	Capital Market Value of Land and Buildings
2. Full Exemptions[a]	Standard	Standard; Total ≤US$41; Selected Dairies, Ranches, Trees, Machinery, Etc.	Standard; Non-Agric. Residential ≤US$15,735; Ag. ≤US$2,524	Standard; Building ≤US$1,899
3. Partial Exemptions and Relief	75% Agric. Reduction; 25% Hotel Reduction; Hardship	Hardship	Misc. for Hotels, Ag. Reform, Man-Made Forests; Localities; Hardship	50% Reduction for New Invest. in East Indo.; Hardship
4. Assessment Ratio	100%	15-80%, Depending on Use and Value	Fiscal Value = ±80% of Market Val.	Now 20%; Can Be Raised to 100%
5. Tax Rate	J$5 flat for first J$6,000; then 1.0-3.0%	0.5-2.0% + 1.0% Special Education Fund	2.0% + 30% Surcharge	0.5%
6. Valuation	Direct Market Value; 5-yr. Revaluation By Land Valuation Department	Self-Declaration; Unit Value Tables; 3-yr. Revaluation By Local Assessor	Self-Decl.; Unit Value Tables; CAV; 10-yr. Revaluation By Internal Tax Service	Self-Decl.; Unit Val. Tables; CAV;3-yr. Reval. By Property Tax Dir.
7. Collection	Annually By Inland Revenue Dept.	Annually By Local Treasurer	Quarterly By Treasury Service via Banks	Annually By Prop. Tax Dir. via Banks

[a]"Standard" refers to real estate used primarily for non-profit social, cultural, educational, diplomatic, charitable, or benevolent purposes.

Source: Compiled by the author.

For example, the Philippines has the largest nominal statutory tax base, comprising land, buildings, and machinery; Chile and Indonesia have a similar base, excluding machinery; and Jamaica's base is the narrowest, confined to unimproved land.

However, special exemptions and assessment ratios ranging from 15 to 80 percent narrow the Philippines' effective statutory tax base, while a 75 percent reduction for agricultural land and a 25 percent reduction for hotel land in Jamaica, miscellaneous partial exemptions in Chile, and a 20 percent assessment ratio in Indonesia all have a similar effect. Tax bases are further eroded through tax roll omissions and inaccuracies, property use and value misclassification, and poor collections.

The inequities of narrow effective tax bases are compounded by mandatory tax payments for low value land in Jamaica and Indonesia, as the poorest property owners are often forced to pay property taxes while far wealthier property owners are not. However, if all property owners were compelled to honor similar statutory tax obligations, fixed minimum tax payments for low value property would increase efficiency and enhance progressivity with negligible revenue loss. They would broaden the property tax base, thereby forcing tax officials to keep property taxation systems simple; this, in turn, would enhance operational cost-effectiveness and administrative accountability. In contrast, the unfairness of excluding high value property from the tax base by adoption of selective exemptions or corrupt administration is somewhat diminished by minimum value thresholds in the Philippines, Chile, and Indonesia (for buildings). This ensures that the most grievous inequity in property taxation cannot occur: payment of tax liabilities by a country's poorest property owners in spite of the *de jure* or *de facto* exemption of the nation's wealthiest property owners. In Chile, however, the explicit desire for fiscal neutrality has resulted in a non-agriculture residential exemption that excludes so much of the potential tax base at nearly US$16,000 that the tax burden might now be too concentrated for political acceptability.

Tax rates range from a flat, uniform 0.5 percent in Indonesia and 2.6 percent in Chile to a maximum 3.0 percent for Philippine cities and highest-value Jamaican land. Again, practice obscures policies, especially in Jamaica, where progressive tax rates have the same effect as progressive assessment ratios in the Philippines: they encourage property misvaluation and misclassification to lower the tax assessment, and thus the effective tax rate.

General revaluations are mandated every three years in the Philippines and Indonesia, every five years in Jamaica, and every ten years in Chile. Nonetheless, Chile, the country with the longest interval between general revaluations has the most buoyant tax base, because it indexes property values to the consumer price index every six months automatically.

Indonesia and the Philippines have *de facto* indexing systems through the periodic issuance of new unit value tables, but their use of an informal "bracket creep" in the interim to try to maintain buoyancy is arbitrary and unfair. Jamaica's tax base has eroded steadily over the past two decades due to persistent undervaluations, long intervals between general valuations, and no effective way of bridging the gap between market and tax values.

Three of the four case study countries separate valuation and collection functions: between Land Valuation and Inland Revenue in Jamaica; between the local assessor and the local treasurer in the Philippines; and between the Internal Tax Service and the Treasury Service in Chile. Indonesia is the only country studied which has a unified valuation and collection system, both under the central Ministry of Finance.

Both Chile and Indonesia make extensive use of their banking systems, and have automated the collection process; Jamaica and the Philippines have done neither. Banks are accustomed to handling cash transactions and leaving clear audit trails, so can adjust with relative ease and minimal expense to receiving and reporting on tax payments. The collection of property taxes through banks can streamline administration, increase accountability, and improve service. It is not surprising that credible enforcement has thus taken place only in Chile and Indonesia, with a commensurate higher collection efficiency than Jamaica and the Philippines.

In sum, statutory provisions vary considerably regarding tax bases, exemptions and relief, assessment ratios and tax rates, valuation techniques and frequency, and collection systems. In practice, however, tax systems converge as operational similarities override statutory differences, and tax officials confront the common problem of generating revenue in an efficient, equitable, and sustainable manner. Constraints are similar: conflicting political pressures both to raise revenue and achieve non-revenue objectives; the tendency for tax bases to contract over time; the proclivity of administrators to compound complexity; and widespread corruption.

Comparison of Property Tax Reform in Case Study Countries

The characteristics of property tax reform in Jamaica, the Philippines, Chile, and Indonesia are very different, including: the nature of reform; key reform activities; reform objectives; the timing and length of reform; reform coverage; the role of foreign assistance; and the principal reform implementor (see Table VI-2).

The most dramatic change was in Jamaica, where reform entailed instituting a completely new system of property taxation: the tax base was shifted from improved to unimproved value and appraisal was changed from self-declaration to external valuation. The changes in Indonesia were somewhat less drastic but even more comprehensive as new legislation consolidated seven different taxes on real property and all administrative subsystems were affected by reform activities. In contrast, reform in the Philippines and Chile essentially entailed better implementation of existing statutes, without introduction of major structural changes.

TABLE VI-2: COMPARISON OF PROPERTY TAX REFORM IN CASE STUDY COUNTRIES

Characteristic	Jamaica	Philippines	Chile	Indonesia
1. Reform Period	1956 to 1974	1972 to Present	1987 to Present	1986 to Present
2. Nature of Reform	Shift from: Improved to Unimproved Value; Self-Declaration to External Valuation	Implementation of Established Property Tax System; No Policy Revision or Structural Change	General Reval. of Non-Agriculture Properties	New Land and Building Tax
3. Key Reform Activities	Comprehensive Data Collection and Revaluation	Comprehensive Data Collection and Revaluation Revaluation	Selective Data Coll. and Compreh. Reform	Compreh. Policy and Adm.
4. Reform Objectives	Redistribute Tax Burden; Improve Land Use; Update Valuations	Increase Financial Capacity of Local Gov.	Improve Equity and Efficiency	More Revenue and Equity
5. Fiscal Neutrality	Ambiguous	Increased Revenue a Key Goal	Explicit	Increased Revenue a Key Goal
6. Reform Coverage to Date	Entire Country, In Stages	±52% of Local Government Units, In Stages	Entire Country, Not Phased	±25% of Local Govt.; ±59% of Rural and Urban Tax Base

(Table VI-2, cont'd)

Characteristic	Jamaica	Philippines	Chile	Indonesia
7. Foreign Assistance[a]	None	±US$35.7m from USAID and World Bank	None	±US$27.0m from ADB and World Bank
8. Principal Reform Implementor	Land Valuation Department	Local Assessors and Local Treasurers	Internal Tax Service	Property Tax Directorate

[a]Data regarding local funds spent on property tax reform are not available.
Source: Compiled by the author.

Key reform activities also varied among the case study countries. Jamaican and Philippine reformers concentrated on improving tax roll accuracy and completeness via comprehensive data collection and revaluation activities. In contrast, Chile and Indonesia focussed their efforts on both valuation and collections, with a strong emphasis on establishing a credible threat to induce greater taxpayer voluntary compliance. Indonesia even dubbed its strategy "collection-led" reform.

Reform objectives were also very different. Philippine and Indonesian reformers were unequivocal in their desire to generate more revenue, hoping to increase efficiency and equity in the process. However, the primary objective of Jamaican and Chilean reformers was to redistribute the property tax burden more equitably; improved land use was a secondary objective in Jamaica, while increased administrative efficiency was a subsidiary goal in Chile. Jamaican reformers were ambiguous about the fiscal neutrality of their efforts, and Chilean reformers placed an explicit limit on increased revenue from their general revaluation activities.

There was considerable variation in the timing and length of property tax reform among the case study countries. Reform activities in Jamaica and the Philippines were decades long: Jamaican reform activities commenced in 1956, and continued for the next 18 years; Philippine reform efforts began in 1972, and have continued to the present. In contrast, Chilean reform activities began in 1987 and are essentially completed, while Indonesian reform efforts commenced in 1986 and are about two-thirds finished.

Reform activities in all of the case study countries were implemented in phases. In Jamaica and the Philippines, the sequencing was geographic; today, all of Jamaica has been covered, and half of the Philippines has been included. In Chile, the phasing was functional, beginning with normalization and continuing with revaluation, but reform activities were always national in scope. Indonesian reform efforts have been implemented in both geographic and functional phases, emphasing collections first, and concentrating on densely populated areas with significant amounts of high-value property; to date, the payment point system has been implemented in one-fourth of Indonesia's local government units and covers two-thirds of its rural and urban tax base.

Jamaican and Chilean reform efforts have been funded entirely with local funds, while foreign assistance has been considerable during implementation of property tax reform in the Philippines and Indonesia: the Philippines has received approximately $35.7 million from USAID and the World Bank, and Indonesia has received about $27.0 million from the Asian Development Bank and the World Bank. Data regarding local funds spent on property tax reform in the case study countries are not available.

In sum, property tax reform activities in Jamaica, the Philippines, Chile, and Indonesia have strikingly different characteristics: some reform efforts entail policy reform, some only administrative reform, and some include both; some include all administrative subsystems, while others focus only on data collection and property revaluation; some try to increase revenue, and others stress fiscal neutrality; some take decades, and others only a few years; although all are phased, the nature of this sequencing is sometimes geographic, sometimes functional, and sometimes both; and some reform efforts are funded completely with domestic resources, while others rely heavily on foreign assistance.

Comparison of Property Tax Performance in Case Study Countries

Property tax performance in Jamaica, the Philippines, Chile, and Indonesia over the past decade exhibits considerable variation, even allowing for dissimilar points of departure. The differences are so striking that this section might better be termed a contrast rather than a comparison of property tax performance in the case study countries (see Table VI-3).

Real property tax revenue in Jamaica actually *declined* from 1980 to 1990 at an average annual rate of 5.5 percent, while rural and urban property tax revenue in Indonesia *increased* at an average annual rate of 10.2 percent during the same period.[1] Revenue generation in the other two case study countries falls between these two extremes: property tax receipts in the Philippines and Chile increased at roughly the same average annual rate, 4.0 and 4.4 percent, respectively.

[1]All figures for Indonesia used in the following cross-country comparison include the rural and urban sectors only; the plantation, forestry, and mining sectors are excluded, as the property tax for these sectors is essentially a proxy for a production tax (see Chapter Five).

TABLE VI-3: COMPARISON OF PROPERTY TAX PERFORMANCE IN CASE STUDY COUNTRIES

Indicator	Jamaica	Philippines	Chile	Indonesia[a]
1. Revenue Generation (1985 US$ millions)				
a. Total: 1980	12.3[b]	105.0	66.8	63.7[f]
b. Total: 1990	7.0[c]	154.9	102.7	167.8[g]
c. Average Annual Change (%)	-5.5	4.0	4.4	10.2
2. Share of Total Tax Revenue (%)				
a. 1980	2.1[b]	2.4[e]	2.5	0.4[h]
b. 1990	1.1[c]	2.4[e]	2.7	0.9
3. Share of GDP (%)				
a. 1980	0.6[b]	0.3	0.6	0.1
b. 1990	0.3[c]	0.4	0.7	0.1[i]
4. Role in Local Government Finance in 1990	All Receipts Credited to the (Central) Consolidated Fund	26% of Total Revenue; 44% of Own-Source Revenue	29% of Total Revenue; 49% of Own-Source Revenue	12% of Total Revenue; 31% of Own-Source Revenue[j]
5. Collection Efficiency in 1990 (%)	55-65	50-60	73	80
6. Administrative Cost Share of Revenue in 1990 (%)	±11[d]	Unknown	±9	Unknown

Notes:

[a]All figures for Indonesia include the rural and urban sectors only; the plantation, forestry, and mining sectors are excluded.
[b]Fiscal year 1979/80. [c]Fiscal year 1989/90.
[d]Fiscal year 1989/90; excludes Inland Revenue collection costs; includes Land Valuation activities unrelated to the property tax.
[e]Share of total revenue. [f]Fiscal year 1980/81.
[g]Fiscal year 1990/91. [h]Figures from 1983.
[i]Figures from 1989. [j]District/municipal level only.

Source: Compiled by the author.

Indonesia's performance remains the best and Jamaica's the worst, with the Philippines and Chile still lying between the two extremes, when trends in property tax revenue are compared with general economic performance in these four countries over the past decade. Indonesian rural and urban property tax receipts rose 19.3 percent, greater than the increase of both GDP (15.6 percent) and revenue (12.1 percent). In contrast, Jamaican property tax receipts increased only 10.5 percent, slightly more than half the increases in GDP (17.9 percent) and revenue (18.2 percent); in the Philippines and Chile, property tax receipts increased by about the same magnitude as GDP and revenue growth (see Table VI-4).[2] In all four case study countries, however, property tax receipts remained a negligible share of both total revenue (roughly one to three percent) and gross domestic product (less than one percent) during the past decade (see Table VI-3).

Indonesia's revenue growth is especially intriguing because the most dramatic increase is after 1986, which coincides with commencement of property tax reform activities. In 1985, the Philippines, Chile, and Indonesia all had about the same property tax revenue: $105 million, $90 million, and $86 million, respectively. However, by 1991, rural and urban property tax receipts in Indonesia had doubled to $168 million, as opposed to increases in property tax revenue of 14 percent in Chile and 48 percent in the Philippines from 1985 to 1990 (see Figure VI-1).[3]

Except in Jamaica, where all property tax revenue is credited to the central government Consolidated Fund, property tax receipts continued to be an important source of local discretionary resources rather than national tax revenue. Property tax receipts ranged from roughly one-third of own-source revenue in Indonesian districts and municipalities (excluding the plantation, forestry, and mining sectors) to almost half of local government own-source revenue in Chile (see Table VI-3).

In another measure of property tax performance, collection efficiency, results have been most disappointing where collection and enforcement activities have been neglected: 1990 collection efficiency was between 55 and 65 percent in Jamaica, and between 50 and 60 percent in the Philippines. In contrast, performance was much more encouraging where reformers have devoted considerable attention to development of a credible threat of sanctions for noncompliance: 1990 collection efficiency was 73 percent in Chile and 80 percent for rural and urban properties in Indonesia (see Table VI-3).

---

[2]All comparisons are based on nominal local currency figures. Due to constraints in data availability, "revenue growth" refers to total tax revenue for Jamaica and Chile, and total revenue for the Philippines and Indonesia; Indonesian revenue figures do not include 1990 data.

[3]Since property tax reform was initiated several decades ago in Jamaica (1956) and the Philippines (1972), it was not possible to obtain pre-reform data; property tax reform commenced much more recently in Indonesia (1986) and Chile (1987), thereby enabling a comparison of pre-reform and post-reform performance. The beginning of each reform effort (except Jamaica) is noted in Figure VI-1.

TABLE VI-4:COMPARISON OF PROPERTY TAX PERFORMANCE WITH GENERAL ECONOMIC PERFORMANCE IN CASE STUDY COUNTRIES

(all figures are nominal)

Country	Property Tax Revenue	Total Tax Revenue or Total Revenue	GDP
1. **Jamaica**			
a. Total: FY 1979/80	J$25m	J$1,175m[b]	J$ 4,293m
b. Total: FY 1989/90	J$67m	J$6,275m[b]	J$22,315m
c. Average Annual Change	10.5%	18.2%	17.9%
2. **Philippines**			
a. Total: 1980	P 821m	P 34,151m[c]	P 264,650m
b. Total: 1990	P4,310m	P178,522m[c]	P1,066,300m
c. Average Annual Change	18.0%	18.0%	15.0%
3. **Chile**			
a. Total: 1980	P4,400m	P 180b[b]	P 707b
b. Total: 1990	P40,000m	P1,485b[b]	P6,055b
c. Average Annual Change	24.7%	23.5%	24.0%
4. **Indonesia**			
a. Total: FY 1980/81	Rp. 49b[a]	Rp.10,405b[d]	Rp. 45,446b[f]
b. Total: FY 1990/91	Rp.286b[a]	Rp.29,093b[e]	Rp.166,330b[g]
c. Average Annual Change	19.3%	12.1%	15.6%

Notes:

[a]Rural and urban sectors only.
[b]Total tax revenue.
[c]Total revenue.
[d]Total revenue; calendar year 1980.
[e]Total revenue; calendar year 1989.
[f]Calendar year 1980.
[g]Calendar year 1989.

Sources: See case studies for full citations.

Data for a third measure of property tax performance, administrative efficiency, are inconclusive due to a combination of incomplete and unreliable information regarding the cost of property tax administration. While expenditure data for foreign assistance are required by donor agencies, there is not yet a comparable client who regularly requests information regarding domestic funds expended on property tax administration.

Evaluation of Property Tax Reform in Case Study Countries

The results of property tax reforms in Jamaica, the Philippines, Chile, and Indonesia can best be evaluated by utilizing the conceptual framework presented in Chapter One (see Figure I-1) to organize and assess results to date (see Figure VI-2):

> *Did reformers in the case study countries enhance the long-term generation of adequate local government discretionary resources in a viable, non-distortive, fair, and enduring manner by changing tax policies, administrative systems, and human behavior?*

Only Indonesia has thus far both articulated an appropriate objective for property tax reform, and made considerable progress in achieving this objective; Jamaica and Chile have misdirected their efforts to attain unreasonable objectives, while the Philippines has misapplied resources to achieve an appropriate tax reform goal.

FIGURE VI-1:
COMPARISON OF PROPERTY TAX REVENUE

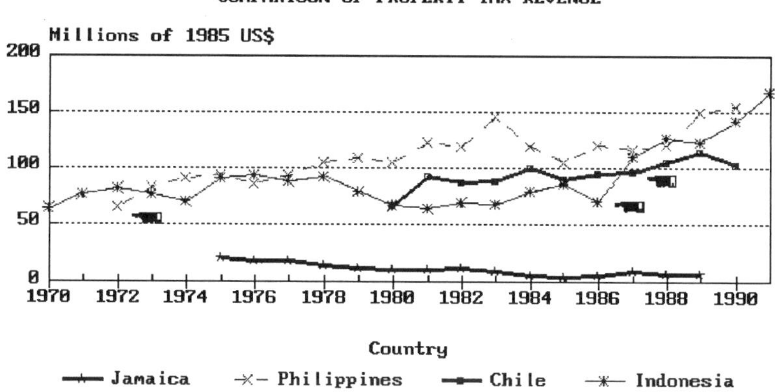

Note: ▬ = Beginning of reform.
(Reform in Jamaica began in 1956.)
Source: Author's calculations.

FIGURE VI-2:

EVALUATION OF PROPERTY TAX REFORM IN CASE STUDY COUNTRIES

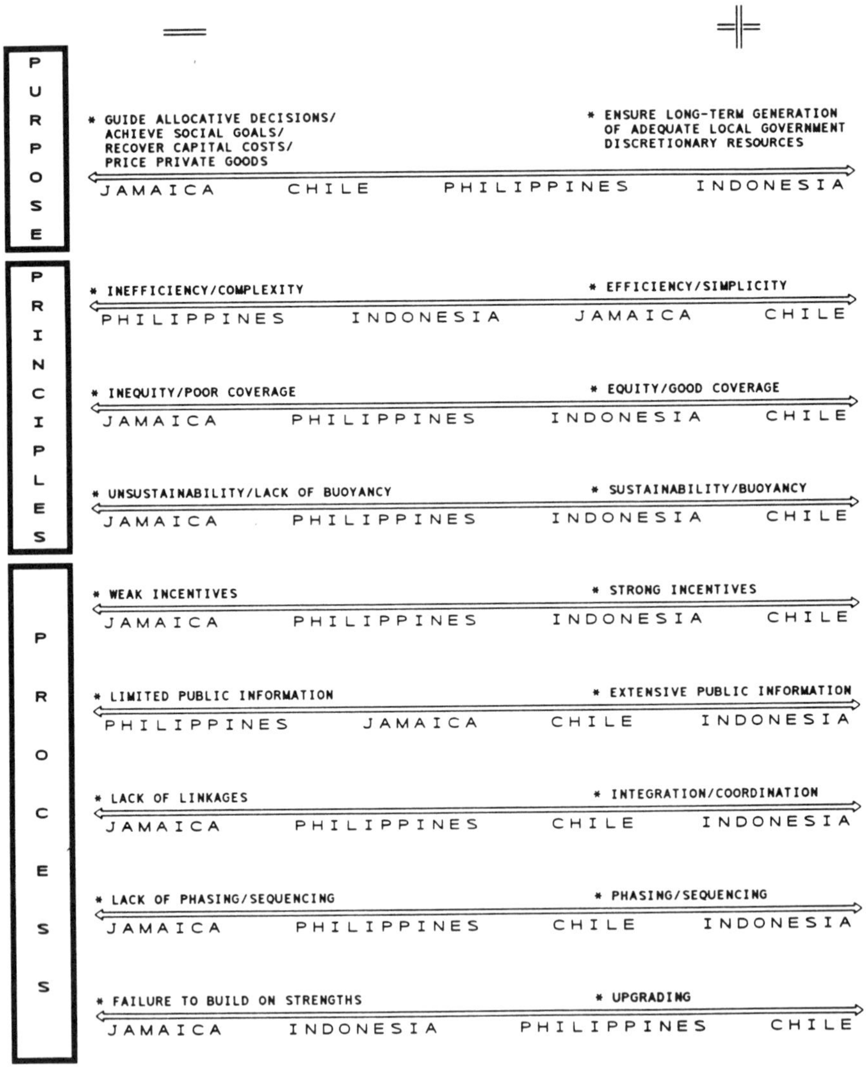

PURPOSE

* GUIDE ALLOCATIVE DECISIONS/ ACHIEVE SOCIAL GOALS/ RECOVER CAPITAL COSTS/ PRICE PRIVATE GOODS ⟷ * ENSURE LONG-TERM GENERATION OF ADEQUATE LOCAL GOVERNMENT DISCRETIONARY RESOURCES

JAMAICA — CHILE — PHILIPPINES — INDONESIA

PRINCIPLES

* INEFFICIENCY/COMPLEXITY ⟷ * EFFICIENCY/SIMPLICITY

PHILIPPINES — INDONESIA — JAMAICA — CHILE

* INEQUITY/POOR COVERAGE ⟷ * EQUITY/GOOD COVERAGE

JAMAICA — PHILIPPINES — INDONESIA — CHILE

* UNSUSTAINABILITY/LACK OF BUOYANCY ⟷ * SUSTAINABILITY/BUOYANCY

JAMAICA — PHILIPPINES — INDONESIA — CHILE

PROCESS

* WEAK INCENTIVES ⟷ * STRONG INCENTIVES

JAMAICA — PHILIPPINES — INDONESIA — CHILE

* LIMITED PUBLIC INFORMATION ⟷ * EXTENSIVE PUBLIC INFORMATION

PHILIPPINES — JAMAICA — CHILE — INDONESIA

* LACK OF LINKAGES ⟷ * INTEGRATION/COORDINATION

JAMAICA — PHILIPPINES — CHILE — INDONESIA

* LACK OF PHASING/SEQUENCING ⟷ * PHASING/SEQUENCING

JAMAICA — PHILIPPINES — CHILE — INDONESIA

* FAILURE TO BUILD ON STRENGTHS ⟷ * UPGRADING

JAMAICA — INDONESIA — PHILIPPINES — CHILE

Source: Author's formulation.

Purpose of Reform

Indonesian reformers have explicitly tried to increase local government revenue, and the rise in property tax receipts for all sectors has been quite dramatic since 1986. Philippine reformers have also tried to enhance the financial resources of local government, but have failed to increase revenue significantly. Thus, these two countries are ranked first and second regarding the purpose of property tax reform: both Indonesia and the Philippines have tried to achieve an objective for which property taxation is well-suited, with Indonesia more successful than the Philippines in attaining this common objective. However, both Indonesia and the Philippines have also tried, and failed, to achieve non-revenue goals through property taxation.

Tax relief in eastern Indonesia has had no discernable effect on promoting investment in light of much more significant competitive disadvantages of the region. Lack of adequate infrastructure, shortages of skilled labor, and distances from large urban markets have been much more important constraints to investment than a tax of 0.1 percent of a property's capital market value. Instead, this tax relief has reduced the most important revenue source of Indonesia's poorest local governments by eliminating tax receipts from investments that would have been made regardless of property tax policy.

Progressive and differential assessment ratios in the Philippines have generated more inequity than they have obviated. Instead of redistributing wealth by forcing rich landowners to pay more taxes per unit of value than their poorer compatriots, these policies have encouraged taxpayers to misreport data and tax officials to undervalue and misclassify property to exploit lower effective tax rates.

In Indonesia and the Philippines, the Asian Development Bank and the World Bank have promoted cost recovery of rural irrigation systems and urban water supply, sewerage, drainage, flood control, and roads systems through the inclusion of project components labeled "local resource mobilization." Such components typically have entailed expensive, map-based fiscal cadastres whose subproject costs alone cannot be recovered by the increased tax revenue they might generate.

These donors should take greater care in analyzing often misleading reports on project progress and results, as well as encourage more rigorous internal evaluation of the returns on such project investments. The proliferation of real property units in the Philippines is a vivid example of misleading data, while high unit valuation costs in Indonesia is clearly something that merits further investigation.

Chilean reformers have been adamant in stressing fiscal neutrality. Their explicit objective has been to improve the equity of tax administration by redistributing the tax burden based on changes in relative and absolute prices.

While the intention of the Chilean reformers has been to enhance the long-term sustainability of property taxation by adapting tax rolls to changed market conditions, the results might well have been counterproductive. Fiscal neutrality in a property market with rapidly increasing values has risked narrowing Chile's effective tax base so much that it has jeopardized future tax revenue adequacy.

Redistribution of the tax burden within revenue ceilings during a period of price escalation has concentrated tax liabilities on ever fewer taxpayers, primarily wealthy and politically influential property owners. This is not politically palatable. Chilean reformers have antagonized their constituency, and have gained little in return, thus discouraging them from continuing to promote reform: why lose votes when you do not even increase revenue?

Chile is thus ranked third regarding the purpose of tax reform. Chilean insistence on fiscal neutrality in property tax reform is not a tenable long-term strategy. Moreover, a byproduct of this approach, low effective tax rates, are sometimes essential during major structural transitions, but these should be universal and temporary.

For example, the maintenance of a 20 percent assessment ratio in Indonesia to encourage broader coverage serves two purposes by imposing a small tax burden for all taxpayers until coverage is relatively complete: it reduces the cost of voluntary compliance, and minimizes the magnitude of current inequities caused by some citizens meeting their tax liabilities while their neighbors pay nothing.

Jamaican reformers have been ambiguous and somewhat inconsistent regarding the fiscal neutrality of their program. They have nonetheless consistently emphasized their desire to redistribute the property tax burden from the poor to the rich, to encourage more efficient land use, and to promote agriculture and tourism. Jamaica is therefore ranked fourth regarding the purpose of tax reform.

The Jamaican experience suggests that property taxation is a poor tool for guiding allocative decisions such as land use. Furthermore, tax relief for hotels and agribusinesses has not enhanced the financial viability or economic competitiveness of these industries - even full property taxes do not significantly affect their profitability. Instead, derating in Jamaica has exacerbated inequity and contributed to substantial foregone revenue.

Finally, the property tax has not been an effective means of pricing private goods in any of the four case study countries. Even in the Philippines, where there is a universal one percent additional levy on property tax bills for the Special Education Fund, it is difficult to disaggregate the effect of local property tax receipts from central government expenditures on the quality of public education. It is even more unlikely a taxpayer can link individual tax payments to educational benefits received.

Principles of Reform

Chile is ranked first regarding the basic principles of property tax reform. By emphasizing simplicity, coverage, and buoyancy, Chile has developed the most efficient, equitable, and sustainable system of property taxation of the four cases:

- Data collection is selective in terms both of quantity of information per property and number of properties included in periodic updating activities.

- Mapping precision is the minimum required for taxation purposes.

- No individual valuations are performed, but rather, tax administrators rely on computer-assisted mass appraisal, including the automatic indexing of property values to consumer price levels.

- Most collection functions are automated, with heavy reliance on the banking system for cashier and accounting functions.

In Chile, sustainability was enhanced by creation of a high level trouble-shooting team that visited field offices regularly. These visits served two key functions: they improved local understanding and implementation of central office tax policies, and they provided a conduit for the concerns of field practioners to affect the reshaping of these policies over time.

Indonesia's uniform tax rate and single assessment ratio decrease opportunities for arbitrary tax administration, its exemption for low-value buildings increases the system's progressivity, and three-year *de facto* indexing provides a measure of tax base buoyancy. However, Indonesia is ranked second behind Chile in terms of equity and sustainability because weaknesses in data collection and property valuation subsystems have tended to benefit wealthy real estate owners (see below), and lack of a formal price indexing system has further undermined fair administration by encouraging arbitrary property reclassification.

In terms of collections, the decision of Indonesian policymakers not to have any minimum property tax exemption for land compelled officials to seek simplicity in property tax system design and administration, and provided a measure of protection against periodic attempts at fine-tuning. The desire to maintain a broad property tax base meant tax officials had an obligation to value, assess, and bill approximately 60 million properties annually for total tax liabilities typically less than $5. To accommodate this desire for broad participation in the property tax system, payment procedures were greatly simplified. Administrative streamlining reduced taxpayer flexibility somewhat by restricting payment options, but at the same time, increased the quality of taxpayer service through automated billing and collection, and improved the equity of tax administration by enabling tax officials to proceed with enforcement based on credible delinquency lists.

A similar tradeoff was made in Chile, based on different policy priorities. Exclusion of approximately two-thirds of taxable properties from the collections system greatly concentrated the tax burden and antagonized a powerful political constituency, but also made it administratively feasible to provide taxpayers with more convenient collection options such as payment in quarterly installments. This decision was based on conventional concepts of vertical equity, while popular perceptions of fairness for property taxation seem to require that all property owners make a contribution based on the relative value of one's property.

Another key element of property tax reform in Indonesia that enhanced sustainability was the upgrading of all levels of the Property Tax Directorate management information system (MIS). This system was streamlined from 48 to 6 basic reporting forms, stratified by level and function, and automated.

Indonesia is ranked third in terms of efficiency and simplicity because of its persistence, aided and abetted by substantial donor funding, in pursuing expensive and complex property valuation systems which are neither cost-effective nor sustainable. Most revenue increases in Indonesia cannot be attributed to extensive and expensive data collection and property appraisal activities.

Likewise, poor revenue performance in the Philippines cannot be blamed on these same activities: periodic property reclassifications, general revaluations using new unit value tables, and a collection-led reform strategy emphasizing both service and sanctions are primarily responsible for increased property tax receipts in Indonesia; widespread undervaluation and misclassification, long intervals between general revaluations, and neglect of collections are the main causes of revenue stagnation in the Philippines.

The difference between project and non-project areas is insignificant in both Indonesia and the Philippines, lending credence to this conclusion. Furthermore, few new properties have been discovered during mapping and appraisal activities, nor have relative value differences been altered very much, undermining the claim that these investments at least have had a major impact on improving the equity of property tax incidence.

Such data and valuation activities decrease both the short-term and long-run efficiency of tax administration. Not only are they quite expensive during project implementation, but the results are produced in forms that rapidly decline in usefulness without follow-on projects to update them. The computer-assisted mass appraisal system being tested in Indonesia requires periodic massive, costly, and unpopular data gathering exercises to maintain the system's currency. In the Philippines, all mapping, data, and appraisal activities are manual, so new property values are often obsolete before they are used for tax billings; they can be updated only by repeating the same time-consuming, expensive, and unpopular exercises.

The experiment conducted in Tangerang, Indonesia regarding utilization of installed electrical capacity as a proxy for high-value property merits further study. Although limited in scope, this exercise demonstrated an approach to data gathering, valuation, and audit activities that focussed scarce resources on investigating real estate with the greatest likelihood of having unmet property tax liabilities. Similar tax compliance monitoring programs could offer immediate and substantial returns for relatively small investments of time and money.

The Philippines is ranked third and Jamaica fourth regarding coverage and buoyancy. In the Philippines, poor coverage and lack of buoyancy characterize property taxation: progressive and differential assessment ratios encourage property misvaluation and misclassification, and thus considerable inequity; poor collections and lack of enforcement exacerbate inequities; and continual postponement of general revaluations and consistent use of gross undervaluations minimizes tax buoyancy. In Jamaica, problems are similar: blanket derating, progressive tax rates, and poor collections result in a very inequitable system of property taxation; and the steady decline in revenue is clear evidence of tax atrophy instead of tax buoyancy.

However, Jamaica is ranked second in terms of efficiency because all reform activities have been funded with relatively routine domestic budget allocations, in contrast to the substantial amount of external assistance received by both Indonesia and the Philippines.

Process of Reform

Chile is ranked first and Indonesia second regarding utilization of incentives for property tax reform. Chilean and Indonesian attempts to balance positive and negative incentives for taxpayers, tax officials, and local government staff have increased taxpayer voluntary compliance and tax administration effectiveness significantly.

In terms of positive incentives for taxpayers, Chilean and Indonesian reformers made considerable efforts to upgrade taxpayer field services: property survey forms were simplified in both countries, and in Chile, they were pre-printed with existing data for confirmation or correction; Indonesia changed the name of its "property tax inspection offices" to "property tax service offices" to highlight a new priority on taxpayer service; and both countries made extensive use of their banking systems for the cashier functions of collections, exploiting the coverage of nationwide networks and the services of consumer-oriented institutions.

Both Chile and Indonesia have also tried to discourage taxpayer noncompliance through the high-profile, widespread application of sanctions. However, Chile has been doing this for several years now, while Indonesia is just beginning.

Chilean and Indonesian reforms have devoted considerable attention to creating a meritocracy for tax officers and local government officials, based on recognition and adequate compensation for good performance, and detection and suitable penalties for poor performance. For example, in Indonesia, senior Ministry of Finance officials made it clear that the Property Tax Directorate would be evaluated primarily on the basis of revenue generated in relation to revenue targets. While revenue targets should eventually comprise all current tax liabilities as higher targets and total tax billings converge, this strategy, when coupled with an organizational structure and reporting system that enabled monitoring of progress in raising tax revenue, has provided an interim strategy of tying career paths to attainment of institutional objectives.

Again in Indonesia, two policy initiatives are now being explored to increase local government institutional and personal incentives: the Ministry of Finance is considering rebating its share of property tax receipts directly to the rural village or urban neighborhood where it was collected to provide the lowest level of local government with a large increase in discretionary resources; and the Ministry of Home Affairs is considering reallocating the property tax collection fee so that a larger share is paid to the lowest levels of local government, to compensate officials for the disproportionate administrative burden they now bear.

In contrast, neglect of taxpayer service and reasonable legal compensation for government officials in Jamaica and the Philippines has created powerful disincentives for voluntary compliance and clean administration. These tendencies have been reinforced by failure to impose sanctions for noncompliance and maladministration.

Reformers in all four case study countries devoted a considerable amount of attention and resources on multi-media public information campaigns:

- The Prime Minister of Jamaica delivered emotional speeches in defense of property tax reform, and posters, pamphlets, and advertisements promoting "One Country, One System, Fair and Square for All" were omnipresent in Jamaica during "LandVal '74."

- The President of the Philippines also rendered explicit and public displays of his support for property tax reform, and local governments prepared brochures explaining the benefits derived from public expenditure of property tax receipts.

- In Chile, a public information campaign designed to mobilize a broad base of popular and political support utilized television, radio, the press, and special presentations to the President, presidential advisors, and legislative commissions.

- The President and Vice President of Indonesia subjected their private homes to high-profile inspections by property surveyors to demonstrate their support for reform, and local government officials prepared printed cartoons and radio dramas in local dialects to encourage cooperation.

Indonesia has the most integrated approach to property tax reform of the case study countries, as it includes not only policy and field operations, but all subsystems of property tax administration. Chile's approach also integrates policy and operations, as well as administrative subsystems, but the gap between normalization and revaluation has created significant coordination problems during implementation. While both the Jamaican and Philippine reforms link policy and operations, they fail to address significant deficiencies in their collections systems.

Indonesia also has the most successful phasing strategy of the case study countries. Indonesian reformers have enhanced their credibility and developed momentum by being very selective both geographically and functionally; they have stressed collections and enforcement first, and have commenced reform activities where the tax potential is greatest. Although Chile's two-step reform (normalization followed by revaluation) has been quite efficient, reformers have not yet been able to convince the government to apply the results of the general revaluation. The main weakness of the Jamaican and Philippine phasing strategy is that two decades is not only an unrealistic time frame for sustaining tax reform, but delays the fruits of reform inordinately.

Chile is ranked first in terms of building on existing strengths: reformers have tried to resuscitate fundamentally sound statutes through improved implementation. Philippine reformers have also tried to enhance administration of existing statutes; unfortunately, property taxation would benefit greatly if these laws were simplified first. Indonesian reformers have tried to accommodate existing practices whenever possible, but have yet to appreciate the benefits of traditional valuation systems. Jamaican reformers started over, with no clear evidence that in abandoning their old system, they had forsaken its main weaknesses as well.

Chile has also been the most successful in enhancing the cost-effectiveness of property tax administration. Chilean reformers have used their own resources to streamline and automate their property tax system. Both Indonesia and the Philippines, however, have relied on substantial external funding to implement property tax reform; donor resources have inflated the price and decreased the sustainability of reform activities, thereby compromising the cost-effectiveness of property tax reform. Nonetheless, much has been accomplished in Indonesia regarding tax policy and tax administration without external assistance; tax reform activities in the Philippines remain closely linked to foreign assistance.

REFORM GUIDELINES

The conceptual framework for property tax reform presented in Chapter One is based on a multidisciplinary literature review. The case studies presented in Chapters Two through Five are based on recent field investigations in Jamaica, the Philippines, Chile, and Indonesia. Together, the conceptual framework and case studies provide considerable reinforcement and dramatic elucidation of this study's principal themes, as noted in the following guidelines for property tax reform in developing countries.

Purpose of Property Tax Reform

GUIDELINE #1:

The purpose of property tax reform in developing countries should be to ensure the long-term generation of adequate local government discretionary resources.

The property tax is best suited to generating money to finance local government facilities and services. Thus, the purpose of property tax reform should be the generation of more money to finance higher quality and more widespread local government facilities and services where revenue adequacy has not yet been attained, and to improve the efficiency, equity, and sustainability of revenue generation whether or not tax receipts are currently sufficient.

The property tax is an appealing tool for local resource generation. The primary store of accumulated wealth in developing countries is real estate, given typically high inflation rates and weak capital markets. Such investments are visible, immobile, and highly concentrated. Property taxation is thus difficult to avoid legally, and if well administered, can be financially efficient and economically non-distortive. As a surrogate for largely ineffectual personal income taxes, property taxation also appeals to popular perceptions of political equity and social justice.

However, the major strengths of property taxation are also its principal weaknesses: a clearly enforceable levy on a relatively universal tax base magnifies the sensitivity of any attempt to apply the property tax more effectively. The beneficiary of property tax reform is an abstract and anonymous "public at large." In contrast, the losers are clearly identifiable: citizens who resent paying more taxes, and tax officials whose standard of living would decline measurably if currently diverted tax payments were redirected from private pockets to the public purse.

This paradox of high revenue potential and explosive political sensitivity places limits on effective property taxation, while providing guidance on how best to proceed within these limits. The primary objective of a government is to stay in power, but a government cannot survive without generating resources to finance itself. *Governments must therefore balance the need to maintain political legitimacy with the fiscal imperative to raise revenue.*

Limits imposed by this delicate balancing act make property taxation an inappropriate policy tool and poor administrative mechanism for:

- guiding allocative decisions;
- achieving social goals;
- recovering the cost of central government capital investments; or
- pricing private goods.

Statutory property tax rates are traditionally less that two percent of capital market value, effective rates are commonly one-tenth of these nominal rates, and in most jurisdictions there are numerous political and social constraints to increasing nominal rates significantly or bridging the gap between statutory and effective rates. It is therefore unrealistic to expect property taxes to play a critical role in the achievement of objectives other than the generation of modest amounts of revenue to meet routine recurrent expenditures:

- Property taxes simply cannot guide allocative decisions when they are inconsequential in investors' cost-benefit analyses.

- Administrative difficulties such as data misrepresentation and manipulation usually make efforts to use property taxation to meet social objectives ultimately counterproductive.

- The incessant desire of donor agencies to justify massive infrastructure investments by anticipated increases in property tax revenue is self-delusion on a truly grand scale.

- Property taxation cannot serve as a credible pricing mechanism for publicly financed private facilities and services when there is seldom a clear link between tax receipts and either provision or consumption of these private goods; cost recovery and conservation objectives for such facilities and services are better met via user charges.

Fundamental Principles of Property Tax Reform

GUIDELINE #2:

The fundamental principles of property tax reform in developing countries should be administrative and allocative efficiency, horizontal and vertical equity, and system sustainability.

Generation of adequate local government discretionary resources is a necessary but not sufficient condition for successful property tax reform in developing countries. Revenue should be raised in an efficient, equitable, and sustainable manner if reform efforts are to be financially viable, economically non-distortive, politically fair, socially just, and temporally enduring. Efficiency minimizes financial and economic costs, while equity minimizes political and social costs; together, they maximize reform longevity.

Otherwise, what might appear to be successful property tax reform could instead produce an ephemeral revenue bonanza, followed by taxpayer resentment, political paralysis, tax administration budget cuts, and a steady decline in tax receipts.

Administrative and Allocative Efficiency

Government officials should evaluate expenditures on tax reform in a manner similar to the way they would assess their return on other financial investments: what is the relationship between revenue generated and the cost of raising these funds? Given the skewed composition of property ownership in most developing countries, it already costs more to tax most properties than the revenue they generate before tax reform. Expensive reform activities, especially when directed at peripheral rather than primary constraints to cost-effective property taxation, only exacerbate these inefficiencies.

Economic efficiency costs should also be minimized. Firms and households should not be encouraged to make socially inefficient decisions based more on tax implications than on inherent economic virtues. Broad tax bases with low tax rates reduce the return on resources spent trying to ease tax burdens or evade tax payments.

Horizontal and Vertical Equity

Government officials must calculate not only the financial and economic return on their investment in property tax reform, but also the political and social ramifications of better property taxation: how can the tradeoff between cost-effective revenue generation and destabilizing popular resentment be minimized? Property taxes are easier to accept if, both in principle and practice, citizens who own real estate of similar value pay comparable property taxes, and tax burdens vary relative to differences in property values.

Considerable discretion in the valuation and classification of property results in arbitrary, subjective, and unfair tax administration. Systems designed to promote equity through progressive tax rates, differential assessment ratios, and multiple classifications instead promote inequity when implemented because valuation and assessment procedures are neither standardized nor objective. However, with formula-driven, computer-based valuation and assessment, if there are appraisal errors, they are at least unintentional, systemic, and universal rather than deliberate, personal, and targeted.

Equity is also undermined by poor collections and lack of enforcement. Failure to establish a credible threat that appropriate sanctions for noncompliance will be applied is especially unjust because those powerful enough to ignore notices of tax liabilities is usually highly correlated with those most able to meet these tax obligations.

System Sustainability

Government officials find it much more appealing to invest money and political capital in endeavors that offer positive returns over extended periods of time rather than in activities that offer momentary gains. To be sustainable, property tax reform must be an ongoing, dynamic activity rather than a singular event followed by static inertia. Although property taxation must be stable, it should also be flexible enough to adapt to unanticipated developments. This requires an effective management information system, so policy makers can monitor field interpretations of their directives, and field officers can shape policy with empirical input.

Subsidiary Principles of Property Tax Reform

==

GUIDELINE #3:

Property tax reformers in developing countries can minimize the costs and maximize the longevity of reform by increasing coverage, enhancing buoyancy, and emphasizing simplicity.

==

The fundamental principles of property tax reform, efficiency, equity, and sustainability, can best be achieved through adherence to the subsidiary principles of coverage, buoyancy, and simplicity.

Coverage

Property tax coverage should be optimized both in terms of statutory provisions and actual administration. The property tax base should be as broad as possible, without incorporating properties of such low current or potential value that their inclusion entails administrative expenses greater than the revenue they currently generate, or could expect to generate if developed. With this caveat, the wider the tax base, the lower the tax rate required to raise a comparable level of revenue, the greater the incentive for voluntary compliance, and the increased tolerance for technical imprecision.

Contrary to the widely held perceptions of government officials and donor agency staff, the valuation rolls in many developing countries appear to be relatively comprehensive. Coverage is not seriously eroded through widespread, blatant omissions, as most properties are identified and recorded by tax authorities in some manner, with accompanying basic data regarding property characteristics. Instead, much of this information is inaccurate, dated, or both, and regardless of data quality, much valuable property is officially either entirely or partially tax exempt.

Progressive tax rates, differential assessment ratios, and a plethora of ill-defined classifications enable the unintentional provision of further concessions through property misvaluation and miscategorization. This is often efficiently achieved by the close cooperation of taxpayers who misreport information and tax officials who knowingly accept and apply bad data. These partners in tax evasion then share the tax savings that result from their joint venture. Coverage is further eroded by poor collections, due primarily to the capitulation of weak tax administration to strong financial, political, and social pressures.

In short, tax officers and local government officials know the location and nature of most property worth taxing, and property owners certainly know the value of their real estate. If statutory provisions offered a legal foundation for taxing all of these properties, technical procedures reinforced rather than undermined the statutory tax base, and incentives for taxpayers and tax officials were greater for voluntary compliance than evasion, then property tax coverage would be relatively broad.

Buoyancy

Regardless of a property tax system's stage of development, progress cannot be maintained without tax base buoyancy. A simple, modest, and predictable price adjustment mechanism is essential to exploit the revenue potential of rapidly increasing land values, and to counteract the tendency of high inflation rates to quickly and substantially erode the value of tax receipts. This is especially vital in urban areas, which tend not only to have the greatest revenue needs, but also the bulk of a nation's high-value real estate.

The alternative to regular, small price adjustments to restore a tax base's real value is occasional, large price corrections. Such measures often result in a dramatic increase in property tax liabilities, which imposes a financial shock and cash-flow hardship on many taxpayers. This both discourages compliance and foments widespread resentment, a lethal combination of poor fiscal policy and bad politics.

The most effective mechanism for regular adjustments in absolute property values is routine indexing to a commonly accepted standard, such as consumer price levels. Relative property values are most easily updated through an objective, formula-driven, computer-assisted mass appraisal system. Manual fiscal cadastres and numerous individual and semi-individual valuations are simply too expensive, subjective, and time-consuming to offer long-term sustainability.

Simplicity

Property tax policies and practices must be simple to balance theoretically ideal systems and procedures with actual institutional capacity and administrative resources. Complicated systems and complex procedures are expensive to implement and difficult to understand. Thus, they are often subjective, arbitrary, and corrupt.

Simple systems and straightforward procedures, however, are relatively inexpensive to administer and easy to comprehend. Transparency is also an effective quality control mechanism, for just as proper operations are clear to taxpayers and tax officials alike, so are deviations from standard policies and procedures.

The Process of Property Tax Reform

===

GUIDELINE #4:

The process of property tax reform in developing countries should entail the cost-effective, integrated, and phased upgrading of existing tax policies and administrative systems.

===

Cost-effective property tax reform, namely reform which strikes a sustainable balance between efficient and equitable revenue generation, can best be achieved through an integrated and phased upgrading of current property tax policies and administrative systems.

Integration

Integrated property tax reform entails coordination of principles and practices, and inclusion of all field operations subsystems. The divergence of policy and performance is most common for collections. Most property tax legislation contains extensive and explicit enforcement measures. However, strong political and social pressures, weak administrative capacity, and insufficient positive incentives for taxpayers and tax officials creates "paper tigers" - few take the threat of sanctions seriously. Collections is also the administrative subsystem most frequently omitted from tax reform programs. This nullifies progress in data and valuation activities by switching tax evasion efforts from reporting and assessment subsystems to billing and payment subsystems.

Phasing

Integrated reform does not mean one should try to change everything at the same time. Although a reformer's policy perspective and field agenda should be comprehensive, scarce resources and risk inherent in change are two compelling reasons for phased implementation of reform.

Selectivity and sequencing can be key variables in the relative success or failure of reform efforts; which activities are tried where, and in what order, are often as important as correlative substantive issues.

Phasing allows reformers to develop credibility by choosing their experiments carefully, controlling their environment more closely, and adapting their reforms to unanticipated taxpayer or tax official responses. Phasing can be geographic (by area or local government unit), functional (by administrative subsystem or reform component), or both geographic and functional.

Upgrading

Wholesale scrapping and complete redesign of property tax systems usually compounds rather than solves the problems that initially motivated property tax reform.

While a clean break with the past is sometimes helpful in destroying the stigma of an unsalvageable system, beginning anew demands far more dramatic behavioral changes from bureaucrats and taxpayers alike, while at the same time fails to exploit familiarity with existing policies and procedures.

Before embarking on such drastic action, reformers should be sure they are dealing with causes rather than symptoms of poor performance. Otherwise, they are greatly increasing the cost, lead-time, and risk of property tax reform unnecessarily.

Incentives for Property Tax Reform

GUIDELINE #5:

Property tax reform in developing countries cannot succeed without utilization of the individual and institutional incentives necessary to induce fundamental behavioral change of taxpayers, central government policymakers, and local government officials.

Successful property tax reform in developing countries requires fundamental behavioral change of several parties, each of whom needs adequate individual and institutional incentives to induce desired responses and discourage unwanted activities.

Principal actors in the drama of property tax reform fall into three groups: taxpayers; central level government officials; and local level government officials. Their respective roles are distinctive: taxpayers provide data and pay taxes on their real estate; central government officials formulate policies; and local level government officials implement policies, whether on behalf of national ministries or local government departments. Incentives for taxpayers and government officials must be compatible with both these institutional roles, as well as the parts individuals play within these institutions; incentives must be both positive and negative as well (see Figure VI-3).

FIGURE VI-3: INDUCING BEHAVIORAL CHANGE THROUGH INCENTIVES

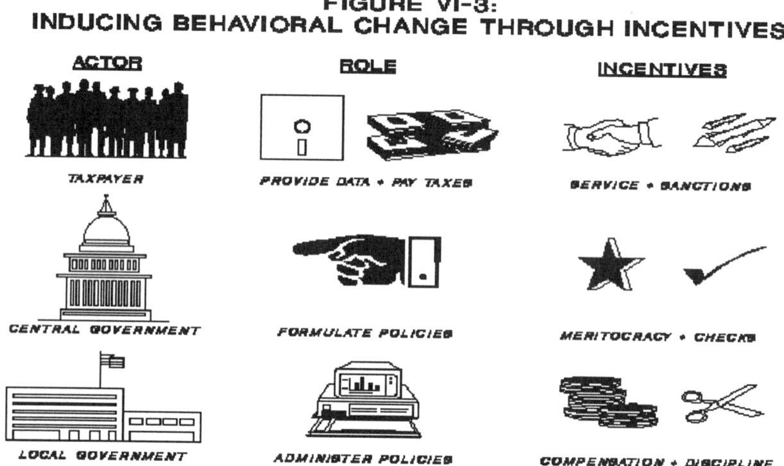

Source: Author's formulation.

The best positive incentive for voluntary compliance is taxpayer service, including:

- easily understood explanations of policy objectives and operational procedures, as well as clear delineation of taxpayer rights and obligations;
- easily accessible taxpayer assistance in protecting taxpayer rights and meeting taxpayer obligations;
- minimum bureaucratic requirements, such as lengthy property survey forms and complex payment requirements; and
- maximum taxpayer convenience, such as requesting verification of data already provided rather than repeated submissions of the same information, and establishing geographically disbursed payment points instead of one central payment location.

The best negative incentive for encouraging taxpayer cooperation is the credible threat that meaningful sanctions will be applied automatically for non-compliance. The price of avoidance must be greater than the price of compliance. Penalties should be certain, swift, and with escalating costs as the delinquency period and magnitude of arrears increase. The cost of sanctions can be both social and financial:

- publication of delinquency lists;
- use of tax clearances to obtain other government services;
- significant penalty payments;
- interest charges greater than the real savings interest rate available at commercial banks;
- payment of disputed amounts while cases are under adjudication; and
- seizure and sale of a taxpayer's assets to clear tax arrears, including auction of a few carefully selected delinquent properties.

While attractive in principle, these sanctions are often very difficult to apply in practice. Publication of delinquency lists is too threatening both politically and socially in many countries, as it would reveal the wealth of those who would prefer to remain anonymous property barons, and cause loss of face for "pillars of society" on whose continued support many governments depend for survival.

Again, although property tax statutes routinely require proof of tax payment, or tax clearances, before services are rendered, these statutes are in fact not usually enforced. Financial penalties are often so low that it is more profitable to deposit one's money in a commercial bank account than to clear tax liabilities in a timely manner, because the return is higher than the sum of all subsequent fines, if ever exacted.

The most dramatic example of application of sanctions for failure to pay property taxes is the seizure and auctioning of delinquent properties. This is most effective if such actions are highly publicized, and properties are selected as much for their demonstration effect as for clearing specific tax arrears.

The best way to encourage central government tax officials is establishment and maintenance of a meritocracy. High-level performances must be recognized and rewarded with better assignments, higher ranks, and more money, while unethical and incompetent performances must be detected and punished. Institutional goals should be clearly articulated, and an internal monitoring and evaluation system should be developed whereby successful efforts to meet these goals can be compensated, and activities which are obstructive can be penalized. In short, central government institutional and personal objectives should be harmonized through the judicious application of positive and negative incentives.

A similar strategy should be followed at the local government level, but the incentives might take a different form. Whether elected or appointed, local government officials are acutely sensitive to the concerns of their constituencies, and would like to offer the most gain for the least pain.

Thus, positive incentives should comprise a combination of reasonable remuneration with enough local discretion and linkages between property tax revenue and local public expenditures to be attractive financially and politically. Negative incentives should reinforce positive incentives by presenting a real threat of reassignment, dismissal, fines, and/or imprisonment for major graft or gross incompetence.

Public Perceptions of Property Tax Reform

GUIDELINE #6:

Property tax reformers in developing countries should devote considerable attention and resources to multi-media information campaigns targeted at both the taxpaying and the tax-exempt general public, senior government elected and appointed officials, and line civil servants.

Public and public servant support is essential for successful property tax reform. Taxpayers and government officials must understand the objectives and nature of reform initiatives if they are to be cooperative participants. Policies will not become practices unless they are bridged by common perceptions.

Public information campaigns should facilitate property tax reform through the enhanced credibility of public exposure and concomitant public accountability. They should increase understanding of, and support for property tax reform by promoting the convergence of public perceptions and reformers' reality.

Marlon Brando's closing ruminations in *The Teahouse of the August Moon* provide a fitting adieu for this study:

Little story now concluded, but history of world unfinished. Lovely ladies, kind gentlemen: go home to ponder. What was true at beginning remains true. Play make man think. Thought make man wise. And wisdom make life endurable.

Appendix

GROSS DOMESTIC PRODUCT/GROSS NATIONAL PRODUCT DEFLATORS AND EXCHANGE RATES/*GDP/GNP DEFLATORS (1985 = 100)*

Year	Jamaica (GDP)	Philippines (GNP)	Chile (GDP)	Indonesia (GDP)
1970	9.7	12.3	—	9.3
1971	10.3	13.8	—	9.6
1972	10.6	14.7	—	10.9
1973	12.5	17.4	0.1	14.5
1974	16.5	22.7	0.4	21.4
1975	19.9	24.6	1.9	24.0
1976	22.1	26.9	6.8	27.5
1977	24.8	28.9	13.8	31.1
1978	31.2	31.6	21.7	34.5
1979	36.4	36.4	31.7	45.7
1980	43.0	42.0	40.9	59.0
1981	46.6	46.6	45.9	69.9
1982	50.9	50.6	52.0	73.5
1983	59.3	56.5	65.9	87.7
1984	80.0	84.6	75.3	95.0
1985	100.0	100.0	100.0	100.0
1986	117.1	101.0	119.2	99.9
1987	131.5	109.2	144.5	115.8
1988	145.4	119.7	175.1	122.7
1989	±173.8	132.3	±192.0	±135.9
1990	n.a.	±149.5	±242.0	±142.9

Source: International Monetary Fund, Bureau of Statistics, *International Monetary Statistics*, monthly issues and yearbooks (Washington, D.C.: International Monetary Fund).

EXCHANGE RATES (PERIOD AVERAGE, PER U.S. DOLLAR)

Year	Jamaica (J$s)	Philippines (Pesos)	Chile (Pesos)	Indonesia (Rupiahs)
1970	0.83	5.91	0.01	362.83
1971	0.83	6.43	0.01	391.88
1972	0.77	6.67	0.02	415.00
1973	0.91	6.76	0.11	415.00
1974	0.91	6.79	0.83	415.00
1975	0.91	7.25	4.91	415.00
1976	0.91	7.44	13.05	415.00
1977	0.91	7.40	21.53	415.00
1978	1.41	7.37	31.66	442.05
1979	1.76	7.38	37.25	623.06
1980	1.78	7.51	39.00	626.99
1981	1.78	7.90	39.00	631.76
1982	1.78	8.54	50.91	661.42
1983	1.93	11.11	78.84	909.26
1984	3.94	16.70	98.66	1,025.94
1985	5.56	18.61	161.08	1,110.58
1986	5.48	20.39	193.02	1,282.56
1987	5.49	20.57	219.54	1,643.85
1988	5.49	21.09	245.05	1,685.70
1989	5.74	21.74	267.16	1,770.06
1990	7.18	24.31	305.06	1,842.83

Source: International Monetary Fund, Bureau of Statistics, *International Monetary Statistics*, monthly issues and yearbooks (Washington, D.C.: International Monetary Fund).

Selected Bibliography

Aaron, Henry J. "A New View of Property Tax Incidence." *American Economic Review* 64 (May 1974): 212-21.

________. *Who Pays the Property Tax? A New View.* Washington, D.C.: The Brookings Institution, 1975.

Aaron, Henry J., and Michael J. Boskin, eds. *The Economics of Taxation.* Washington, D.C.: The Brookings Institution, 1980.

Aaron, Henry J., and Harvey Galper. *Assessing Tax Reform.* Washington, D.C.: The Brookings Institution, 1985.

Aaronson, J. Richard., and John L. Hilley. *Financing State and Local Governments.* 4th ed. Washington, D.C.: The Brookings Institution. 1986.

Adams, F.G., *et al.* "Underdeveloped Land Prices During Urbanization: A Micro-Empirical Study Over Time." *Review of Economics and Statistics* 50 (May 1968): 248-58.

Ahmad, E., and N. Stern. *The Analysis of Tax Reform for Developing Countries: Lessons from Research on Pakistan and India.* Development Research Programme Discussion Paper no. 2. London: London School of Economics, 1986.

Alonso, William. *Location and Land Use.* Cambridge, Mass.: Harvard University Press, 1964.

Alm, James, and Larry Schroeder. *The Land Development Tax in Bangladesh.* Occasional Paper no. 84. Syracuse: Maxwell School of Citizenship and Public Affairs, Syracuse University, 1985.

American Institute of Real Estate Appraisers. *The Appraisal of Real Estate.* 9th ed. Chicago: AIREA, 1987.

________. *Appraisal Terminology and Handbook.* Chicago: AIREA, 1967.

Andic, Suphan. *Some Aspects of Taxation in Less Developed Countries.* Baden-Baden: Nomos Verlagsgesellschaft, 1982.

Asher, Mukul. "Tax Reforms in East Asian Developing Countries: Motivations, Directions, and Implications." *Asian-Pacific Economic Literature*, 3 (March 1989): 39-62.

Askari, Hossein, John Thomas Cummings, and Michael Glover. *Taxation and Tax Policies in the Middle East.* Butterworths Studies in International Political Economy. London: Butterworth Scientific, 1982.

Asociacion de Corredores de Propiedades de Chile A.G. COPROCH). *Boletin Informativo*, Mayo de 1991.

Bahl, Roy W. *Property Taxation in the 1980s.* Tax Policy Roundtable Property Tax Papers Series no. 2 (TPR-2). Cambridge, Mass.: Lincoln Institute of Land Policy, 1979.

________. *Urban Government, Financial Structure and Management in Developing Countries.* Metropolitan Studies Program Monograph no. 11. Syracuse: The Maxwell School of Citizenship and Public Affairs, Syracuse University, December 1982.

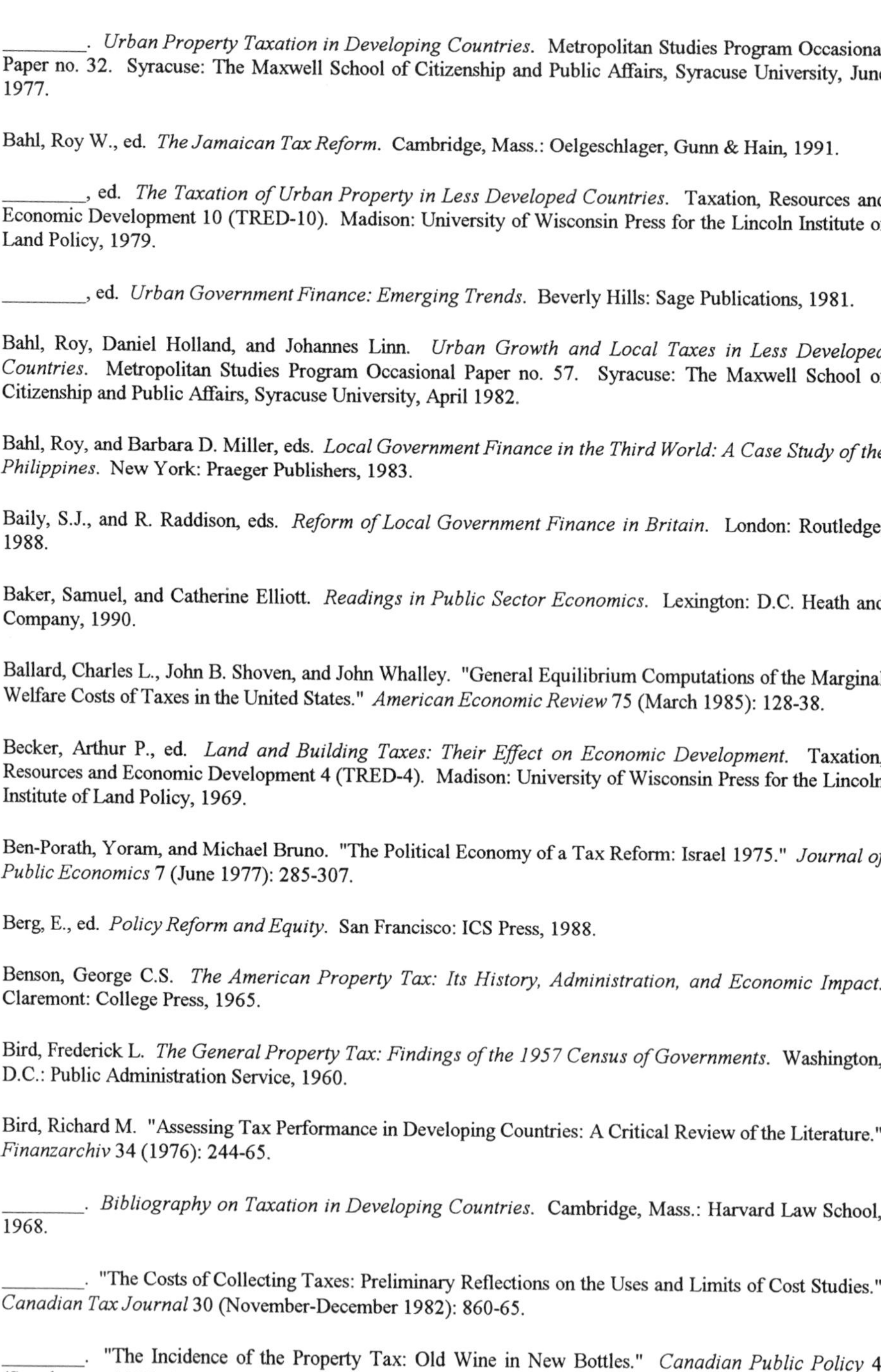

________. *Urban Property Taxation in Developing Countries.* Metropolitan Studies Program Occasional Paper no. 32. Syracuse: The Maxwell School of Citizenship and Public Affairs, Syracuse University, June 1977.

Bahl, Roy W., ed. *The Jamaican Tax Reform.* Cambridge, Mass.: Oelgeschlager, Gunn & Hain, 1991.

________, ed. *The Taxation of Urban Property in Less Developed Countries.* Taxation, Resources and Economic Development 10 (TRED-10). Madison: University of Wisconsin Press for the Lincoln Institute of Land Policy, 1979.

________, ed. *Urban Government Finance: Emerging Trends.* Beverly Hills: Sage Publications, 1981.

Bahl, Roy, Daniel Holland, and Johannes Linn. *Urban Growth and Local Taxes in Less Developed Countries.* Metropolitan Studies Program Occasional Paper no. 57. Syracuse: The Maxwell School of Citizenship and Public Affairs, Syracuse University, April 1982.

Bahl, Roy, and Barbara D. Miller, eds. *Local Government Finance in the Third World: A Case Study of the Philippines.* New York: Praeger Publishers, 1983.

Baily, S.J., and R. Raddison, eds. *Reform of Local Government Finance in Britain.* London: Routledge, 1988.

Baker, Samuel, and Catherine Elliott. *Readings in Public Sector Economics.* Lexington: D.C. Heath and Company, 1990.

Ballard, Charles L., John B. Shoven, and John Whalley. "General Equilibrium Computations of the Marginal Welfare Costs of Taxes in the United States." *American Economic Review* 75 (March 1985): 128-38.

Becker, Arthur P., ed. *Land and Building Taxes: Their Effect on Economic Development.* Taxation, Resources and Economic Development 4 (TRED-4). Madison: University of Wisconsin Press for the Lincoln Institute of Land Policy, 1969.

Ben-Porath, Yoram, and Michael Bruno. "The Political Economy of a Tax Reform: Israel 1975." *Journal of Public Economics* 7 (June 1977): 285-307.

Berg, E., ed. *Policy Reform and Equity.* San Francisco: ICS Press, 1988.

Benson, George C.S. *The American Property Tax: Its History, Administration, and Economic Impact.* Claremont: College Press, 1965.

Bird, Frederick L. *The General Property Tax: Findings of the 1957 Census of Governments.* Washington, D.C.: Public Administration Service, 1960.

Bird, Richard M. "Assessing Tax Performance in Developing Countries: A Critical Review of the Literature." *Finanzarchiv* 34 (1976): 244-65.

________. *Bibliography on Taxation in Developing Countries.* Cambridge, Mass.: Harvard Law School, 1968.

________. "The Costs of Collecting Taxes: Preliminary Reflections on the Uses and Limits of Cost Studies." *Canadian Tax Journal* 30 (November-December 1982): 860-65.

________. "The Incidence of the Property Tax: Old Wine in New Bottles." *Canadian Public Policy* 4 (Supplement, 1976): 323-34.

________. *Intergovernmental Finance in Colombia.* Cambridge, Mass.: Harvard Law School International Tax Program, 1984.

________. "Perspectives on Wealth Taxation." *Bulletin for International Fiscal Documentation* 32 (November 1978): 479-88.

________. "Tax Reform and Tax Design in Developing Countries." *Revista di Diritto Finanziario e Scienza delle Finanze* 36 (1977): 297-306.

________. *Taxation and Development: Lessons from the Colombian Experience.* Cambridge, Mass.: Harvard University Press, 1975.

________. *Taxing Agricultural Land in Developing Countries.* Cambridge, Mass.: Harvard University Press, 1974.

Bird, R.M., and O. Oldman, eds. *Taxation in Developing Countries.* 4th ed. Baltimore: The Johns Hopkins University Press, 1990.

Bird, R.M., and N.E. Slack. *Residential Property Tax Relief in Ontario.* Toronto: Ontario Economic Council Research Studies, 1978.

Bogart, William T., and David F. Bradford. *A Short Treatise on the Property Tax.* Department of Economics and Woodrow Wilson School of Public Affairs Discussion Paper no. 24. Princeton: Princeton University, August 1988.

Bonbright, James Cummings. *The Valuation of Property: A Treatise on the Appraisal of Property for Different Legal Purposes.* 2 vols. New York: McGraw-Hill Book Company, 1937.

Booth, A. "Ipeda - Indonesia's Land Tax." *Bulletin of Indonesian Economic Studies* 10 (March 1974): 55-81.

Boskin, Michael J., and Charles E. McLure, Jr., eds. *World Tax Reform: Case Studies of Developed and Developing Countries.* San Franciso: ICS Press for the International Center for Economic Growth, 1990.

Bradford, D.F., and U.S. Treasury Department Staff. *Blueprints for Basic Tax Reform.* Arlington: Tax Analysts, 1984.

Brazer, Harvey E., *et al.* "The Property Tax: Progressive or Regressive?" Symposium discussion. *American Economic Review* 64 (May 1974): 230-35.

Break, George F., and Bruce Wallin, eds. *Taxation Myths and Realities.* Menlo Park: Addison-Wesley Publishing Company, 1978.

Bridges, Benjamin. "Income Elasticity of the Property Tax Base." *National Tax Journal* 17 (September 1964): 253-64.

Brown, J. Bruce. "The Incidence of Property Taxes Under Three Alternative Systems in Urban Areas in New Zealand." *National Tax Journal* 21 (September 1968): 237-52.

Case, Karl E. *Economics and Tax Policy.* Boston: Oelgeschlager, Gunn & Hain, in association with the Lincoln Institute of Land Policy, 1986.

________. *Interim Evaluation of the Tangerang Pilot Project and Report on Compliance Monitoring Program.* Jakarta: Harvard Institute for International Development, January 1990. Photocopied.

________. *Property Taxation: The Need for Reform.* Cambridge, Mass.: Ballinger Publishing Company, 1978.

Chelliah, R.J., H.J. Baas, and M.R. Kelly. "Tax Ratios and Tax Effort in Developing Countries, 1969-71." *International Monetary Fund Staff Papers*, no. 22, 187-205. Washington, D.C.: IMF, 1975.

Clark, W.A. *The Impact of Property Taxation on Urban Spatial Development.* Institute of Government and Public Affairs Report no. 187. Los Angeles: University of California, 1974.

Cnossen, Sijbren, ed. *Comparative Tax Studies: Essays in Honor of Richard Goode.* Amsterdam: North-Holland Publishing Co., 1983.

Coffman, J. *Alternatives in Property Tax System Design.* Paper presented at the Real Property Taxation Conference: A Community of Interests, Vancouver, British Columbia, May 12, 1989.

Cook, Charles, and Arlo Woolery. *Real Property Tax Valuation in Jamaica: Recommendations for Change.* Jamaica Tax Structure Examination Project Staff Paper no. 34. Syracuse: Metropolitan Studies Program, Syracuse University for the Government of Jamaica Board of Revenue, July 1987.

Crommelin, M., and A.R. Thompson. *Mineral Leasing as an Instrument of Public Policy.* Vancouver: University of British Columbia Press, 1977.

Datta, Abhijit, ed. *Property Taxation in India.* New Delhi: Centre for Urban Studies, Indian Institute of Public Administration, 1983.

Davis, L.H. *Economics of the Property Tax in Rural Areas of Colombia.* Land Tenure Center Research Paper no. 25. Madison: University of Wisconsin, 1967.

Dillinger, William. Urban Property *Tax Reform: The Case of the Philippines' Real Property Tax Administration Project.* Report INU-16. Washington, D.C.: World Bank, May 1988.

________. *Urban Property Taxation: Lessons from Brazil.* Report INU-37. Washington, D.C.: World Bank, April 1989.

________. *Urban Property Taxation in Developing Countries.* Background paper for the 1988 World Development Report. Washington, D.C.: Office of the Vice President, Development Economics, World Bank, August 1988.

Doebele, William A., ed. *Land Readjustment: A Different Approach to Financing Urbanization.* Lexington: Lexington Books, 1982.

Doebele, W.A., O.F. Grimes, and J.F. Linn. "Participation of Beneficiaries in Financing Urban Services: Valorization Charges in Bogota, Colombia." Land Economics 55 (February 1979): 73-92.

Due, John F. *Taxation and Economic Development in Tropical Africa.* Cambridge, Mass.: The M.I.T. Press, 1963.

Dunkerly, Harold B., ed. *Urban Land Policy: Issues and Opportunities.* New York: Oxford University Press for the World Bank, 1983.

Ebel, Robert D., and James Ortbal. "Property Tax Relief: Current Status, Future Issues." *Tax Notes*, July 10, 1989, 223-28.

Eckert, Joseph K. "Evaluation of the CAV to Date and Recommendations for Simplification and Implementation." Memorandum PBB/91/DPRT/385, June 28, 1991. Photocopied.

Eckert, Joseph K., Robert J. Gloudemans, and Richard R. Almy, eds. *Property Appraisal and Assessment Administration.* Chicago: International Association of Assessing Officers, 1990.

Feldstein, Martin. "On the Theory of Tax Reform." *Journal of Public Economics* 6 (July-August 1976): 77-104.

Fiscal Services (EDP) Limited. *Revenue Services Project Description.* Kingston: Fiscal Services (EDP) Limited, no date. Photocopied.

Fisher, Ronald C. *State and Local Public Finance.* Glenview: Scott, Foresman and Company, 1988.

Follain, J.R., and T.E. Miyake. *Land versus Property Taxation: A General Equilibrium Analysis.* Metropolitan Studies Program Staff Paper no. 13. Syracuse: The Maxwell School of Citizenship and Public Affairs, Syracuse University, 1984.

Garnaut, R., and A. Clunies-Ross. *Taxation of Mineral Rents.* Oxford: Oxford University Press, 1983.

Garzon, Hernando. *The Property Tax Systems Applied in Selected Latin American and Caribbean Nations.* Metropolitan Studies Program Occasional Paper no. 131. Syracuse: The Maxwell School of Citizenship and Public Affairs, Syracuse University, January 1989.

Garzon-Lopez, Hernando R. *The Property Tax: An Evaluation and an International Comparison for Less Developed Countries, with Emphasis on the Case of Peru.* Dissertation submitted in partial fulfillment of

the requirements for the degree of Doctor of Philosophy in Social Science in the Graduate School of Syracuse University, February 1988.

Gemmell, J.T.E. *Immovable Property Tax Reform in Thailand.* ADAB/IBRD Thailand Land Titling Project Report no. 6. Bangkok: BHP Engineering *et al.* for Royal Thai Government, September 1985.

George, Henry. *Progress and Poverty: An Inquiry into the Cause of Industrial Depressions and of Increase of Want with Increase of Wealth . . . The Remedy.* Author's edition. San Francisco: W.M. Hinton and Company, 1879.

Ghandi, Ved P., ed. *Supply-Side Tax Policy: Its Relevance to Developing Countries.* Washington, D.C.: International Monetary Fund, 1987.

Gillis, Malcolm. "Evolution of Natural Resource Taxation in Developing Countries." *Natural Resources Journal* 22 (July 1982): 619-48.

________. *The Indonesian Tax Reform After Five Years.* Draft manuscript, November 1989.

________. "Micro and Macroeconomics of Tax Reform: Indonesia." *Journal of Development Economics* 19 (December 1985): 221-54.

________, ed. *Tax Reform in Developing Countries.* Durham: Duke University Press, 1989.

Gillis, Malcolm, *et al.* *Taxation and Mining: Nonfuel Minerals in Bolivia and Other Countries.* Cambridge, Mass.: Ballinger, 1978.

Goode, Richard. *Government Finance in Developing Countries.* Washington, D.C.: The Brookings Institution, 1984.

________. "Limits to Taxation." *Finance and Development* 17 (March 1980): 11-13.

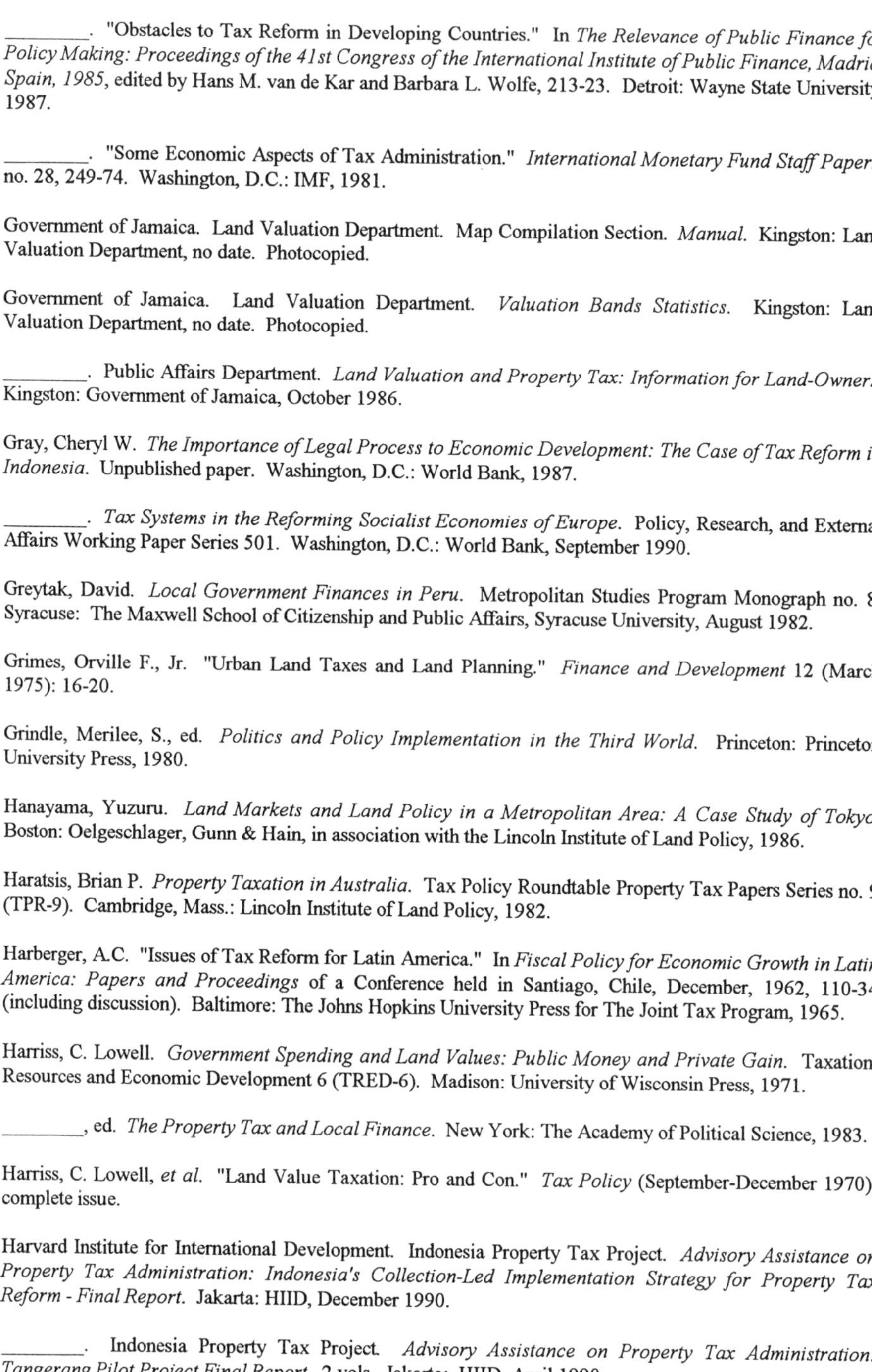

________. "Obstacles to Tax Reform in Developing Countries." In *The Relevance of Public Finance for Policy Making: Proceedings of the 41st Congress of the International Institute of Public Finance, Madrid, Spain, 1985*, edited by Hans M. van de Kar and Barbara L. Wolfe, 213-23. Detroit: Wayne State University, 1987.

________. "Some Economic Aspects of Tax Administration." *International Monetary Fund Staff Papers*, no. 28, 249-74. Washington, D.C.: IMF, 1981.

Government of Jamaica. Land Valuation Department. Map Compilation Section. *Manual*. Kingston: Land Valuation Department, no date. Photocopied.

Government of Jamaica. Land Valuation Department. *Valuation Bands Statistics*. Kingston: Land Valuation Department, no date. Photocopied.

________. Public Affairs Department. *Land Valuation and Property Tax: Information for Land-Owners*. Kingston: Government of Jamaica, October 1986.

Gray, Cheryl W. *The Importance of Legal Process to Economic Development: The Case of Tax Reform in Indonesia*. Unpublished paper. Washington, D.C.: World Bank, 1987.

________. *Tax Systems in the Reforming Socialist Economies of Europe*. Policy, Research, and External Affairs Working Paper Series 501. Washington, D.C.: World Bank, September 1990.

Greytak, David. *Local Government Finances in Peru*. Metropolitan Studies Program Monograph no. 8. Syracuse: The Maxwell School of Citizenship and Public Affairs, Syracuse University, August 1982.

Grimes, Orville F., Jr. "Urban Land Taxes and Land Planning." *Finance and Development* 12 (March 1975): 16-20.

Grindle, Merilee, S., ed. *Politics and Policy Implementation in the Third World*. Princeton: Princeton University Press, 1980.

Hanayama, Yuzuru. *Land Markets and Land Policy in a Metropolitan Area: A Case Study of Tokyo*. Boston: Oelgeschlager, Gunn & Hain, in association with the Lincoln Institute of Land Policy, 1986.

Haratsis, Brian P. *Property Taxation in Australia*. Tax Policy Roundtable Property Tax Papers Series no. 9 (TPR-9). Cambridge, Mass.: Lincoln Institute of Land Policy, 1982.

Harberger, A.C. "Issues of Tax Reform for Latin America." In *Fiscal Policy for Economic Growth in Latin America: Papers and Proceedings* of a Conference held in Santiago, Chile, December, 1962, 110-34 (including discussion). Baltimore: The Johns Hopkins University Press for The Joint Tax Program, 1965.

Harriss, C. Lowell. *Government Spending and Land Values: Public Money and Private Gain*. Taxation, Resources and Economic Development 6 (TRED-6). Madison: University of Wisconsin Press, 1971.

________, ed. *The Property Tax and Local Finance*. New York: The Academy of Political Science, 1983.

Harriss, C. Lowell, *et al.* "Land Value Taxation: Pro and Con." *Tax Policy* (September-December 1970): complete issue.

Harvard Institute for International Development. Indonesia Property Tax Project. *Advisory Assistance on Property Tax Administration: Indonesia's Collection-Led Implementation Strategy for Property Tax Reform - Final Report*. Jakarta: HIID, December 1990.

________. Indonesia Property Tax Project. *Advisory Assistance on Property Tax Administration: Tangerang Pilot Project Final Report*. 2 vols. Jakarta: HIID, April 1990.

Harvey, David. *Social Justice and the City.* Baltimore: The Johns Hopkins University Press, 1973.

Heinberg, J.D., and Wallace Oates. "The Incidence of Differential Property Taxes on Urban Housing: A Comment and Some Further Evidence." *National Tax Journal* 23 (March 1970): 92-8.

Herber, B.P., and P. Pawlik. "An Efficient and Fair Delinquent Real Estate Tax Collection Model for Local Governments." *Property Tax Journal* 7 (March 1988): 129-44.

Herschel, Federico J. "Tax Evasion and its Measurement in Developing Countries." *Public Finance* 33 (1978): 232-68.

Hicks, Ursula K. *Development from Below: Local Government and Finance in Developing Countries of the Commonwealth.* Oxford: Clarendon Press, 1961.

Holland, Daniel M. *The Assessment of Land Value.* Taxation, Resources and Economic Development 5 (TRED-5). Madison: University of Wisconsin Press, 1971.

________. *Report on the Revenue Structure of the City of Jakarta.* Jakarta: Mimeograph of the Jakarta Real Estate Tax Project, 1971.

Holland, Daniel, and James Follain. *The Property Tax in Jamaica.* Jamaica Tax Structure Examination Project Staff Paper no. 16. Syracuse: Metropolitan Studies Program, Syracuse University for the Government of Jamaica Board of Revenue, January 1985.

Holland, Daniel, Michael Wasylenko, and Roy Bahl. *The Real Property Tax Administration Project.* Metropolitan Studies Program Monograph no. 9. Syracuse: The Maxwell School of Citizenship and Public Affairs, Syracuse University, October 1980.

Institute of Property Taxation. *Property Taxation.* Washington, D.C.: IPT, 1987.

International Association of Assessing Officers. *Improving Real Property Assessment: A Reference Manual.* Chicago: IAAO, 1978.

________. *Property Assessment Valuation.* Chicago: IAAO, 1977.

________. *Property Tax Reform.* Chicago: IAAO, 1973.

International Conference on Property Taxation and Its Interaction with Land Policy: Plenary Session Papers. Cambridge, Mass.: Lincoln Institute of Land Policy, September 1991.

International Conference on Property Taxation and Its Interaction with Land Policy: Resource Manual. 2 vols. Cambridge, Mass.: Lincoln Institute of Land Policy, September 1991.

International Land Information Services. *Pajak Bumi dan Bangunan Improvement Plan (PBBIP) Advisory Assistance for Property Valuation: Completion Report on Contracts 1164, 1264, 1547 and 144.* ILIS: Jakarta, May 1991.

________. *Pajak Bumi dan Bangunan Improvement Plan (PBBIP) Advisory Assistance for Property Valuation: 50.000 High, 10.000 Top Value Properties, Jakarta, Medan, Bandung - Main Report.* ILIS: Jakarta, March 1991.

International Monetary Fund. Bureau of Statistics. *International Financial Statistics.* Monthly issues and yearbooks. Washington, D.C.: International Monetary Fund.

________. Fiscal Affairs Department. Tax Administration Division. *Tax Administration in Developing Countries: Strategies and Tools of Implementation.* Policy, Planning, and Research Working Paper Series 43. Washington, D.C.: World Bank, August 1989.

Ishi, Hiromitsu. "The Impact of the Shoup Mission." In *The Relevance of Public Finance for Policy-Making: Proceedings of the 41st Congress of the International Institute of Public Finance, Madrid, Spain, 1985*, edited by Hans M. van de Kar and Barbara L. Wolfe, 237-49. Detroit: Wayne State University Press, 1987.

Jackson, Ira A. "Amnesty and Creative Tax Administration." *National Tax Journal* 39 (September 1986): 317-23.

James, Simon, and Christopher Nobes. *The Economics of Taxation.* 3rd ed. Oxford: Philip Allan, 1988.

"Japanese Finance." *Economist,* special survey, 8 December 1990.

Jeffries, A. *The Design and Implemenation of a System of Market-Based Urban Property Valuation in Surabaya.* Jakarta: Ministry of Finance, Government of Indonesia, 1980.

Jensen, Jens P. *Property Taxation in the United States.* Chicago: University of Chicago Press, 1931.

Kaldor, Nicholas. "The Role of Taxation in Economic Development." In *Fiscal Policy for Economic Growth in Latin America: Papers and Proceedings* of a Conference held in Santiago, Chile, December, 1962, 70-109 (including discussion). Baltimore: The Johns Hopkins University Press for The Joint Tax Program, 1965.

Keith, John H. *Property Tax Assessment Practices.* Monterey Park: Highland Publishing Company, 1966.

Kelly, Roy. "Property Taxation: The Indonesian Experience." Paper prepared for The 9th International Symposium on the Property Tax, Barcelona and Seville, November 21-30, 1988.

________. *Property Taxation in Indonesia: An Analysis of the New Property Tax Law of 1986.* Development Discussion Paper no. 271. Cambridge, Mass.: Harvard Institute for International Development, July 1988.

Kelly, Roy, and Marco Montes. *Property Taxation in Dominican Republic: A Preliminary Proposal.* Manuscript, April 1990. Photocopied.

Khalilzadeh-Shiraz, Javad, and Anwar Shah, eds. *Tax Policy in Developing Countries.* Papers presented at the World Bank Conference on Tax Policy in Developing Countries. Washington, D.C.: World Bank, March 1990.

Kinnard, William N., Jr., ed. *1984 Real Estate Valuation Colloquium.* Boston: Oelgeschlager, Gunn & Hain, in association with the Lincoln Institute of Land Policy, 1986.

Kinnard, William N., Jr, and Byrl N. Boyce. *Appraising Real Property.* Lexington: D.C. Heath, 1984.

Kurnow, Ernest. "On the Elasticity of the Real Property Tax." *Journal of Finance* 18 (March 1963): 36-38.

Ladd, Helen F., and John Yinger. *America's Ailing Cities: Fiscal Health and the Design of Urban Policy.* Baltimore: Johns Hopkins University Press, 1989.

Lent, George E. "Experience with Urban Land Value Tax in Developing Countries." *Bulletin for International Fiscal Documentation* 32 (February 1978): 75-83.

________. *Taiwan's Land Tax Policy*. Working paper FAD/76/2. Washington, D.C.: Fiscal Affairs Department, International Monetary Fund, 1976.

________. "The Urban Property Tax in Developing Countries." *Finanzarchiv*, Neue Folge 33 (1974): 45-72.

Leonard, Herman B., and Richard J. Zeckhauser. "Amnesty, Enforcement, and Tax Policy." In *Tax Policy and the Economy*, ed. Lawrence H. Summers, vol. 1, 55-85. Cambridge, Mass: The National Bureau of Economic Research and The Massachusetts Institute of Technology, 1987.

Lerche, D. "Notes on Land and Property Taxation in Indonesia." *In Land Taxation in Indonesia: Report of the Jakarta Real Estate Tax Project*. Jakarta: JRETP, 1974.

Lewis, Alan. *The Psychology of Taxation*. Oxford: Martin Robertson & Company Ltd., 1982.

Lewis, Stephen R., Jr. "Agricultural Taxation in a Developing Economy." In H.M. Southworth and B.F. Johnston, eds., 453-92, *Agricultural Development and Economic Growth*. Ithaca: Cornell University Press, 1967.

________. *Taxation for Development: Principles and Applications*. New York: Oxford University Press, 1984.

Lindauer, John, and Sarjit Singh. *Land Taxation and Indian Economic Development*. New Delhi: Kalyani Publishers, 1979.

Lindenberg, Marc, and Benjamin Crosby. *Managing Development: The Political Dimension*. West Hartford: Kumarian Press, 1981.

Lindenberg, Marc, and Noel Ramirez. *Managing Adjustment in Developing Countries*. San Francisco: ICS Press for the International Center for Economic Growth and the Instituto Centroamericano de Administracion de Empresas, 1989.

Lindholm, Richard W., ed. *Property Tax Reform: Foreign and United States Experience with Site Value Taxation*. Lincoln Institute Monograph no. 77-11. Cambridge, Mass.: Lincoln Institute of Land Policy, December 1977.

________, ed. *Property Taxation - U.S.A.* Taxation, Resources and Economic Development 2 (TRED-2). Madison: University of Wisconsin Press, 1965.

Lindholm, Richard W., and Arthur D. Lynn, Jr., eds. *Land Value Taxation: The Progress and Poverty Centenary*. Taxation, Resources and Economic Development 11 (TRED-11). Madison: University of Wisconsin Press, 1982.

Linn, J.F., R.S. Smith, and Wignjowijoto. *Urban Public Finances in Developing Countries: A Case Study of Jakarta, Indonesia*. World Bank Report no. 80-7. Washington, D.C.: World Bank, 1976.

Lissner, Will. "On the Centenary of *Progress and Poverty*." *The American Journal of Economics and Sociology* 38 (January 1979), reprint.

Local Revenue Administration Project. *Grenada Tax Project Comprehensive Fiscal Reforms for Grenada: Directions for Research and Technical Assistance*. Metropolitan Studies Program Monograph no. 16. Syracuse: The Maxwell School of Citizenship and Public Affairs, Syracuse University, September 1984.

Local Revenue Administration Project. *Local Revenue Administration in Burkina Faso, Phase II: Final Report.* Metropolitan Studies Program Monograph no. 17 (revised). Syracuse: The Maxwell School of Citizenship and Public Affairs, Syracuse University, January 1986.

Local Revenue Administration Project. *Local Revenue and Service Provision in Upper Volta, Phase I: Final Report.* Metropolitan Studies Program Monograph no. 13. Syracuse: The Maxwell School of Citizenship and Public Affairs, Syracuse University, August 1983.

Local Revenue Administration Project. *A Plan for Increased Resource Mobilization by Local Governments in Bangladesh, Volume I: Executive Summary; Volume II: Policy Recommendations, Final Report.* Metropolitan Studies Program Monograph no. 14. Syracuse: The Maxwell School of Citizenship and Public Affairs, Syracuse University, May 1984.

Local Revenue Administration Project. *Syracuse University Technical Assistance to the Integrated Regional Development Project (Peru): Final Report.* Metropolitan Studies Program Monograph no. 15. Syracuse: The Maxwell School of Citizenship and Public Affairs, Syracuse University, May 1984.

Lynn, Arthur D., Jr., ed. *The Property Tax and its Administration.* Taxation, Resources and Economic Development 3 (TRED-3). Madison: University of Wisconsin Press, 1969.

________, ed. *Property Taxation, Land Use, and Public Policy.* Taxation, Resources and Economic Development 8 (TRED-8). Madison: University of Wisconsin Press, 1976.

MacAndrews, Colin. *Land Policy in Modern Indonesia: A Study of Land Issues in the New Order Period.* Boston: Oelgeschlager, Gunn & Hain, in association with the Lincoln Institute for Land Policy, 1986.

________, ed. *Central Government and Local Development in Indonesia.* Kuala Lumpur: Oxford University Press, 1986.

Macon, Jorge, and Jose Merino Manon. *Financing Urban and Rural Development Through Betterment Levies: The Latin American Experience.* New York: Praeger Publishers, 1977.

Mansfield, C.Y. "Tax Administration in Developing Countries: An Economic Perspective." *International Monetary Fund Staff Papers*, no. 35, 181-97. Washington, D.C.: IMF, 1988.

Mathew, E.T. *Agricultural Taxation and Economic Development in India.* London: Asia Publishing House, 1968.

McIntyre, M.J., and O. Oldman. *Institutionalizing the Process of Tax Reform.* Amsterdam: International Bureau of Fiscal Documentation, 1975.

McLure, Charles E., Jr. "The Interstate Exporting of State and Local Taxes: Estimates for 1962." *National Tax Journal* 20 (March 1967): 49-77.

________. "The New View of the Property Tax: A Caveat." *National Tax Journal* 30 (March 1977): 69-75.

________. "Taxation and the Urban Poor in Developing Countries." *World Development* 5 (March 1977): 169-88.

McLure, Charles E., Jr., and Wayne R. Thirsk. "A Simplified Exposition of the Harberger Model I: Tax Incidence." *National Tax Journal* 28 (March 1975): 1-27.

McSwain, Robert, and Arlo Woolery. *Appraisal for Property Tax Purposes.* Taoyuan: Land Reform Training Institute, 1987.

Meade, J.E., *et al.* *The Structure and Reform of Direct Taxation.* London: Allen & Unwin, 1978.

Meadows, George R. "Taxes, Spending and Property Values: A Comment and Further Results." *Journal of Political Economy* 84 (August 1976): 869-80.

Mieszkowski, Peter. "The Property Tax: An Excise Tax or a Profits Tax?" *Journal of Public Economics* 1 (April 1972): 73-96.

Montes, Marco. "Chile Case Study." Presentation at the International Conference on Property Taxation and Its Interaction with Land Policy, Cambridge, Mass., September 22-28, 1991. Photocopied.

Montes, Marco, and Roy Kelly. "Observations and Recommendations for Improving the Property Tax Administration in Indonesia Based on the Chilean Experience." Memorandum PBB/89/DPRT/153, March 7, 1989. Photocopied.

Musgrave, Richard A. "Equity Principles in Public Finance." In *The Relevance of Public Finance for Policy-Making: Proceedings of the 41st Congress of the International Institute of Public Finance, Madrid, Spain, 1985*, edited by Hans M. van de Kar and Barbara L. Wolfe, 113-23. Detroit: Wayne State University Press, 1987.

________. *Fiscal Reform in Bolivia: Final Report of the Bolivian Mission on Tax Reform.* Cambridge, Mass.: Harvard Law School International Tax Program, 1981.

________. "Is a Property Tax on Housing Regressive?" *American Economic Review* 64 (May 1974): 222-29.

________. *The Theory of Public Finance.* New York: McGraw-Hill, 1959.

Musgrave, Richard A., and Malcolm Gillis. *Fiscal Reform for Colombia.* Cambridge, Mass.: Harvard Law School International Tax Program, 1971.

Musgrave, Richard A., and Peggy B. Musgrave. *Public Finance in Theory and Practice.* 5th ed. New York: McGraw-Hill, 1989.

Musgrave, Richard, and Alan Peacock, eds. *Classics in the Theory of Public Finance.* New York: Macmillan, St. Martin's Press, 1967.

Namsiripongpu, Wiriya. *Property Tax Reform for Thailand.* Mimeograph, 1983.

Netzer, Dick. *Economics of the Property Tax.* Washington, D.C.: The Brookings Institution, 1966.

________. *Impact of the Property Tax: Its Economic Implications for Urban Problems.* Research report supplied by the National Commission on Urban Problems to the Joint Economic Committee, Congress of the United States. Washington, D.C.: U.S. Government Printing Office, 1968.

________. "The Incidence of the Property Tax Revisited." *National Tax Journal* 26 (December 1973): 515-35.

Newbery, David, and Nicholas Stern. *The Theory of Taxation for Developing Countries.* New York: Oxford University Press for the World Bank, 1987.

Nimeiri, Sayed. *Taxation and Economic Development: A Case Study of the Sudan.* Khartoum: Khartoum University Press, August 1974.

Oldman, Oliver. "Tax Reform in El Salvador." *Inter-American Law Review* 6 (1964): 379-420.

Oldman, Oliver, and Daniel Holland. *Jakarta Real Estate Tax Study: Final Report.* Jakarta: Ministry of Finance, Government of Indonesia, 1972.

Oldman, Oliver, and F. Schoettle. *State and Local Taxes and Finance: Text Problems and Cases.* Mineola: The Foundation Press, 1974.

Oldman, Oliver, *et al. Financing Urban Development in Mexico City.* Cambridge, Mass.: Harvard University Press, 1967.

Organisation for Economic Co-operation and Development. *Taxes on Immovable Property.* Paris: OECD, 1983.

Organization of American States Joint Tax Program. *Problems of Tax Administration in Latin America.* Baltimore: John Hopkins University Press, 1965.

Palmer, K.F. "Mineral Taxation Policies in Developing Countries: An Application of Resource Rent Tax." *International Monetary Fund Staff Papers*, no. 27, 517-42. Washington, D.C.: IMF, 1980.

Pardo, Erlito. *Local Government Finance: The Philippine Experience (1973-1990).* Manila: Bureau of Local Government Finance, September 1991. Photocopied.

Paul, Diana B. *The Politics of the Property Tax.* Lexington: Lexington Books, 1975.

Paul, Samuel. *Managing Development Programs: The Lessons of Success.* Boulder: Westview Press, 1982.

Peacock, Alan. "Some Gratuitous Advice to Fiscal Advisers." In *The Relevance of Public Finance for Policy-Making: Proceedings of the 41st Congress of the International Institute of Public Finance, Madrid, Spain, 1985*, edited by Hans M. van de Kar and Barbara L. Wolfe, 265-76. Detroit: Wayne State University Press, 1987.

Pechman, Joseph A. *World Tax Reform: A Progress Report.* Washington, D.C.: The Brookings Institution, 1988.

Pechman, Joseph A., and Benjamin A. Okner. *Who Bears the Tax Burden?* Washington, D.C.: The Brookings Institution, 1974.

Perkins, Dwight H., and Michael Roemer, eds. *Reforming Economic Systems in Developing Countries.* Cambridge, Mass.: Harvard Institute for International Development, 1991.

Peterson, George, ed. *Property Tax Reform.* Washington, D.C.: The Urban Institute, 1973.

Phares, Donald. *Who Pays State and Local Taxes?* Cambridge, Mass.: Oelgeschlager, Gunn & Hain, 1980.

Pickard, Jerome. *Changing Urban Land Uses as Affected by Taxation.* Research Monograph 6. Washington, D.C.: Urban Land Institute, 1962.

Pigou, A.C. *A Study in Public Finance.* 4th ed. London: Routledge and Kegan Paul, 1954.

Polinsky, A. Mitchell, and Steven Shavell. "The Optimal Tradeoff between the Probability and the Magnitude of Fines." *American Economic Review* 69 (December 1979): 880-91.

Prentice, P.I. "Urban Financing for Jobs, Profits and Prosperity: The ABCs of Property Tax Reform with Questions and Answers." *The American Journal of Economics and Sociology* 35 (July 1976), reprint.

Pressman, Jeffrey L., and Aaron Wildavsky. *Implementation.* 3rd ed. Berkeley: University of California Press, 1984.

Prest, Alan R. "Land Taxation and Urban Finances in Less-Developed Countries." In *Proceedings of the World Congress on Land Policy, 1980*, edited by Matthew Cullen and Sharon Woolery, 369-406. Lexington: D.C. Heath, 1982.

________. *Public Finance in Developing Countries.* 3rd ed. New York: St. Martin's Press, 1985.

________. *The Taxation of Urban Land.* Manchester: Manchester University Press, 1981.

Przeworski, Adam, and Henry Teune. *The Logic of Comparative Social Inquiry.* Reprint. Malabar: Robert E. Krieger Publishing Company, Inc., 1982.

Public Administration Service, and Sycip, Gorres, Velayo & Co. *Impact Evaluation of the Local Resource Management/Real Property Tax Administration (LRM/RPTA) Project.* Manila: U.S. Agency for International Development, Philippine Mission, September 1990.

Radian, Alex "On the Difference between the Political Economy of *Introducing and Implementing Tax Reforms: Israel 1975-1978."* *Journal of Public Economics* 11 (April 1979): 261-71.

________. *Resource Mobilization in Poor Countries: Implementing Tax Policies.* New Brunswick: Transaction Books, 1980.

Radian, Alex, and Ira Sharkansky. "Tax Reform in Israel: Partial Implementation of Ambitious Goals." *Policy Analysis* 5 (Summer 1979): 351-66.

Ragin, Charles C. *The Comparative Method: Moving Beyond Qualitative and Quantitative Strategies.* Berkeley: University of California Press, 1987.

Real Property Tax Administration (RPTA) Regional Project Management Office. *Terminal Report: LRM-RPTA Project Phase III, Region VI.* Iloilo City: RPTA Regional Project Management Office, August 1991.

Reeves, H. Clyde, ed. *Measuring Fiscal Capacity.* Boston: Oelgeschalager, Gunn & Hain, in association with the Lincoln Institute of Land Policy, 1986.

Report of the Commission on the Reform of Property Taxation in Ontario. Toronto: Ontario Government Bookstore, 1977.

Republic of the Philippines. Department of Finance. Bureau of Local Government Finance. *Local Finance Window VI.* Iloilo City: Bureau of Local Government Finance, Region VI, 1990.

________. Ministry of Finance. Office of Local Government Finance. *The Real Property Tax Administration and You.* Manila: Ministry of Finance, no date.

Ricardo, David. *On the Principles of Political Economy and Taxation.* 2nd American ed. Washington, D.C.: John B. Bell, 1830.

Richman, Raymond L. *The Theory and Practice of Site-Value Taxation in Pittsburgh.* Proceedings of the Fifty-Seventh Annual Conference on Taxation. Harrisburg: National Tax Association, 1965.

Riew, J. "Property Taxation in Taiwan: Merits, Issues, and Options." *Industry of Free China* 68 (July, August 1987): 7-28, 17-32.

Risden, O. St. Clare. *An Analysis of Alternative Strategies for the Period 1977 to the Decade of the 1980s.* Kingston: Land Valuation Office, April 1977. Photocopied.

________. "A History of Jamaica's Experience with Land Taxation based on the Site Value System." Paper prepared for the Conference of the Committee on Taxation, Resources and Economic Development, Lincoln Institute of Land Policy, Cambridge, Mass., October 1976.

________. "A Re-Examination of the Site Value System as the Base for Property Taxation in Jamaica." Paper prepared for the Conference of the International Union for Land-Value Taxation and Free Trade, Vancouver, May 1986.

Rosen, Harvey S. *Public Finance.* Homewood: Richard D. Irwin, Inc., 1985.

Rosengard, Jay K. *The Dilettante Development Dance: A Critical Assessment of In Absentia Project Management through Site Visits.* Cambridge, Mass.: Kennedy School of Government, Harvard University, January 1980.

________. *Property Tax Reform in Developing Countries: A Literature Survey.* TMs [photocopy]. Cambridge, Mass.: January 1991.

Rosengard, Jay K., and George H. Honadle. "Management Improvement in Developing Countries: Beyond a Formal Focus." Prepared for *World Bank World Development Report VI*, Washington, D.C., November 1982.

Rosengard, Jay K., and George H. Honadle. *Politics Versus Culture: An Assessment of 14 Mini-Cases of Management Improvement in Developing Countries.* Presented to Frontier of Development Management in Africa Panel at the National Conference of the American Society for Public Administration, New York, April 1983.

Rosengard, Jay K., and George H. Honadle. "Putting 'Projectized' Development in Perspective." *Public Administration and Development* 3 (October-December 1983): 299-305.

Roth, Jeffrey A., John T. Scholz, and Ann Dryden Witte, eds. *Taxpayer Compliance.* 2 vols. Philadelphia: University of Pennsylvania Press, 1986.

Saint-Vil, Jean. *Comment Améliorer les Articulations Entre la Production Foncière Urbaine et la Fiscalité en Côte d'Ivoire?* Abidjan: Direction et Controle des Grands Travaux, Avril 1990.

Saxton, Terri A. "Forecasting Property Values: A Comparison and Evaluation of Methods." *National Tax Journal* 40 (1987): 47-59.

Schroeder, Larry. *An Assessment of the Revenue Generation Capabilities of Villages, Districts and Arusha Region: Some Policy Options.* Metropolitan Studies Program Monograph no. 10. Syracuse: The Maxwell School of Citizenship and Public Affairs, Syracuse University, July 1981.

Servicio de Impuestos Internos. *Resumen de Antecedentes Tributarios.* Información para el Director Nacional del Servicio de Impuestos Internos, Mayo 1991.

Shome, Parthasarathi, ed. *Fiscal Issues in South-East Asia.* Singapore: Oxford University Press, 1986.

Shoup, Carl S., C. Lowell Harriss, and William S. Vickrey. *The Fiscal System of the Federal District of Venezuela: A Report.* Baltimore: Garamond Press, 1960.

Shoup, Carl S., *et al.* *The Fiscal System of Venezuela: A Report.* Baltimore: The Johns Hopkins Press, 1959.

Shoup, Carl S., *et al. The Tax System of Liberia: Report of the Tax Mission.* New York: Columbia University Press, 1970.

Sinha, K.P. *Property Taxation in a Developing Economy.* New Delhi: Puja Publications, 1981.

Sicat, Gerardo P. "Tax Reform in the Philippines." Presented at the Conference on Tax Policy and Economic Development Among Pacific Asian Countries, Taipei, January 1990.

Skinner, Jonathan. *Prospects for Agricultural Land Taxation in Developing Countries.* TMs [photocopy], February 1991.

Slemrod, Joel. "Optimal Taxation and Optimal Tax Systems." *Journal of Economic Perspectives* 4 (Winter 1990): 157-78.

Smith, Adam. *An Inquiry into the Nature and Causes of the Wealth of Nations.* 2nd ed. London: W. Strahan and T. Cadell, 1778.

Smith, R.S. "Financing Cities in Developing Countries." *International Monetary Fund Staff Papers*, no. 21, 329-88. Washington, D.C.: IMF, July 1974.

Smoke, Paul J. *Is Local Government Finance Theory Relevant for Developing Countries?* Development Discussion Paper no. 316. Cambridge, Mass.: Harvard Institute for International Development, November 1989.

________. *Local Government Fiscal Reform in Developing Countries: Lessons from Kenya.* Development Discussion Paper no. 321. Cambridge, Mass.: Harvard Institute for International Development, January 1990.

Stair, Elizabeth. "A Position Paper on The Property Taxation System." Kingston: Land Valuation Department, August 1990. Photocopied.

Stiglitz, Joseph E. *Economics of the Public Sector.* 2nd ed. New York: W.W. Norton and Company, 1988.

Stinchcombe, Arthur L. *Constructing Social Theories.* Chicago: University of Chicago Press, 1968.

Strasma, J. "Market-Enforced Self-Assessment for Real Estate Taxes." *Bulletin for International Fiscal Documentation* 19 (1965): 353-65, 397-414.

Strasma, J., *et al. Impact of Agricultural Land Revenue Systems on Agricultural Land Usage.* Burlington: Associates in Rural Development, 1987.

Study Group on Asian Tax Administration and Research. *Property Valuation Practices in Selected Countries in Asia and the Pacific.* Manila: SGATAR, 1983.

Surjowibowo, Karsono. "Kebijaksanaan Pajak Bumi dan Bangunan, Aspek Administrasi dan Manajemen Operasional Bagi Hasil Pajak." Jakarta, no date. Photocopied.

________. "Land and Building Tax: The Indonesian Experience." Paper prepared for the International Conference on Property Taxation and Its Interaction with Land Policy, Cambridge, Mass., September 22-28, 1991. Photocopied.

________. "The Property Tax in Indonesia." Paper prepared for the Municipal Finance Seminar, Cipanas, December 1990.

Surrey, S.S. *Pathways to Tax Reform.* Cambridge, Mass.: Harvard University Press, 1973.

________. "Tax Administration in Underdeveloped Countries." *University of Miami Law Review* 12 (1957-1958): 158-88.

Tait, A.A. *The Taxation of Personal Wealth.* Urbana: University of Illinois Press, 1967.

Tait, Alan, Wilfred Gratz, and Barry Eichengreen. "International Comparisons of Taxation for Selected Developing Countries." *International Monetary Fund Staff Papers*, no. 26, 123-56. Washington, D.C.: IMF, March 1987.

Tanzi, Vito. *The IMF and Tax Reform.* IMF Working Paper WP/90/39. Washington, D.C.: International Monetary Fund, Fiscal Affairs Department, April 1990.

________. "A Review of Major Tax Policy Missions in Developing Countries." In *Proceedings of the World Congress on Land Policy, 1980*, edited by Matthew Cullen and Sharon Woolery, 225-36. Lexington: D.C. Heath, 1982.

________. *Tax Reform in Economies in Transition: A Brief Introduction to the Main Issues.* IMF Working Paper WP/91/23. Washington, D.C.: International Monetary Fund, Fiscal Affairs Department, March 1991.

________. "Tax System and Policy Objectives in Developing Countries: General Principles and Diagnostic Test." *Tax Administration Review* 3 (January 1987): 23-34.

Tanzi, Vito, and Parthasarathi Shome. *The Role of Taxation in the Development of East Asian Economies.* Prepared for Conference on the Political Economy of Tax Reforms and their Implications for Interdependence, Seoul, 14-16 June 1990.

Taylor, Milton C., ed. *Taxation for African Economic Development.* New York: Africana Publishing Corporation, 1970.

Taylor, Milton C., and Raymond L. Richman. *Fiscal Survey of Colombia: A Report Prepared Under the Direction of The Joint Tax Program.* Baltimore: The Johns Hopkins Press for The Joint Tax Program, 1965.

Thirsk, Wayne. *Lessons from Tax Reform: An Overview.* Policy, Research, and External Affairs Working Paper Series 576. Washington, D.C.: World Bank, January 1991.

Thirsk, W.R., and J. Whalley, eds. *Tax Policy Options in the 1980s.* Toronto: Canadian Tax Foundation, 1982.

Toye, J.F.J. *Taxation and Economic Development: Twelve Critical Studies.* London: Frank Cass, 1978.

Turvey, Ralph. *The Economics of Real Property.* London: Allen and Unwin, 1957.

United Nations. *Manual of Land Tax Administration.* New York: United Nations, Department of Economic and Social Affairs, 1968.

United States Department of the Treasury. *Tax Reform for Fairness, Simplicity and Economic Growth: The Treasury Department Report to the President.* 3 vols. Washington, D.C.: Office of the Secretary, Department of the Treasury, November 1984.

Uphoff, Norman. *Local Institutional Development: An Analytical Sourcebook with Cases.* West Hartford: Kumarian Press, 1986.

Vance, Mary A. *The Property Tax: A Bibliography.* Monticello: Vance Bibliographies, 1981.

Virmani, A. *Tax Evasion, Corruption, and Administration: Monitoring the People's Agents under Symmetric Dishonesty*. Development Research Department Discussion Paper no. DRD 271. Washington, D.C.: World Bank, 1987.

Wagner, Richard E., ed. *Charging for Government: User Charges and Earmarked Taxes in Principle and Practice*. New York: Routledge, 1991.

Wald, H.P. *Taxation of Agricultural Land in Underdeveloped Economies*. Cambridge, Mass.: Harvard University Press, 1959.

Wang, N.T., ed. *Taxation and Development*. New York: Praeger Publishers, 1976.

Wasylenko, Michael. *Tax Burden in Jamaica Before and After Tax Reform*. Jamaica Tax Structure Examination Project Staff Paper no. 37. Syracuse: Metropolitan Studies Program, Syracuse University for the Government of Jamaica Board of Revenue, October 1987.

Wead, James K. *The Property Tax: A Primer*. Lexington: Council of State Governments, 1978.

Weidner, Edward, ed. *Development Administration in Asia*. Durham: Duke University Press, 1970.

Welch, R.B. "Measuring the Optimum Size of a Field Audit Staff." *National Tax Journal* 32 (1979): 143-56.

Wolfson, Dirk J. *Public Finance and Development Strategy*. Baltimore: The Johns Hopkins University Press, 1979.

Wong, John, ed. *The Cities of Asia: A Study of Urban Solutions and Urban Finance*. Papers presented at the International Seminar on Urban Land Use Policy, Taxation, and Economic Development, Singapore, 1974. Singapore: Singapore University Press for the Economic Society of Singapore, 1976.

Woolery, Arlo. *Property Tax Principles and Practice*. Taoyuan: The Land Reform Training Institute, 1989.

Woolery, Arlo, and Sharon Shea, eds. *Introduction to Computer Assisted Valuation*. Boston: Oelgeschlager, Gunn & Hain, in association with the Lincoln Institute for Land Policy, 1985.

World Bank. Asia Regional Office. Country Department II. Infrastructure Division. *Staff Appraisal Report: Philippines Second Municipal Development Project*. Report No. 7873-PH. Washington, D.C.: World Bank, November 17, 1989.

________. Asia Regional Office. Country Department II. Infrastructure Division. *Staff Appraisal Report: Third Municipal Development Project*, draft.

________. East Asia and Pacific Projects Department. Urban and Water Supply Division. *Staff Appraisal Report: Indonesia Urban Sector Loan*. Report No. 6598-IND. Washington, D.C.: World Bank, April 23, 1987.

________. East Asia and Pacific Projects Department. Urban and Water Supply Division. *Staff Appraisal Report: Philippines Municipal Development Project*. Report No. 5027-PH. Washington, D.C.: World Bank, May 10, 1984.

________. Latin America and the Caribbean Region. Technical Department. Public Sector Management Division. *Assessing Tax Administration in Latin America. Volume I: Main Report*. Washington, D.C.: World Bank, March 12, 1991.

________. *Lessons of Tax Reform*. Washington, D.C.: World Bank, 1991.

________. *World Development Report 1991: The Challenge of Development.* New York: Oxford University Press, 1991.

Yinger, John, *et al. Property Taxes and House Values: The Theory and Estimation of Intrajurisdictional Property Tax Capitalization.* Cambridge, Mass.: Academic Press, 1988.

Yoingco, Angel. *Property Taxation in Asian Countries.* Manila: Republic of the Philippines, Joint Legislative-Executive Tax Commission, no date.

Youngman, Joan M. "Defining and Valuing the Base of the Property Tax." *Washington Law Review* 58 (1983): 713-812.

________. "The Property Tax as an Income Tax." Chapter 17 in *New York University Proceedings of the Third Annual Institute on State and Local Taxation and Conference on Property Taxation.* Albany: Matthew Bender and Company, Inc. for NYU, 1985.

Index

The art of taxation consists in so plucking the goose as to obtain the largest amount of feathers with the least possible amount of hissing.

Attributed to J.B. Colbert, Louis XIV's Controller-General of Finance, c. 1665